THE LD CHILD AND THE ADHD CHILD

ALSO BY SUZANNE H. STEVENS

The
LD Child
and the
ADHD Child

WAYS PARENTS

AND PROFESSIONALS

CAN HELP

by Suzanne H. Stevens

JOHN F. BLAIR, PUBLISHER

WINSTON-SALEM, NC

Designed by Liza Langrall

Third Printing, 2000

*The paper in this book meets the guidlines
for permanence and durability of
the Committee on Production Guidelines
for Book Longevity of the Council on Library Resources.*

Library of Congress Cataloging-in-Publication Data

Stevens, Suzanne H., 1938–
    The LD child and the ADHD child : ways parents and
professionals can help / by Suzanne H. Stevens.
        p.   cm.
    Rev. ed. of: The learning-disabled child. c1980.
    Includes bibliographical references and index.
    ISBN 0-89587-142-4 (alk. paper)
    1. Learning disabilities—United States. 2. Attention-deficit
hyperactivity disorder—United States. 3. Learning disabled
children—Education—United States. 4. Learning disabled children—
Services for—United States. 5. Attention-deficit-disordered
children—Education—United States. 6. Attention-deficit-disordered
children—Services for—United States. 7. Child rearing—United States.
8. Special education—Parent participation—United States.
I. Stevens, Suzanne H., 1938–   Learning-disabled child. II. Title.
LC4705.S75   1996
371.93—dc20   95-26401

This book is lovingly and gratefully dedicated to
MY FATHER, JAMES A. "FIREBALL" HURT.
He believed his greatest gift was
his boundless energy.
His motto was "Do it now."

Contents

PREFACE
to the Revised and Expanded Edition

When this book first came out in 1980, its title was *The Learning-Disabled Child: Ways That Parents Can Help*. The term *attention deficit disorder* was not yet in use. Hyperactivity and distractibility were recognized as part of a learning disability but were not seen as elements of an entirely different (but related) condition. Much has changed!

In the 1980 edition of *Diagnostic and Statistical Manual of Mental Disorders*, Attention Deficit Hyperactivity Disorder was first recognized as a distinct disorder that often co-occurs with a learning disability. At that time, this internationally recognized reference manual classified ADD as a *behavior* problem, while learning disabilities were categorized as disorders in cognitive, or thinking, function. With that simple change of labels, the terminology jumble began. At first, it was common to hear of ADD as a problem with paying attention, and Attention Deficit Disorder with Hyperactivity as a concentration problem *combined* with overactivity. Each year, new variations appeared for use in schools and clinics. The current "correct" label is Attention-Deficit/Hyperactivity Disorder, with three different types possible within the one general ADHD category: Predominantly Inattentive Type, Predominantly Hyperactive/Impulsive Type, and Combined Type. As research continues, the defining characteristics and descriptive terminology will continue to be revised.

For the purposes of this book, ADD will be applied to adults and children whose behavior patterns include problems with attention, organization, and impulse control. Some of them will also have a problem with energy level or pace; some will not. When hyperactivity or hypoactivity is a significant issue, it will be pointed out. Unless specified as being of particular importance to one of these subcategories, ADD will be applied to all those who have the characteristics of an attention deficit disorder whether or not they are hyperactive.

Since research indicates that the majority of those with a learning disability also have an attention deficit disorder, there will be times when the two terms will be combined for the sake of clarity, and abbreviated LD/ADD for brevity.

In current usage, the proper way to write the full titles of these two disorders requires capital letters: Learning Disability and Attention-Deficit/Hyperactivity Disorder. On the theory that such a practice gives the idea of defectiveness more emphasis than it deserves, this book will not treat LD and ADD as proper names that require initial capital letters. This book will deal with attention deficit disorders and learning disabilities.

Since the vast majority of those with an attention deficit disorder also have most of the characteristics associated with a learning disability—and since almost all LD individuals have difficulty with concentration—the suggestions in this book will usually apply to adults and children in both categories. For those with a diagnosis of ADD, problems with attention, impulsive behavior, and hyperactivity or hypoactivity will probably be of primary significance. For those with a diagnosis of LD, problems with basic academic skills will be the most important aspect of the problem.

Unfortunately, the majority of those diagnosed as having an attention deficit disorder have been evaluated with only checklists and questionnaires, with no in-depth testing to determine the degree of learning difficulty. Thus, those who read this book with the intention of gaining knowledge about attention deficit disorders are likely to be surprised by the frequency with which LD issues apply to adults and children who had previously been considered just ADD.

A further word about usage is in order for this revised edition. As standard American English moves away from gender-biased language, the consistent use of male pronouns no longer feels comfortable. As much as is possible, this book avoids gender-specific language. However, in those cases where adjusting the pronouns compromised clarity, the traditional form *he* will be used to refer to an LD and/or ADD individual.

This choice is based on fact, not sexism. Experts used to say that seven out of ten of those with learning disabilities were male. With more sophisticated testing and a clearer understanding of how the characteristics are manifested in girls, it is now obvious that females make up a larger percentage than previously suspected—but they are still in the minority.

Current figures on attention deficit disorders suggest that 70 to 80 percent of those affected are male.

Likewise, *she* will be used to refer to a teacher, a psychologist, or a learning-disabilities specialist. Here again, facts support the usage. While there are many men who work in various capacities with LD and/or ADD adults and children, most of the specialists these children see for help—especially if they are in elementary school—are women.

Various forms of the term *learning disability* crop up so often that they are abbreviated as LD much of the time. That's convenient and logical, but often confusing. Sometimes it's proper to use the abbreviation, sometimes it's not. And sometimes LD may seem to stand for two different terms at once. The following explanation should help in keeping the terminology straight.

Learning disability will not be abbreviated when the term is used as a noun. Nobody has an LD. Instead, it is correct to say, "John has a learning disability." Also note that learning disabilities come one to a customer. A child may have many different learning problems, but they go together to make his own personal learning disability. Thus, no matter how many problems he has, John does not have learning disabilities; he has *a* learning disability. These phrases are correct: his learning disability, some learning disabilities, a learning disability, John's learning disability.

The abbreviation *LD* may be used as an adjective to indicate that a person has a learning disability; that is, it may be used to mean *learning-disabled*. For example, we say either "the learning-disabled child" or "the LD child"; "the learning-disabled students" or "the LD students."

LD may also serve as an abbreviation when the term is used as an adjective. It is correct to say "the LD teacher" for "the learning-disabilities teacher"; "the LD class" for "the learning-disabilities class"; and so on.

ACKNOWLEDGMENTS

No book is ever written entirely alone. From those who share ideas in casual conversation to those who check a manuscript comma by comma, words published as the work of one author really represent a composite of influences from past experience and opinions actively sought in the process of completing the project.

And this book is no exception.

To my mentors and trainers, I offer my sincere thanks. I'm particularly grateful to Dr. Lucia R. Karnes and June Lyday Orton for the patient instruction that established a body of knowledge and a set of attitudes that prepared me to explore alternative educational techniques from a previously unexamined perspective. Their faith in me provided inspiration, motivation, and courage. Their wisdom and methods are remembered and appreciated.

To those who carefully scrutinized the new material incorporated into my original 1980 book, *The Learning-Disabled Child: Ways That Parents Can Help*, I'm deeply appreciative. The lovingly offered criticism of well-informed colleagues supplied a greatly expanded body of current information to draw upon in updating a work that still held many valid opinions but no longer fit the reality of the situation in schools. The observations of Dr. Barbara Guyer, director of the learning-disabilities program at Marshall University, were tremendously helpful in areas where my opinion differs from others in the field. The comments and suggestions of C. Wilson Anderson, author, educational consultant formerly associated with the Menninger Clinic, and past president of the Orton Dyslexia Society, guided me in presenting a balanced set of ideas based on recent research as well as many years of experience. Kathy Hopkins, director of the National Institute for Learning Disabilities, and Shirley M. R. Minster of Home Education and Family Services graciously scrutinized the revised manuscript to be sure its language and style of presentation is compatible with the beliefs and sensibilities of Christian educators. For editorial advice and direction on homeschooling, I'm indebted to Maureen E. Westcott, editor of *The Homeschool ADDvisor*, as well as Shirley M. R. Minster. Their years of experience as trained educators teaching their own children offered insights and counsel otherwise unavailable.

I'm particularly grateful to those who evaluated the manuscript from a medical perspective. Without their patient guidance, this edition would have contained many personal biases and much misinformation. Henry Harvey, M.D., pediatrician with the Developmental Evaluation Clinic in West End, North Carolina; Ed DeWindt-Robson, Ph.D., clinical psychologist with Kernersville (N.C.) Psychological Associates; and Kenneth Guyer, Ph.D., biochemist with Marshall University Medical School and past president of the Learning Disabilities Association of West Virginia, graciously shared their knowledge about current practices and the most recent research findings aimed at solving difficulties faced by adults and children who are dealing with learning disabilities and attention deficit disorders.

LD therapy is an interactive process. As students grow, surprising strengths and weaknesses emerge in both the pupil and the teacher. The fun part of the remedial process is the observing, the learning, the speculating and comparing. To all my students who have taught me so much about the intricacies of the human mind, I am forever indebted. All the anecdotes in this book are based on their real-life experiences. Always, the names and key descriptive details have been changed to protect the privacy of the adults who outgrew our silly, academically convenient labels.

While others have pursued research and degrees, my time has been spent with students and in the library. Always, there has been such generosity of spirit from those who have done the studies and analyzed the data. Their willingness to share is a constant source of delight and amazement.

To all those who helped me analyze and understand—it's a privilege to call you colleagues and friends.

INTRODUCTION

For those who are interested in learning about learning disabilities and/or attention deficit disorders, there are five kinds of books on the market:

1. Inspirational books.

Famous men of tremendous talent who succeeded despite their difficulties with learning and attention are held up as examples. These biographies are designed to encourage LD/ADD children and adults (and those who love them) to take heart.

2. Self-help books.

These sell like those well-known hot cakes. The parents of LD and/or ADD children are desperate—they'll try anything! LD and ADD adults are even more desperate. Many of them are consumed with a passionate determination to find answers to problems that have plagued them all their lives. A lot of authors (most of them well meaning, some of them out-and-out quacks) make a great deal of money writing workbooks, reading-improvement courses, self-analysis programs, and other do-it-yourself at-home materials that are of no help to those with a learning disability and/or an attention deficit disorder.

3. Scholarly presentations by highly trained professionals.

Some of these would be helpful if the untrained nonprofessionals who need them could only understand them. Most of these books, however, present findings and theories of such a highly technical nature that they are of little value to LD/ADD adults or parents.

4. Success stories.

Usually, these are biographies written by LD teachers or mothers of children with an attention deficit disorder and/or a learning disability. "My son didn't learn to read until he was twelve years old and now he's a brain surgeon." It's never, "My son the plumber" or "My son the drugstore clerk." The main character is almost always a great success. Such stories are an inspiration to others. And that's good. But not all LD/ADD children grow up to be great successes. Most blend into society as average people.

5. Dire-warnings-of-what-can-happen books.

Prisons and welfare rolls are filled with those who never overcame a learning disability and/or an attention deficit disorder. It's important to hear their stories. It's frightening to see the figures that tell what becomes of children who fail in school. Such books arouse public interest. They point out the fact that LD/ADD youngsters don't merely need help—they *must* have it.

None of the books ever seems to talk about LD/ADD people who are just plain okay. And there are many such individuals.

Whether they're LD/ADD or not, most youngsters are not going to grow up to be judges, brain surgeons, or senators. Every minority group (and to have a learning disability and/or an attention deficit disorder is to be part of a minority) has its outstanding successes. We need the encouragement we get from those examples. But most of us grow up to be ordinary. We find pleasure and satisfaction in just being "normal." We can cope—we live, we love, we enjoy—and we're okay.

The object of this book is to help parents raise their LD and/or ADD children so that they, too, can grow up to be okay—so that they will be happy, well-adjusted, and successful adults despite the learning and behavior patterns that make them different.

And for the LD and ADD adults who read this book, the object is to give you control. With knowledge and understanding, it is possible to take charge of your mental processing and direct your physical energy so that differences that have long been handicaps are converted to assets.

THE LD CHILD AND THE ADHD CHILD

SOME OF THE BASICS:

Let's Be Sure We're Talking about the Same Thing

What is a learning disability? There is no commonly accepted definition. The experts simply do not agree.

There are only four points that all the professionals accept as true of all learning-disabled individuals. These points of general agreement are that

1. The learning-disabled individual does not learn satisfactorily from standard methods of instruction

2. The basic cause for this failure to learn is not a lack of normal intelligence

3. The basic cause is not a psychological problem

4. The basic cause is not a physical handicap

Thus, to classify a person as learning disabled is to place him in a particular group while giving only a limited amount of information. Within this group, there is a long and varied list of types of individuals and types of difficulties. The term *learning disabled* covers a very broad range of learning problems and says nothing about the special talents commonly found among this segment of our population.

1. HE DOES NOT LEARN SATISFACTORILY

A learning disability prevents a child from successfully mastering one or more of the basic skills: reading, writing, spelling, and mathematics. These skills, of course, affect all areas of schoolwork. A general lack of success in school results. The key to the failure almost always lies in the three R's—reading, 'riting (including spelling), and 'rithmetic.

Dyslexia is a medical term which originally meant the impaired use of words. Many think of dyslexia as a reading disability. The original Greek word implies a broader problem. The most accurate translation is provided in the commonly used term *specific language disability*, or just *language disability*. Discovered by medical researchers in the early 1900s, dyslexia is the most commonly seen and widely known kind of learning disability. The dyslexic child is the one who shows up at school a completely normal six-year-old. He's eager and ready to learn to read. But he quickly amazes everybody with his lack of success. (He can't write or spell either, but the reading is the main issue.) The poorly informed call this type of youngster a "mirror reader" or "one of those kids who reads backwards."

Originally, the word *dyslexia* described a very specific problem with clearly defined symptoms. A handful of doctors (mostly American and British) did research. A tiny group of educators developed methods of therapy. Specially trained teachers worked in clinics and a few of the most exclusive private schools. (Until the late 1960s, a learning-disabled child could seldom get help unless his parents had the money and influence to get him into a top-notch private school. To a lesser extent, that tradition continues today. The best LD therapy still tends to be found in clinics and in private country-day-type schools. There are also a number of extremely competent therapists working one-to-one in small tutoring businesses out of their homes.)

During the years when no one knew much about dyslexia, the word kept a definite meaning because only experts used it. But then, in the mid-1960s, the general public became interested in the subject. Women's magazines, bridge-table conversations, people eager to make money, neighbors chatting over the backyard fence—all contributed to the talk about the new fad topic. It was "in" to know about dyslexia, and even more "in" to have it.

In 1966, Mrs. Grisson was having difficulty with one of her four children. Walter, her fourth-grade son, was always in trouble at school. His grades were not very good. He had a reputation as a bully, a fighter, a petty thief. Everybody thought of him as a destructive, unmanageable, undesirable child. Most of the mothers in the Grissons' neighborhood preferred that their children not play with the boy. He seemed bright enough, but he had a terrible attitude.

Mrs. Grisson took Walter to a doctor for testing. It was discovered that he had mixed dominance (see page 22–24); therefore, he was diagnosed as having dyslexia.

These two "facts" supplied Walter's mother with a juicy conversational topic. Her son's dyslexia added a wonderful element of excitement to her life. The doctor's diagnosis provided Walter with a perfect excuse for not succeeding, not trying, and not behaving. Nothing was done to help him in school. Nothing was done to correct his basic learning problem—if there was one. Nothing was done to help him become better adjusted.

Sticking the label *dyslexia* on this boy did not help him at all.

During the 1960s, everybody thought he knew about dyslexia. The label was stuck onto almost any child with almost any kind of problem. Dyslexia meant different things to different people. It could mean anything and everything. It soon reached the point where the word meant nothing at all. Some of the old-time experts kept using the word with its original definition, but many of them began searching for a new term. And a new generation of experts was divided over the issue.

Some wanted a new labeling word. They sought a mutually acceptable name for a clearly definable condition. Much new research had been done. The situation had become more complicated than in the past. Many children were failing to learn to read, but they didn't seem to have much in common. Their symptoms didn't fall into nice, neat, totally predictable patterns. For a while, the only widely accepted label for the problem was *reading deficiency*. The term said nothing more than "The kid can't read."

Others in the new generation of experts believed the whole theory of dyslexia was a bunch of baloney. They did research. They studied and argued. They claimed, "Children who are mentally, physically, and emotionally normal will not fail to learn. No one is 'just made that way.' Something other than the child himself must be causing the problem." Their mission was to find those outside causes and correct them. Teaching methods, parents' attitudes, the educational environment—everything and everybody fell under their accusing gaze. Children were failing to learn, and it had to be somebody's fault. They used the term *reading deficiency* and searched for someone to blame.

> In the summer of 1971, I took a graduate course in remedial reading. The term *learning disability* was not yet "in."
>
> The instructor was a young, dedicated, well-trained professional. At the first class meeting, he introduced himself by saying, "Good morning. I'm George Deal. And there is no such thing as dyslexia."

The word and the original theory behind it had fallen almost totally out of favor, especially among the professionals in the field. Since then, it has returned to wide acceptance and gone back out of favor several times. Some of those who believed in a clearly definable condition called *dyslexia* gradually shifted to calling it a *specific language disability*. Over time, many of them gave in to using the vague but generally accepted term *learning disability*. Some held out to the very end, refusing to stick the label *disabled* on any child. Within this group, it is popular to substitute the word *difference* for the D part of the LD label. Unfortunately, making LD stand for *learning differences* gives even less information than the more generally accepted terminology.

The type of learning problem described by the word *dyslexia*, a long list of similar problems, and a whole group of seemingly unrelated learning difficulties got lumped into the general term now used to include them all: *learning disability*.

Dysgraphia is the medical term originally used to indicate a writing disability. Dysgraphia is most often seen as a part of dyslexia. Along with his trouble in learning to read, the student is unable to control a pencil or develop reasonable skill in forming letters and numbers. Most therapists treat dysgraphia as a side issue of little importance. Almost all their teaching is aimed at improving reading and spelling. They merely shrug at papers that are a jumbled mess of unreadable scratches. They believe that once the student learns to spell, penmanship will take care of itself.

This is not true. And it's not fair to the child. The inability to produce a decent-looking paper causes him much humiliation. Most people with dyslexia learn to live with their reading problem. But their writing problem is a constant source of embarrassment.

> Kenneth was an extremely bright eight-year-old. He had done very well in the first and second grades in public school. But when placed in the third grade in a private school, he fell apart.
>
> His happy, playful outlook on life suddenly disappeared. Homework became an unbearable chore. Lying, screaming, crying, hiding—Kenneth did everything possible to get out of sitting down to study at home. As matters grew worse, he began refusing to do his classwork as well. Normally a cheerful and cooperative little boy, he was rapidly becoming a serious behavior problem both at home and at school.
>
> Testing indicated that Kenneth had a combination of dyslexia and dysgraphia. He was so smart that he had taught himself to work around his reading difficulties. It was the dysgraphia that was causing most of his trouble.
>
> Put a pencil in his hand and Kenneth froze. He could not recall what the different letters looked like. His hand refused to remember how to form them. And his high IQ was no help in overcoming the problem. Any assignment requiring writing put the boy into a panic. He'd do anything rather than even try to write.
>
> For Kenneth, the answer was in therapy aimed mainly at his dysgraphia. Other areas needed work. But it was the handwriting problem that was crippling him.

Therapy for dysgraphia is a long, slow process. Many youngsters are highly resistant to any attempt to get them to change their pencil grip or style of script. Most specialists let it go because it doesn't seem worth all the effort. The majority of LD teachers have no training in handwriting therapy anyway.

Dysgraphia is one of the learning disabilities that is not taken very seriously. Experts tend to think of it as so common that it is unimportant. Yet children who do succeed in transforming an illegible scrawl into lovely, flowing cursive take tremendous pride in their accomplishment. It provides them with proof that they can learn successfully, and that they do have a chance to overcome other aspects of their learning disability. Much more study and research is needed in the field of writing difficulties.

Dysgraphia is very commonly seen in students with ADD. Unless their academic difficulties spread to a much broader area, it is usually ignored as just part of the pattern to be expected from children who are always in a hurry and not willing to take the time to pay attention to details.

Dyscalculia is the medical term originally used to indicate a math disability. Dyscalculia usually appears as part of a larger learning problem. Sometimes, math is the only area in which an individual has difficulty. That used to be considered rare but is now recognized as common among LD girls. It is also seen quite often among youngsters with an attention deficit disorder, but it is rarely given any attention as the learning problem it really is.

Most LD specialists know very little about dyscalculia. They are usually neither trained nor experienced in methods of diagnosis and therapy for math disabilities. Appropriate teaching materials are hard to find. On this topic, also, there is a need for more study and research.

Experts have begun to believe that dyscalculia is much more common than previously suspected. It is possible that the condition is not at all rare. It could be that it just goes unrecognized.

> Linda was a normal, bright fourth-grader. All her schoolwork was excellent—except math. She knew her basic addition and multiplication facts. Her papers were neat, her attitude

good. Yet her answers to arithmetic problems always turned out wrong.

Linda's mother had been to the school repeatedly. No one would take her daughter's math problem seriously. She kept hearing, "Linda's a great little kid. She's just not very good with numbers. Lots of little girls are that way."

At the beginning of the fourth grade, Linda's mother formally requested that her daughter be tested. School officials were cheerful and cooperative. Testing would be done if she insisted, but they felt the mother's fears were totally groundless. The school's LD teacher was called in. Even she felt there was no reason to suspect a learning disability. With the very best of intentions, the teachers and principal talked Linda's mother out of pushing for a diagnosis.

Nothing was done. The situation did not improve. Linda was still a great little kid. But she still could not do arithmetic.

Two of Linda's brothers had severe learning disabilities. In a conference with one of their therapists, the mother happened to mention her daughter's problem with math. The wheels were set in motion, a diagnosis was made, and Linda was found to have dyscalculia.

No one had considered this math problem important until an LD specialist recommended testing. In most cases like Linda's, the inability to succeed at arithmetic is noticed but left uninvestigated and uncorrected.

Within these three major areas of disability (dyslexia, or language disability; dysgraphia, or writing disability; and dyscalculia, or math disability) are many specific types of problems. Some of these are described in terms of what the child cannot do:

Decoding problems—difficulty with the mechanical process of reading. This problem tends to show up at a young age and is relatively easy to remedy with an appropriately designed, multisensory program of instruction in word-attack skills. Those with a high IQ often overcome weaknesses in decoding without special instruction. When youngsters with ADD have problems with decoding, it's usually blamed on careless errors and rarely taken seriously.

Encoding problems—difficulty with the mechanical process of spelling and writing. Youngsters who have trouble acquiring skill in decoding almost always have even more difficulty with encoding. Those with a high IQ and/or ADD often manage to work around encoding limitations until third or fourth grade, when the problem is blamed on laziness and lack of motivation. Teaching children to get their ideas into a correctly written form is a very complicated process that requires great patience and extensive training. Such help is rarely provided unless the problem is extensive enough to carry over into other academic areas.

Expressive language problems—difficulty putting ideas into any form of spoken or written language. Most LD and ADD children are very talkative and only have expressive trouble when putting their thoughts into writing. When a child has difficulty with all forms of verbal expression, parents and teachers usually assume the reluctance to share thoughts and feelings is caused by a personality trait or psychological problem. Children with expressive language difficulties often end up with psychiatrists rather than the language therapists they need.

Retrieval problems—difficulty remembering words to fit ideas. Youngsters with this problem often forget what they wanted to say, or insist they know the answer but can't explain. Most LD/ADD children do *not* have difficulty with word retrieval. Those who do often develop some rather strange-looking eye movements and glances as they fish around in their minds for the words they need. Sometimes, they get in the habit of parroting back the words just spoken to them. They almost always look like they have a reading comprehension problem.

Other specific types of disabilities are described in terms of a particular weakness that causes the learning problems:

Poor auditory discrimination—trouble telling the difference between sounds despite the fact that there is no physical problem with hearing.

Poor visual memory—inability to remember what has been seen despite the fact that there is no problem with vision.

Visual/motor problems—poor eye/hand coordination that makes copying and writing extremely difficult.

All these difficulties, plus many more like them, are closely related. A child with dyslexia usually has problems with poor visual memory. A child with an encoding problem can usually be said to have dysgraphia. How a particular learning problem is described depends on who is doing the labeling.

Most LD and ADD children have learning problems similar to the types listed above. It is to these children that the suggestions in this book will apply. (There are youngsters with less common types of learning disabilities. Their parents and teachers will find that some of the material in this book will be helpful and some will not.)

As trends change within the educational system, the ability to recognize and appropriately diagnose LD and ADD students varies. In the late 1960s and early 1970s, the United States Department of Health, Education, and Welfare estimated that over 17 percent of our schoolchildren had reading difficulties severe enough to require remedial work. At that time, the terms *learning disability* and *attention deficit disorder* had not yet been coined. Throughout the 1980s, a federal law (PL 94-142) forced public schools to provide appropriate special services for all exceptional children. At that time, learning disabilities became an official "handicapping condition." (This legislation did not apply to those who are now considered to be ADD.) The federal government subsidized these programs with funding but only allowed for 3.9 percent of a student body to be classified as learning disabled. What happened to the other 13 percent?

With public schools shifting toward "inclusion," learning disabilities and attention deficit disorder are thought of as typical of the many possible learning styles that can be taken care of within the regular classroom. The vast majority of LD children will never be officially diagnosed or provided with remedial instruction. Many are considered to have attention deficit disorder, with no further investigation necessary. More than ever, it has become the parents' responsibility to figure out what's causing their child's academic problems and to see to it that the needed special services are provided through the schools or by private tutors and therapists.

The purpose of this book is to offer sound advice that will apply to the *majority* of LD and ADD children. None of the situations described or recommendations made will fit every one of these youngsters.

2. HE HAS NORMAL INTELLIGENCE

LD children are not mentally retarded. The learning disabled have normal intelligence. However, a diagnosis of attention deficit disorder gives absolutely no indication of the student's level of mental ability.

The child with low mental ability cannot learn as quickly as his classmates. If not recognized as a slow learner, he falls behind, gets discouraged, loses interest, and gives up. Many become behavior problems; a few keep trying but continue to fail. Almost all such failing students develop deep and lasting feelings of inferiority. These children are not learning satisfactorily in school, but they are *not* learning disabled.

Years ago, classes for the mentally retarded were the catchall. In many school systems, they were the only type of special education classes provided. All sorts of non-learners were put into these classes by mistake. Improved screening and testing have reversed the situation. Today, it is very difficult to get a student into an MH class (a class for the mentally handicapped) even when the need is obvious and desperate.

> Average IQs range from 90 to 110 (see page 192). Sharon was in an LD class but had an IQ of only 78. She was definitely not learning disabled, but her low mental ability made it impossible for her to learn in a regular class.
> The school system she was in had a hard-and-fast rule: MH (mentally handicapped) classes were available for those children whose IQs tested *no higher* than 75. No exceptions were allowed. Sharon could not get into any class that could really help her. By the time she was fourteen, her life was a mess!

This policy is typical of programs, classes, and clinics designed to help the mentally retarded. Programs for the mentally handicapped are no longer the dumping ground for all of a school's non-learners.

The children who are most neglected in our schools are those with IQs between 75 and 90. An IQ in that range is below average but not low enough to classify a child as mentally retarded. A child who falls into that gap is too smart for an MH class. But he can't keep up in a regular class. If all goes well, he will make about three years of progress for every four years in school. From the very beginning, he is doomed to fail because his limited level of intelligence places him in a never-never land where no special programs are provided.

If such a child has many symptoms of a learning disability and/ or attention deficit disorder in addition to his below-average IQ, he's got big problems. He will never learn to read without LD therapy—but he won't fit in an LD class.

In spite of that fact, children with IQs between 75 and 90 are often placed in LD programs, especially in the public schools. Regular LD children have IQs of 90 or more, often much more. Thus, even in LD classes, these "in-between" children can't think as fast as their classmates and so stand out as failures.

What should be done with this group of children? It's a thorny issue. The laws say they have a right to an appropriate education. But our educational system does not have any niche appropriate for them! Whether they're learning disabled or not, children with "in-between" IQs don't fit anywhere.

LD children are now seldom mistakenly placed in special classes for the mentally handicapped, although many children with severe attention deficit disorder do get placed in classes designed for those with behavior disorders. LD youngsters still get grouped with the slow learners within their regular classes, especially if they're not recognized as learning disabled. Spending years in the "low group" with children not nearly as bright as he is has a numbing effect on an LD child. Information that he is perfectly capable of understanding is not presented to him because the rest of the slow group could not handle it. He doesn't get the chance to be a part of good group discussions in which he could learn from the ideas of other students. His work is watered down and presented slowly. This is *not* what the LD student needs. It isn't that he can't think—it's that he can't read (or write, or spell, or whatever).

On the other hand, how can an LD child function in a regular class when he can't read the book? Even if the school agrees to let him do all his work orally, he's going to have a hard time keeping up. Getting all of a student's assignments read aloud to him takes a lot of time, energy, and money.

The question constantly comes up: Is it better to place an LD student according to how well he can think or according to how well he can read?

To truly fit the needs of their LD students, school systems would have to revamp their programs entirely. In addition to the courses already taught in each subject—one for slow learners, one for average students, and one for bright students—schools would have to offer specially designed courses appropriate to the way LD students learn. There would have to be parallel classes in biology, chemistry, history, math—parallel everything. Such a system would meet the needs of more than the 3.9 percent of the student body officially labeled as learning disabled. And, if provided as a choice available to all the ADD students, as well as to the many others who want a more hands-on approach to learning, it would provide an excellent option for the hordes of students struggling to survive in spite of unrecognized learning disabilities. We know that about 25 percent of our adult population is functionally illiterate. An alternative track that placed less emphasis on reading and writing would give them an opportunity to achieve academic success. Under the present system, some very good minds are going to waste. There must be a better way.

3. HE DOES NOT HAVE A PSYCHOLOGICAL PROBLEM

Learning-disabled children are not emotionally disturbed. No hang-ups or mental blocks keep them from learning successfully. They are psychologically normal—at least until after they start to fail. Many children with ADD have such severe behavior problems that they are categorized as BD (behavior disorder) or ED (emotionally disturbed) and placed in classes with other such hard-to-manage youngsters. In such cases, it is extremely difficult to determine whether or not a child has a genuine psychological problem.

Children who are caught up in their own disturbed emotions cannot put much mental energy into learning. They fail in school because they're trapped in their own private world of anger, fear, fantasy, guilt, shame, or hatred. Emotionally disturbed youngsters often appear to have standard behavior problems. Sometimes, they merely seem a little strange. It is alarming how many children have severe psychological problems that are not noticed by family, teacher, or physician. They are not learning satisfactorily in school, but they are *not* learning disabled.

It is often very difficult to tell the difference between a learning-disabled child and an emotionally handicapped child, especially among older children. Trouble with concentration and hyperactivity are common in both groups. Their behavior problems and failure patterns are very similar. LD classes often become a school system's dumping ground for pupils with behavior problems. (And EH classes end up with a few LD students, too.) Even a well-trained, experienced psychologist occasionally has trouble deciding whether a particular child's difficulty is caused by a learning disability, an attention deficit disorder, or an emotional disturbance.

An LD class of fourteen fifth- and sixth-graders contained the following mix of students:

> Eight children who were purely learning disabled; they had the normal behavior problems typical of such students

> Four students who were clearly learning disabled, but who had developed severe emotional problems

> One boy who was definitely learning disabled, but who had such severe behavior problems that he probably could have been helped more by being placed in an EH class

> One child who really belonged in a class for the emotionally handicapped; this youngster showed no sign of a learning disability, and this class did not help him at all

Every child in the class had an attention deficit disorder. Half were hyperactive. Two were hypoactive.

All these students had been tested by a good psychologist. Out of fourteen youngsters, one diagnosis was wrong, one questionable. The psychologist had done a better-than-average job of identifying students to be placed in this LD class. It is not unusual to see LD classes in which up to half the students have been diagnosed incorrectly. Some of the misclassified children will be emotionally disturbed, some mentally retarded, and some merely in need of remedial reading.

Having emotionally disturbed children placed in LD classes is not always harmful to the correctly placed students—though it is very rough on the teacher. However, it does mean that a pupil who can't benefit from the class is taking up a space that could otherwise be filled by a student who really needs the special type of instruction available. Or worse yet, an already crowded class could be pushed up to an unmanageable size by the presence of non-LD students. (Some school systems do not strictly limit the size of LD classes. Too large a class turns a good LD specialist into a policeman, rather than a teacher.)

On the other hand, LD children are often incorrectly placed in classes for the emotionally handicapped. It isn't a question of whether or not such children have emotional problems. Students who spend several years dealing with the frustration caused by an unrecognized learning disability will develop some pretty strange patterns of behavior. Youngsters who cannot control their focus of attention and act on every impulsive urge have many traits in common with those who have severe psychological problems. As often as not, by the time LD and ADD students get to the sixth or seventh grade, they really *are* emotionally disturbed. But merely working to correct their psychological difficulties and build their self-esteem will not help them. Their failure pattern is feeding their emotional problem. They won't feel better about themselves or their world until they stop failing! They need to get control of their focus of attention. They may need counseling in addition to LD therapy. But first and foremost, they need to succeed at thinking and learning.

4. HE DOES NOT HAVE A PHYSICAL PROBLEM

Learning-disabled children are not physically handicapped. No physical problem keeps them from learning successfully.

Bodily malfunctions can prevent a child from learning. Some of these are easily recognized. Arthritic fingers obviously cannot hold a pencil. Cataract-dimmed eyes cannot be expected to read a page of normal print. Unfortunately, many physical problems are hard to recognize. Blood-sugar disorders can make a student sleepy or unable to concentrate, but the youngster won't appear to be sick. He'll look as if he's just lazy. Eyes that have perfect vision sometimes refuse to stay focused—but to parents and teachers, the child with this problem simply seems unwilling to concentrate. Major hearing losses occasionally go unnoticed for years. To those who don't know the cause of the learning failure, the hard-of-hearing merely appear to be slow. Physical problems have a strong effect on learning. And the list of impairments that can affect a child's ability to learn is nearly endless.

> Gil was in a regular fifth-grade class. He seemed to be very bright but was constantly wiggling, roaming around the room, and asking permission to go to the bathroom. He never got much work done because he never stayed in his seat. He was definitely not learning satisfactorily.
>
> In a conference with his mother, it was revealed that the boy was a bed-wetter. On the theory that he would eventually outgrow it, his parents had never consulted a doctor about the problem. The bed-wetting didn't appear to be directly related to Gil's classroom behavior. But his mother agreed that it was time to look into the matter. Gil was taken to a urologist.
>
> The doctor found that the boy had a chronic bladder ailment. Gil always felt as if he had to go to the bathroom. Physical irritation and discomfort kept him on edge. Fear that he would have an accident kept him uptight.
>
> The doctor prescribed medicine. Adjustments were made at home and at school to help Gil live with his problem. Slowly, the situation improved.
>
> To an uninformed observer, this student looked as if he were LD, ADD, or emotionally disturbed. Gil's frequent trips to the restroom looked like an excuse to get out of doing classwork. It took a doctor to prove that he did not have a learning problem; he had a physical problem.

Doctors believe there is a chemical and functional problem in the brains of those who have trouble controlling their focus of attention. In labeling a youngster ADD and prescribing medication, that physical component of an attention deficit disorder is supposed to be helped or corrected. In some children, drugs increase the ability to concentrate and make a significant difference in controlling impulsive behavior. For many youngsters, prescription medications seem to make no difference at all. For others, the attempt to chemically adjust the ability to pay attention adds new nervous habits like nail-biting, lip picking, and shirt chewing to the list of behaviors the drugs were intended to overcome. A diagnosis of attention deficit disorder does not imply that some physical malfunction might not be causing the difficulty with concentration and impulse control.

OTHER REASONS CHILDREN FAIL TO LEARN

Within almost every normal classroom, there are some students who are failing. They are not *all* LD or ADD. Many things can keep a child from learning successfully. In diagnosing a child as learning disabled, experts check to eliminate the possibility of failure due to below-average intelligence, a physical problem, or a psychological problem. (These three factors do *not* have to be eliminated in order for a child's academic problems to be blamed on an attention deficit disorder.)

There are several causes of failure in school that are very hard to detect. The most common of these are listed below.

1. Poor instruction. From the tiniest rural schools to huge, big-city school systems to the fanciest private schools, there are poor teachers. They are a minority, but they do exist—everywhere.

Students will not learn much from a bad teacher. Very young children (in grades one, two, and three) can have the rest of their school career damaged if they have a bad teacher and miss out on an important stage in their background.

The teacher is not always the one to blame for poor instruction. Overcrowded classrooms, poor materials (many school systems *force* teachers to use methods and materials that do not work), a shortage of books, uncooperative principals, horrible working conditions (schools with inadequate facilities often stick a class or two on the stage in the auditorium!), incompetent supervisors and administrators, too many nonteaching duties for teachers, mountains of government forms and administrative paperwork—many conditions can work together to cause an otherwise good teacher to provide poor instruction.

Regardless of the cause, students who survive a whole year of poor instruction suffer greatly later on. They start to fall behind, and a failure pattern sets in. It is rare that anyone figures out the reason for the learning problems in youngsters who have such a gap in their background.

2. Frequent or prolonged absences. Students who miss a lot of school will fall behind. Sometimes, they never catch up. In fact, they usually get farther and farther behind because they cannot overcome the gaps in their background. Unless the problem is corrected quickly, failure patterns begin. After two or three years, these children join the ranks of other non-learners.

3. Lack of readiness. Perfectly normal six-year-olds are often not ready to learn to read and write. Large numbers of them are not ready to be asked to sit still and pay attention in the regimented manner required by primary classrooms. Many areas of mental and physical ability must be well developed before a child has a chance to learn successfully in school. It has nothing to do with being smart or stupid—it's a question of growth and maturation.

> Henry had an IQ well into the genius range. By the time he was five, he had taught himself to read and could do some pretty impressive math in his head. He was incredibly smart.
>
> A psychologist (well meaning, but using poor judgment) suggested that the parents enter the boy in the first grade a year early. A good private school agreed to the plan.
>
> Even though he was a year younger than his fellow first-graders, Henry could read and think circles around his classmates. He was dynamite.
>
> But he had one problem. He could not make a pencil do what he wanted. He was not learning disabled. He had no trouble with concentration or behavior. He was simply not yet to the stage of development where he could learn to write. Bright as he was, he was being expected to do something that he was not yet physically able to do.

By the end of the second grade, Henry was such an emotional wreck that psychiatry was needed. Being placed in a situation where he could not succeed had caused severe emotional damage—needlessly.

When children are not ready to learn, all attempts to teach them will fail. Through no fault of their own, the failure pattern will be set into motion. To avoid such problems, it is wise to hold off on placing a youngster in the first grade until at least three months after the sixth birthday. (Despite the fact that laws force us to put six- and seven-year-olds in school, many perfectly normal children are not ready for formal academic instruction until after they turn eight.)

4. Being turned off. Every child enters school eager to learn. If the enthusiasm for learning is gone by fourth or fifth grade, somebody killed it!

By asking the impossible, not praising the successes, showing no enthusiasm, criticizing needlessly, forcing conformity, discouraging creativity, we adults systematically kill children's natural desire to learn. Instead of seeing school as a challenging, rewarding process of discovery, youngsters find school to be a pointless hassle. They turn off and tune out. Once their interest is gone, it is very difficult to change their attitude.

STICKING TO THE BASICS

In dealing with all non-learners, the secret is to discover the basic problem, then work to correct or overcome it. It is always a matter of asking, "Which is cause and which is effect?"

If the *basic* problem is a learning disability (and not one of the other problems discussed above), then that's where you start. With or without a diagnosis of ADD, the student's ability to pay attention must be considered an important aspect of the investigation and remediation.

2

RECOGNIZING THE LD/ ADHD CHILD:
Quick Appraisals for the Amateur

Most LD and ADD children can be recognized fairly easily without the use of tests. All teachers should be capable of screening their students to find those who have the characteristics of a learning disability or an attention deficit disorder. Parents are even better qualified to check their own children for signs of these problems.

In considering the symptoms associated with learning disabilities and attention deficit disorders, it is important to remember six things:

1. No one will have all of the characteristics. An LD child may have six or eight or even ten of them, but no individual will have them all.

2. Among LD and ADD students, some of these problems are more common than others. A few are even typical. But there is not a single symptom that is always found in every LD child. And except for the difficulties with concentration, no one trait applies to all youngsters with an attention deficit disorder.

3. All people have at least one or two of these characteristics to some degree. However, unless there is a *group* of symptoms, there is no reason to suspect a learning disability.

4. The academic problems associated with a learning disability are usually fewer in number and less pronounced among those whose main problems are in the areas of concentration and behavior than among those whose problems lie in other areas.

5. It is possible for a young child to have many of the first nine traits and still have no trouble learning to read, write, spell, or do math. It takes a large battery of tests administered by a qualified psychologist to give a truly accurate diagnosis of a learning disability in a young child.

6. The number of symptoms seen in a particular child does *not* give an indication as to whether the disability is mild or severe. In order to determine the severity of a disability, one must also consider personality, intelligence, and attitude.

The following list introduces the seventeen characteristics most commonly associated with learning disabilities and attention deficit disorders. Next to each of these symptoms is a one- or two-word description of how often the particular problem is seen. The descriptions used are *typical, common, not common*, and *rare*. These terms give a rough estimate of how often I have seen the symptom in my own work with LD and ADD children.

1. MIXED DOMINANCE—COMMON

It is considered "normal" for a human being to consistently prefer to use one side of the body rather than the other. Usually, a right-handed person is also right-footed and right-eyed. It isn't that the left foot or eye is defective; it's just that it feels more natural to use the right. Normally, by the age of six or seven, a child has developed a strong tendency to use one side of the body almost exclusively.

Those with mixed dominance do not do this—ever. There are many variations, but the pattern is always the same: the person does not have a same-side preference for handedness, "eyedness," and "footedness."

It used to be thought that this one symptom could separate LD individuals from all others. This has been found to be wrong. Many LD students do not show any sign of mixed dominance. It is common to see this trait among those with ADD. And although it is unusual, mixed dominance is occasionally seen in those who have no difficulties with learning or attention.

Specialists use complicated tests to check for mixed dominance. (They sometimes say they're checking for "laterality.") If a child does have mixed dominance, it is usually easy to recognize.

Teachers and parents should *not* attempt to "cure" mixed dominance in a youngster. Experts believe that any attempt to change laterality compounds the problem. Mixed dominance should only be noted as a possible symptom of a learning disability; it is not something to be corrected. It's simply the way the child is wired. (If left alone, most children learn to take advantage of their mixed dominance, or at least to work around it.)

Parents and teachers also should be very careful not to be critical because a child with mixed dominance doesn't do some task in the "normal" way. Their role should be one of helping the child find the best way to succeed at what he's trying to accomplish.

> Lucy was a darling, bright, mildly LD girl in the fifth grade. She had mixed dominance. Though her lovely penmanship was done right-handed, she was the best artist in her class with her left hand. Had she been criticized for this rather odd hand-switch, she might have been deprived of the great pleasure she got from her success in art. It was strange and she knew it. But she was secure in her faith that *different* doesn't mean *wrong*.

> George was the fastest man on his high-school track team, but he kept losing races because of his mixed dominance. He could never remember which foot to start with. The other runners were two strides ahead of him before he even got moving.
> The mixed dominance couldn't be corrected, so his coach figured out a way around it. When George crouched in the starting blocks, the coach would squat behind him and lightly hold the trailing foot. That hand on his ankle was enough to

get George to spring forward with the proper foot at the sound of the starting gun.

It looked pretty odd. Sometimes, the crowd hooted. Officials usually demanded an explanation. But his family, friends, and teammates were understanding, rather than critical. George had a different way of doing it, but he brought home the ribbons. It's hard to argue with success.

2. DIRECTIONAL CONFUSION—TYPICAL

Many LD and ADD children have difficulty telling right from left. If asked which hand they write with, they'll hold up the appropriate one. If asked, "Which way should I turn at the corner?" they'll point quickly and accurately, yet fumble to decide which word to use to identify the direction. When told, "Touch your left ear," most of them will have to pause to think before acting—and after careful thought, many won't be able to decide at all, especially the younger ones. In a game of Simon Says, the LD or ADD child looks like a real klutz!

Directional confusion causes LD and ADD children a great deal of embarrassment. Parents and teachers usually make matters worse by insisting that they could overcome this difficulty if they'd only put their mind to it. Teachers often protest with a comment like, "My gosh, even a mule can tell 'Gee' from 'Haw'!"

Adults who have a learning disability or an attention deficit disorder tend to be deeply ashamed of their inability to tell right from left. They believe it proves that they are stupid.

Very often, this problem does *not* go away. Sometimes, it seems to be outgrown, and a few researchers are working to develop methods of therapy. But usually the individual learns to live with his directional confusion and develops ways to compensate.

> At twenty-five years of age, Carol had a master's degree in physical education and was highly respected as a coach and teacher. Wearing her wristwatch on her left arm was the clue she used to tell right from left. Carol thought everybody had to do something like that.
>
> In coaching her college volleyball team in the finals of the national championships, Carol's instructions from the bench in-

cluded many hand signals. In the heat of a game, she didn't have time to decide between the words *right* and *left*. Her players knew to ignore the direction she named and move the way her hands indicated.

Mr. Smitherman was a successful and prosperous furniture manufacturer. His severely LD and ADD son was having trouble at school. This father had never realized he himself was learning disabled until his son's symptoms were explained to him in a conference.

He said marine boot camp had been the worst experience of his entire life. His inability to tell right from left kept him in trouble with his drill sergeant. He spent several miserable weeks being punished for constantly marching out of step!

By the age of eleven or twelve, most youngsters have pretty well adjusted to their directional problems. But people with directional confusion cannot automatically tell right from left with speed and certainty. Pressure only makes it worse. Careful, patient instruction sometimes helps. Usually, the person learns to use gimmicks and memory tricks to help compensate. Most also learn to keep the problem so carefully concealed that no one ever notices.

People with directional confusion should avoid jobs where they must respond instantly to directional commands—as must jet pilots, military gunners, and the like.

3. SIMILAR LEARNING PROBLEMS IN OTHER FAMILY MEMBERS—TYPICAL

When first hearing an explanation of their child's learning disability or attention deficit disorder, parents often gasp, "Good heavens, what you've just described sounds like Uncle Charlie." There is usually some family member who has had the same types of problems the child is experiencing.

During a conference with the Nelsons, all the LD symptoms listed here were discussed, along with predictions of the difficulties their fourth-grade daughter might face in the future. The family was warned to keep an eye out for difficulties with the foreign language her private school required of all older students.

It was at that point that a realization hit the father. Dr. Nelson said that he had nearly flunked out of medical school because of his trouble with Latin. As he explained his own academic problems, it became more and more evident that he was a highly intelligent man with a learning disability. The doctor concluded by saying, "I've always been a slow reader, and in college and med school, I had to work a lot harder than everybody else. I always assumed I just wasn't as smart as they were."

Of the doctor's four extremely bright children, two had mild attention deficit disorders and some learning problems, and his one daughter was clearly learning disabled.

Researchers have clearly established that learning disabilities are genetic. If there is one LD child in a family, there is probably another. In large families, it is rare to see just one child who is learning disabled while all the others are not, though it does happen. Every combination is possible. But the usual pattern is for some or all of the boys to have trouble with reading, writing, spelling, and concentration, while their sisters show signs of problems with reading comprehension and math. (The term *ADD* is too new to have a body of research available to prove or disprove genetically transmitted patterns. Experienced professionals believe attention deficit disorders run in families in much the same way learning disabilities do.)

Three large families stand out from my own experience. In one family of six children, one of the older boys was not recognized as learning disabled until he was out of high school, one brother had problems with concentration and behavior, two of the children had no problems, one of the younger girls had a math disability, and the youngest boy was severely disabled. I saw the same type of pattern in a family of five children: the oldest boy was severely LD, the next boy was fine, the two girls were okay, and the youngest boy had a disability. The third family is explained below.

The Bakers had four boys, three of whom were in private school. The youngest child was still a preschooler. As the three oldest brothers entered school, each was found to be more severely learning disabled than the one before him. The third one required two years of intensive therapy in addition to two years in the first grade before he could read well enough to try the second grade. The father was spending a fortune getting his children to read.

When Mr. Baker asked for a prediction about the youngest one, he knew the odds were definitely against him. The best he could hope was that by watching the little one closely, delaying his entry into school as long as possible, and seeking professional help at the first sign of trouble, a disaster might be avoided. There was no guarantee that the youngster would be disabled, but it seemed likely that he would.

4. EXTREME DIFFICULTY WITH SEQUENCING—TYPICAL

Those with learning disabilities and attention deficit disorders have a very hard time remembering a series of things in order. Perhaps that doesn't seem to be a particularly great handicap. In reality, though, it proves to be a constant source of embarrassment from early childhood to adult life.

Starting in kindergarten or first grade, LD and ADD youngsters stand out as the ones who can't learn to say the alphabet. For many of these students, their inability to say the alphabet in correct order remains into high school unless they are given special instruction. The same thing happens with memorizing the months of the year. The second- or third-grade class quickly masters the simple sequence and moves on to something else. But the LD/ADD student hasn't learned the material, and it's never taught again. Unless special help is provided, the sequence of the months remains a jumble into adulthood.

LD and ADD children are usually ashamed of their inability to remember things in order. To them, it is further proof of just how stupid they really are. The following example is typical of a scene that takes place in LD classes every year.

"How many of you can say the months of the year—in order?" I asked my fifth- and sixth-grade LD students.

Most of the hands in the class went up. Comments such as "Shoot, that's easy" came from most of the boys.

Two brave souls left their hands down and made apologies. "Ms. Jones tried to teach me that last year. Ain't no way I'm ever gonna learn that," Bobby drawled.

"Oh, man, that's too hard," Pete agreed.

"Most of you feel like you can do it," I observed. "Who'll go first and give it a try?"

Some of the hands dropped immediately, and a few more lowered slowly after moments of careful consideration. One hand continued to wave confidently above a beaming face.

"All right, Richard. Take your time."

Clear, precise, quick—the twelve words were rattled off with pride.

It's a touchy situation. As often as not, there isn't a single child in the class able to do it. I was relieved at Richard's success and openly showed my delight. "Perfect. Absolutely perfect."

None of his classmates seemed impressed. They were still pretending they could do it, too. They didn't know that I already knew their secret.

"Who else is ready to give it a try?" I searched the faces of the seven who wanted me to think they could do it. The boys were no longer making cocky remarks. Now, they sat very quietly, hoping they'd be invisible.

"No point askin' me." Bobby tossed his words casually into the silence. He'd already confessed his inability and was becoming comfortable with the fact that it was now public knowledge.

Reluctantly, one of the younger students volunteered. "I think I can," Doug said hesitantly. "Sometimes, I get mixed up. . . ." His voice trailed off as his courage wavered.

I offered, "You go as far as you can. If you get stuck, I'll help you out."

It was as though he'd been given permission to be less than perfect. Confident that he wasn't going to get shot down, Doug began. "January, February . . ." A brief pause interrupted. "March, April, May . . ." He paused again, then asked in a puzzled tone, "July?"

"No, but it does start with a *J*."

"January," he fired back, then scratched his head to ponder. "Oh, I know. I know. June. Then comes July."

"Right. Right." I was nodding my head to encourage him.

"June . . . July . . . What comes next?"

I gave him the first syllable: "Au . . ."

"Oh, yeah." And he rattled off August, September, November, December. (If calendars were made by the learning disabled, we'd miss out on a lovely month in the fall. Probably due to the way the brain groups information into chunks, LD/ADD children invariably omit October.)

"You left out the month that has Halloween in it," I told Doug.

"I did?" He seemed surprised. But the clue didn't help him. "October," I explained. "You know, fall and pumpkins and witches and trick or treat. You wouldn't want to leave out all that candy, would you?"

Doug grinned. "My mom makes me throw most of it out anyway."

All of us laughed with him. The tension was eased. Everybody was relieved.

By the end of the hour, each of the boys willingly demonstrated how much he could or could not do with the months. Except for Richard, none of them could do it perfectly. Three of the pupils couldn't do it at all—didn't even know how to begin.

The session drew to a conclusion with my announcement: "For our next big project, we're going to work on it every day until every one of you guys can say them, read them, and write them—with all the abbreviations spelled correctly!"

The word *spell* brought a few gasps. The idea that I actually believed I could teach them this shocked all but one into silence. Bobby shook his head in amazement, and his eyes widened as though watching the cavalry crest the hill on the way to his rescue. "If anybody can pound it into our heads, Ms. Stevenson, you can." (My name is Stevens, but LD/ADD children always seem to improvise. As long as it isn't done with deliberate disrespect, I let it go.)

It took nearly three months of daily repetition and drill. All but two mastered the skill completely. Ken was absent so much that he showed little improvement. Bobby learned to read all twelve and could spell and write through June in order. Each of the boys was delighted with his success. Even Bobby was proud of the fact that he'd gone halfway to his goal, and he knew he'd finish the task next year.

It takes an incredible amount of time, patience, and determination, but the learning disabled can learn the specific sequences necessary for survival. However, keeping the digits of phone numbers straight is often a lifelong problem.

Those with an attention deficit disorder but no significant learning disability almost always have difficulty with sequencing, but not to the extent seen in their LD classmates. ADD children typically have trouble following any kind of directions that include more than two or three steps. In their personal lives, tasks like getting dressed and ready for school confuse them because of the many steps involved in the process. It's very common for ADD youngsters to grab their book bag and say they're ready for school, even though they've forgotten to brush their teeth, comb their hair, or put on their socks. Little children with ADD often have a rather rumpled look.

In adult life, those with ADD tend to have continuing difficulty with organizing and remembering anything sequentially. They have to use memory tricks and organizational systems in order to work around this weakness.

5. SLOW OR DELAYED SPEECH DEVELOPMENT— NOT COMMON

Some children have a developmental lag in all language areas. They learn to talk at a later age than other children and often continue to use baby talk longer than would normally be expected. Sometimes they lisp, have pronunciation problems, stutter, or show other speech difficulties. Such developmental patterns sometimes prove to be part of a learning disability.

> A mother once told me, "My daughter was talking before she was one and a half and could carry on a conversation before she was three. My son didn't learn to talk until he was three—and he hasn't shut up since."
>
> In the sixth grade, her son wasn't as good a reader as his intelligence suggested he should be. His spelling was poor, and the mechanics of grammar and punctuation were hard for him. Yet he was excellent in math, science, and all his other subjects except French.
>
> It was decided that the boy was so well adjusted and so mildly disabled that therapy would be singling him out needlessly. He was placed in a special English class during one year of junior high school. In addition to help with spelling and grammar, he was given instruction in study skills, time management, and memory techniques. From then on, he and his family accepted his weakness with language and made the best of it. Nothing further was needed.

6. DIFFICULTY WITH TIME AND TIME RELATIONSHIPS—TYPICAL

Most LD and ADD individuals are so ashamed of their difficulty with telling time that they don't admit it even to themselves. As a general rule, LD youngsters have extreme problems learning to read a clock. By the fifth or sixth grade, they've developed all kinds of tricks to hide the fact that on a round-faced timepiece, they can't tell nine o'clock from six-fifteen. When using digital clocks, they can read out the numbers accurately but get very little meaning from them. This problem adds to their belief in their own stupidity but causes surprisingly little difficulty. They learn to rely on others and avoid situations where their secret might be revealed.

Even without special instruction, most LD and ADD children do master the skill eventually. But they rarely develop the kind of ability that allows others to glance at a clock and know the time instantly. Many LD adults look at the little hand, look at the big hand, then count it out by fives. Most learn to do it quickly. Some never realize that their method is different.

Other problems with comprehending time are not so easy to recognize or understand. Time relationships often cause confusion and make the individual look foolish. LD and ADD youngsters are often slow in understanding the difference between before and after, sooner and later, yesterday and tomorrow, etc. And once they do master the idea, they often express it incorrectly.

> During testing of a bright, mildly LD sixth-grader, his inability to deal with time relationships showed up clearly. Hal read a paragraph aloud. It was about a girl who had gone to camp for two weeks in July. It told how the little girl sailed, fished, swam, etc. There was no question that Hal recognized these as summer activities.
>
> One of the comprehension questions asked the student to identify the time of year during which the story took place. Instantly, Hal replied, "Winter." But he quickly realized his own error and said, "No, no. Summer."
>
> Most people probably would have thought this a slip of the tongue and of no importance. To the person who understands learning disabilities, this kind of mistake can be very significant.

Most human beings seem to have an inner sense of time. We can easily judge the amount of time that passes in half an hour without looking at a clock. We feel the difference between five minutes and one hour. Even though deeply involved in conversation or some other activity, we have a good idea how much time has gone by. Not so for those with learning disabilities and attention deficit disorders. It often seems that they were made without mental clocks inside their heads. Time seems to slip by them unnoticed. Even if they are careful to wear a watch to fight the problem, they forget to use it. LD and ADD adults are almost always late!

> Thirty-eight-year-old Kermit owned a chain of department stores and employed staffs of secretaries, lawyers, accountants, managers, and clerks. Although he was a college graduate, he was working with me to improve his poor spelling. He wanted the lessons and was paying for the therapy out of his own pocket. Yet he was always at least half an hour late for our sessions.
>
> I was very strict about charging him for his scheduled lesson time whether he was there or not. He cheerfully paid for the hours he missed because of his tardiness. The penalty had no effect on his habit at all.
>
> When asked about it, he said, "I'm always late. My girlfriend is constantly mad at me. I'm never on time for business appointments or dinner reservations."
>
> Kermit believed he had a good reason for his behavior. "I hate to wait," he explained. "When I'm ready to do something, I want to do it right away. If I'm the last one to arrive, everybody is ready and I don't have to wait."
>
> It made a good story, and he probably believed it, but the habit made him a most inconsiderate guest. I made two suggestions: that he face the fact that his lack of promptness was part of his learning disability and not a personality trait, and that he buy a digital wristwatch with an alarm on it.
>
> I rather doubt that he did either.

For LD and ADD children, the purchase of a watch (digital or not) isn't always the solution. They go out to play with their mom's words in their ears: "Be back for dinner" or "Be home in an hour." They fully intend to do as told. But their inner clock has no concept of how much time is involved—so they're out until dark, or until someone else's mother sends them home, or until their angry father goes searching the neighborhood. A watch isn't much help because they forget to look at it, and the numbers don't mean much to them anyway. Since they are very observant of what's going on around them, they're more likely to head for home if told to do so when the streetlights come on or when the news comes on TV. But of course, events don't always occur at helpful moments to serve as reminders. A digital wristwatch with an alarm is sometimes helpful, but it's often not practical or is beyond the parents' means.

Two goals need to be set up in dealing with this problem. The child needs to be made aware of his lack of an inner clock without being made to feel guilty about it. He's got enough problems trying to fit in with the schedule of the rest of the world without feeling that it's his fault when he doesn't. And the adults in the child's life need to help devise creative solutions that will bring the desired promptness, while avoiding asking the youngster to do something he is not capable of doing.

How do you live in peace with children who have no mental clock? One firm policy almost always helps: from the very earliest age, teach children to keep their family informed about where they are. (This is not the same as asking permission.) Even six-year-olds are capable of remembering to tell their mother where they're going (and of being where they said they'd be until telling her otherwise). A simple announcement of a destination ("I'm going to the park") should be expected every time they leave the house. When no one is home to get the information in person, they can leave a note (poor spelling accepted), draw a picture, or leave a message on the answering machine or with a friend or neighbor. It is vitally important that LD and ADD children be taught to make sure someone knows where they are at all times.

No matter what system is used, LD and ADD youngsters are often going to fail to be home on time. Their families must understand and accept this, but they should not be willing to put up with delayed meals, missed appointments, and long periods of worry and waiting. Search parties should not be needed. Parents should always be able to locate a child with just *one* phone call!

Along with this one basic rule, there are many procedures that can help children live without a reliable mental clock. Large, old-fashioned dinner bells, ranch-type triangles, and whistles can be used to call youngsters when playing in the neighborhood. (Of course, it is perfectly fair to insist that they respond quickly when the signal is heard.) Many young children arrive at a friend's house with a note pinned to a shirt or collar: "Please send Sally home at five-thirty." As youngsters get older, they can deliver this kind of message themselves. When my own children were small, it was common for one of their friends to seek me out when first arriving in our house and tell me, "My mommy says I'm to be home by six." I didn't mind being made responsible for watching the clock. In fact, it made me feel good to know that my children had playmates whose mothers kept track of them.

LD and ADD children often think up their own ways of telling time without using a clock. This should be encouraged.

> Ken, a severely LD and ADD twelve-year-old, had five brothers and sisters. In his house, the TV was almost always on. He developed a clever way of telling time based on what was on television. For example, he knew he had to be out the door for his school bus before a particular morning show began, he knew he had to be home for dinner before the start of the evening news, etc.
>
> Ken and his mother often had conversations like the one that follows.
>
> Ken gave his mother the simple message, "Aunt Louise called while you were out."
>
> "What did she have to say?" his mother asked.
>
> Ken reported a minute or two of family news.
>
> "Does she want me to call her back?"
>
> "Yeah. She said she wants to ask you about something."
>
> "Was she at work?"
>
> "I don't know if she'd still be there now. She said she'd be at the office for about an hour; then she was going out somewhere." Ken shrugged and gave a weak grin. Details often leaked out of his memory. He'd relayed the message, but it didn't make much sense to him.
>
> Glancing at her watch, his mother asked, "What time did she call?"
>
> "During *Gilligan's Island*" was his reply.
>
> Most people would have to consult the TV listings to get

any information out of Ken's answer. But a mother of six TV-watching children is up on such things. Mrs. Williams reached for the phone with a matter-of-fact, "Oh, good. She's still at work then."

People lived without clocks for centuries. It can still be done today.

Many children balk at going to bed on time or living within other time limits placed on them. LD and ADD youngsters are especially prone to this. If adults make it a point always to give a five-minute warning before, say, bedtime, then strictly enforce the deadline, this problem can be totally eliminated. Do not announce out of the blue, "Okay, troops. It's nine o'clock. Everybody to bed." Instead, give a warning that bedtime will arrive in so many minutes. Then, when the time comes, announce bedtime (or dinnertime, or time to leave for Granny's) and do *not* take no for an answer.

> When my LD class went outside for physical education, I took responsibility for watching the clock. Whether they were in the middle of a football game or scattered over the playing fields, I always gave them advance notice by holding up the appropriate number of fingers and shouting out the number of minutes left before we had to go in. If some were too far off to hear me, the others spread the word. Then, when I held my hand up to call them in, I demanded that they come on the run. And they did. (They knew slow movers would get no sympathy.)

LD and ADD people have a strong tendency to let time slip through their fingers. They dawdle. It seems to be part of their lack of a mental clock. Kermit, the thirty-eight-year-old department-store owner, was such a person. It took him at least an hour and a half just to get dressed! He would piddle around shining his shoes, brushing lint off his sports coat, selecting a tie, etc. He thought everybody moved through life that way—by just letting time slip past unnoticed. And he really believed others were selfish and inconsiderate when they got angry with him for being so slow.

In dealing with youngsters who have problems with time, it's usually best to find a way to work around the difficulty, rather than to meet it head-on. ("You'll be home on time or you'll go without dinner!" rarely helps.) It *is* important to be punctual. If this can't be accomplished in the regular way, other methods can be almost as effective. Creative solutions help LD and ADD children understand a weakness that they have to learn to live with.

7. RETRIEVAL PROBLEMS—COMMON

Everyone has experienced the frustration of having a word or phrase "on the tip of the tongue." Those with retrieval problems deal with this aggravating block constantly. They'll have an idea in their head but will not be able to find the words to say it. The difficulty usually carries over into written expression as well. They simply cannot generate language.

Children with retrieval problems can't hold their own in an argument, so they tend to punch a lot. Since they can't express their anger in words, they hit.

Retrieval problems are extremely hard to recognize and are often misunderstood by teachers as well as parents.

> Nine-year-old Norman looked like a little professor. This extremely intelligent fourth-grader was a strange little kid. He had so many social and behavioral problems that he had begun seeing a psychiatrist in the third grade. But the counseling didn't help much.
>
> Norman had already been diagnosed as learning disabled, but his retrieval problem was not recognized as important. This part of his disability needed to be dealt with before his behavior could be expected to improve.
>
> None of Norman's classmates liked him. He had a quick temper and got into a lot of fights. In addition to that, he was a pest in class. Norman was famous for raising his hand to answer and then, when called on, saying, "I forgot what I wanted to say." His teachers thought he was just trying to get attention. So instead of sympathy, understanding, and guidance, he'd get anger and criticism. Nobody realized that what looked like a bothersome habit was really a part of his learning disability. A great deal of emotional damage was done by whose who didn't understand.

Children who have trouble putting their ideas into words rarely recognize their difficulties with generating language. Since their skill with inner-self talk seems to be equally limited, they do not spend a lot of time analyzing the way their minds work. They are usually not in touch with their feelings and seem secretive and reluctant to be honest and open. When asked what they think, their typical response is, "I don't know. I hadn't thought about it." If asked to think about it now, their answer is likely to be short and superficial—and it will probably be based on parroting back the exact words that were used to state the question. They may talk on and on about the routine activities of their daily life, but when serious verbal thinking is required, they have little to say. To express their deep thoughts and innermost feelings, they need a medium other than words.

Isadora Duncan, the renowned dancer of the early 1900s, often told reporters it was impossible for her to explain what her dances meant. When asked to interpret one of her pieces, she would say, "If I could tell you what I mean, I wouldn't have to dance it." Beethoven gave a similar response to a friend who heard him play one of his piano sonatas and asked for an explanation. Rather than trying to verbally describe his ideas, the maestro simply played the piece a second time, finished with a flourish, and said, "That's what it means." Albert Einstein often claimed that he did all his thinking in pictures and only translated his visual thoughts into words when he wanted to share them. Many creative people find it easier to put their ideas into words after they've first expressed them through their preferred medium.

Children who have difficulty putting their thoughts and feelings into words are almost always misunderstood. Since they can successfully take in language through reading and hearing (decoding), it is hard to believe they are not able to put their ideas into words for writing and speaking (encoding). They look lazy or stubborn. They read a story with ease but somehow never manage to get around to doing the written questions. But it doesn't seem as if they *can't* do the written work.

Teachers have a hard time believing these children have a real problem with written work. They frequently express their suspicions by saying some of the following things:

> He just doesn't want to do it.
> He's a perfectly normal child and has no trouble with reading.
> He's just too busy daydreaming (or horsing around, or drawing, etc.).
> He's just got a mental block.
> He just thinks he can't do it.
> He has no trouble doing things he likes to do.
> He may have you fooled, but he isn't fooling me!

Children with expressive problems are often in trouble for failing to finish their written classwork. As a result, they miss recess a lot. And they are famous for not doing their homework. Since their parents and teachers keep blaming them for bad habits and laziness, serious emotional damage is done. The child does *not* understand his problem and grows to believe he is a worthless good-for-nothing. But the terrible psychological damage is totally unnecessary. This type of difficulty can be corrected to some extent, and there are many things that can be done to help the child compensate for his weakness. It is just as often found among children diagnosed as ADD as among those categorized as LD.

> Andy was diagnosed as learning disabled at the end of the first grade. With tears and hysteria, his parents sent him to a therapist, put him in a different school, and hoped for the best. After nine months of private instruction with a trained specialist, he was reading well above grade level. All his skills were satisfactory. Therapy was stopped. In a long conference, his parents were told how to guide their son through the future pitfalls he would face because of his expressive language problem.
> They were given the following advice:
>
> **A.** When Andy is babbling at the dinner table, trying to tell you about his day, don't tell him to shut up. Help him sort out his ideas. Listen to what he's attempting to say, not how he's saying it.
> **B.** Encourage Andy to tell you of the events in his life. Keep him talking. Give him practice. If he goes to a movie, take time to let him tell you about it. He'll have trouble relating

the story in the right sequence. Don't criticize him with "Can't you keep the story straight?" Rather, when he gets confused with the order of events, help him straighten them out with questions like these: "What happened first?" "What happened next?" "How did it end?"

C. When Andy has a word on the tip of his tongue but can't get it out, show that you care and understand. Help him face the fact that he is learning disabled while also encouraging him to keep trying. When he fumbles for a word and gives up on the whole story with "Oh, never mind," say something such as "Slipped away, huh?" If he's still discouraged, add, "Hey, don't quit without telling me how it finally worked out. You were just getting to the best part." In dealing with retrieval problems, be patient and sympathetic. Help Andy realize this is part of his learning disability. Remember that he needs extra time in expressing himself. And keep him talking.

D. Help Andy find outside activities that he enjoys. Sports are often a good outlet. But from what he's said and the work he's done so far, it looks like art might be his bag. It would be well worth your time and money to encourage him in this area. Sign him up for some of the children's art classes available around the community. He needs something in which he can find both success and pleasure.

E. Be prepared to fight for Andy against teachers and principals who don't understand. He is *not* lazy. He is *not* stupid. Don't ever let anyone try to convince him that he is. As he gets older, be prepared to fight for special adjustments in his assignments if and when they're needed. If he's flunking social studies in junior high because he can't write a good answer to an essay question, get them to test him some other way. He will have to do lots of things that are hard for him. See that he's not asked to do things that are *impossible* for him. But don't jump to his rescue too soon. Let him try before you decide he can't do it.

Both of Andy's parents followed these recommendations very carefully.

By the time the boy finished the fourth grade, he was an excellent student in every way. And he was very proud of his success. But most important, he was a perfectly normal, well-adjusted little boy. He knew he sometimes had trouble expressing himself, but it didn't bother him in the least. Friendly, outgoing, full of self-confidence, he showed no shame or embarrassment when he occasionally fumbled for a word or forgot what he wanted to say. Best of all, Andy didn't think of himself as learning disabled. He knew he was a little different. But he also knew he wasn't inferior.

Every year, LD therapists see a miracle or two. Andy certainly shines as one such case. But it was not the therapy that brought about the wonder of his success. It was his parents. They got him the best help available, then made sure that he did not become an emotional cripple. They adjusted their own actions to fit his needs. Their investment of time and energy is paying off handsomely.

8. POOR MOTOR CONTROL—COMMON

Some LD and ADD children are awkward or clumsy. They have trouble learning to skip or ride a bike, can't catch or throw a ball as well as their playmates can, never quite catch on to swinging a bat or a tennis racket. This poor motor control in large muscles shows up most clearly on the playground. They are usually the last ones picked for a team.

Kathy was in the fourth grade before her learning disability was recognized. As the pattern of her symptoms was explained to her family, her father shook his head and smiled. "Of our four kids, Kathy's always the one who spills her milk at the dinner table." She indeed had poor control of her large muscles.

Kathy's parents took a great interest in this area of her development. They left the schoolwork and the therapy to the school and concentrated their efforts on love, understanding, and sports. Fighting mixed dominance and extreme directional confusion in addition to poor motor control, they struggled to help their daughter find physical activities at which she could be successful.

By the time she entered junior high school, Kathy was winning medals and ribbons as a swimmer. And early in her high-school years, she took up tennis. Under the supervision of a good coach, she played successfully in many tournaments.

After high school, Kathy got an athletic scholarship to a large state university. After graduation, she became an outstanding physical education teacher. Her gentle, loving attitude helped children so much that she returned to college and got a master's degree in counseling.

The area that caused Kathy the most difficulty became the one in which she found the most success and pleasure.

The child with poor coordination in large muscle movement will not necessarily have trouble with fine motor movement. In the fourth grade, Kathy was awkward at sports but very good with her hands. She had excellent handwriting, loved to paint and draw, used scissors well, etc. Many LD and ADD children are in just the opposite situation. Some cannot control a pencil or work well with their hands but are poetry in motion on the athletic field. And a few youngsters have poor motor control in both large and small muscles. It is very hard for such children to find any activities at which they can be successful in either school, sports, art, or music. Yet even these children can be helped to find outlets they enjoy. The therapist will deal with the problems in schoolwork. It is up to the parents to help their child succeed in other areas.

> Ron was an eleven-year-old with a severe learning disability and attention deficit disorder. He was unusually large for his age, and his muscular build made him look as if he'd be a natural athlete. He had a passionate love of football, but unfortunately, he had very poor large and small muscle control, along with poor eye/hand coordination and extreme directional confusion. He never figured out a way to catch a ball. He either dropped it or let it plop to the ground beside him.
>
> But Ron was lucky. He came from a large, loving family that understood his problem and was determined to help him. Although he couldn't kick or catch or throw, his family encouraged him in his love of sports. By the time he entered junior high, he'd had several successful seasons in children's football leagues. He did well in defensive positions where he had to run and tackle. As long as he didn't have to handle the ball, he was terrific.

Many LD and ADD youngsters show no signs of difficulty with motor control, yet in real-life situations, they are klutzy. They can be talented little ballerinas, but when not moving gracefully to music, they will trip over their own feet. They can be the star of the football team, but when not flashing down the field evading tacklers, they will bump into doorjambs and corners of buildings. The problem is usually blamed on poor motor control but looks suspiciously like they're just not paying attention.

9. PROBLEMS WITH ATTENTION—COMMON

In 1980, an inability to focus was *rare* among LD students. Now, it is seen so often, it must be considered *common*.

LD children almost always have trouble paying attention. Their minds wander. The least little distraction will capture their attention and keep them from getting their work done. It is extremely common for students to be categorized as LD *and* ADD. No matter how they are labeled, the learning difficulties can't be resolved until something is done to help the students pay attention in class.

Youngsters who are classified as just plain ADD almost always have many of the characteristics associated with a learning disability. Most of them have difficulty with spelling, handwriting, sequencing, following directions, organizing time and materials, and expressing ideas in writing. Merely dealing with their attention problem will not solve all their academic difficulties.

Getting a youngster labeled ADD can usually be done quickly and inexpensively with one or two visits to the family physician. But getting a child diagnosed as learning disabled requires a complete evaluation by a psychologist. Such testing is time-consuming and extremely expensive.

Research studies show that LD and ADD children have little or no difficulty paying attention when taught one-to-one. Traditional techniques that have successfully helped these students since the early 1920s tend to require intense, close, private contact between pupil and teacher. In the schools of the 1990s, medication is more popular.

SHORT ATTENTION SPAN—TYPICAL

LD and ADD children tend to have an extremely short attention span. Their thinking works like a machine gun—in short spurts. They will tune into one thing briefly but quickly lose interest and let their thoughts move to something else. A book, a row of math problems, a conversation, a ball game, a TV program—few things hold their attention for very long. They can't seem to stick with any one activity.

Yet when playing Nintendo or building with Legos, they go into an overfocus that keeps them involved for hours. This superconcentration allows them to sustain their attention long after others would lose interest and move to something else—provided they are doing something they love. They will slip into the basement to do a little woodworking or duck out to the garage to tinker with the lawn mower and not emerge for hours. When called for dinner, they fail to show up at the table after repeated warnings and promises of "I'll be there in just a minute." It's like they've stepped into a time warp. The overfocus tends to kick on during whole-body, hands-on activities that the individual enjoys. It keeps musicians playing and actors performing long into the night. It's what gives authors, composers, artists, and craftsmen their persistence.

When parents watch their child spend hours contentedly building a go-cart, they find it hard to believe this same youngster can't generate more than three minutes of concentration for studying a spelling list. Abstract, verbal tasks require a narrow focus of attention that is entirely different from the wide-angle approach needed for artistic creativity or hands-on activities. Very few students learn how to use their overfocus on schoolwork.

DISTRACTIBILITY—TYPICAL

Most LD and ADD children are easily distracted. The least little noise or disturbance breaks their concentration. When they are working, they can't tune out tiny background disturbances. Almost any student will look up when someone walks into the classroom. LD and ADD students look up when someone walks down the hall, when a garbage can rattles two blocks away, or when a truck rumbles up a street halfway across town. Those with an attention deficit disorder and/or learning disability notice *everything* that's going on around them. Everything that can be seen, heard, smelled, or felt will draw their attention away from what they are doing.

Typically, LD and ADD individuals have a short attention span *and* are easily distracted, especially in their younger years. In school, they need to be in small, very structured classes. Parents need to provide them with a study place where they can work undisturbed by noise or interruptions from brothers and sisters. Many find it helpful to have a fan or quiet music in the background to screen out environmental sounds that would be distracting. Even things in their line of vision can draw their attention away from the task at hand. Placing their desk or study table so that it faces a blank wall is often beneficial.

HYPOACTIVITY—COMMON

Many LD and ADD youngsters are *underactive*. They move through life at an excruciatingly slow pace. No amount of pressure can get them to speed up their unhurried style of acting and thinking. Sharpening a pencil, doing their homework, walking down the hall—everything they do takes *much* longer than feels appropriate to others. The drummer they march to rarely matches the beat of any of those around them. Just getting these children out of bed and off to school can be an incredibly difficult chore.

> Eleven-year-old Matt was downright poky. Oozing along while being totally oblivious of time was a major aspect of his learning disability. He was bright, cute, and eager to please. Yet every morning, he got his widowed father and older brother into an uproar as they tried to get him dressed and fed and out of the house before the school bus left him behind.
>
> His family tried a whole list of solutions. It seemed that Matt just could not be made to move faster. Finally, in desperation, his father decided to let him skip breakfast at home. This freed the child to use all his time to get dressed, make his bed, brush his teeth, find his shoes, and catch the bus. Then, when he got to school, he would go to the cafeteria and buy breakfast. (If a morning meal had not been available at his school, he could have brought a sandwich and a piece of fruit to eat in homeroom.)

Hypoactive people are particularly prone to lapsing into a time warp when they get near water. They are famous for tying up a bathroom for hours. Washing cars, doing dishes, hosing off the driveway, watering the garden—tasks of this type tend to draw them into a dream world where they disconnect from the reality of reasonable time limits and schedules.

Hypoactive parents often have hyperactive children. It's a deadly combination! The slow-moving adult thinks it's a virtue to do everything with painstaking precision. In packing a school lunch, such a parent will take the time to neatly fold and crease the lunch bag, then carefully staple it closed at the top. On the day the hyperactive child packs up the noon meal without help, the sandwich gets thrown together, stuffed into a baggie, and tossed into the book bag—and the gooey knife is left right next to the open peanut butter jar, to be cleaned up by someone who isn't in such a hurry. Parents who move to their own drummer usually have children who do the same. But it's rarely the same drummer. Extreme differences in activity level can keep a family in a constant state of conflict.

HYPERACTIVITY—COMMON

Hyperactive children cannot sit still. They are constantly in motion—wandering around the room, wiggling, bouncing, hanging out of their seat, running instead of walking, always on the move. They are particularly prone to having something to fiddle with in their hands—especially as they get older.

Some LD and ADD children are hyperactive; most are not. Some children are hyperactive without being learning disabled. This is occasionally seen among those with a high level of intelligence. They seem to learn successfully even though they're hanging from the rafters. They drive their teachers and classmates crazy, but somehow they get the gist of what's going on. Others cannot learn while all their energy is channeled into physical activity but begin to succeed in school after being put on medication to help them control their focus of attention. And some can be drugged to a near stupor and still not be able to learn.

In highly structured classrooms with teachers who use multisensory teaching techniques and hands-on activities, most hyperactive students can thrive without medication. However, these high-energy youngsters have an extremely low tolerance for boredom. If the instructor runs a disorganized classroom, talks in a monotone, or fails to make the subject interesting, even the most highly motivated hyperactive students will be unable to keep their restlessness under control.

In general, medication tends to be grossly overused. A few

pediatricians no longer prescribe drugs for their hyperactive patients. Instead, these doctors recommend counseling with a psychologist trained to help overactive youngsters deal with their need to be in motion. In the hands of the right therapist, the results of such counseling can be very impressive.

There are times when carefully supervised medication produces remarkable results.

> Twelve-year-old Tommy had a severe learning disability, plus a condition that caused him to have convulsions. With the drugs he was taking to control his seizures, he was bounding around the classroom in a state of perpetual restlessness. His pediatrician assured his family that hyperactivity was a common side effect of his anticonvulsant medication and offered to prescribe another drug to counteract it. Tommy's parents decided that as long as their son's constant activity didn't prevent him from learning, they'd let the school work around it.
>
> Tommy was seated in the back of the classroom, where he could wiggle, bounce, lean, sprawl, pace, stand, or lie on the floor without bothering his classmates. He was allowed to move around the back half of the room as much as he wanted, provided he didn't disturb anyone else, didn't do anything dangerous, and gave his schoolwork his full *mental* attention.
>
> For more than a semester, this arrangement worked beautifully. Walking along the top of the cabinets or crawling under the furniture, he managed to stay tuned to what was going on in the class. No matter where he was in the room, he was always one of the most active participants in class discussions. He did all his work and was making good progress.
>
> Suddenly, in midwinter, Tommy started having trouble paying attention. He couldn't seem to get his work down, and he was often so lost during class discussions that he didn't even know what subject was being talked about. His mind wandered vaguely.
>
> The doctor added two pills to the handful Tommy was already taking daily. For the first few days, he was quiet and sleepy. He yawned a lot and even dozed off in class once or twice. But by the end of the first week, Tommy was back to normal—hyperactive and always on the move, but paying attention and learning.

As with Tommy, the medications usually used to control the difficulties associated with attention deficit disorder act to enhance concentration while also changing the level of activity. The hyperactive will still be in a hurry; the hypoactive will continue to be slow-moving. For those who find the drug effective, there is a noticeable difference in the ability to control the focus of attention and stay on task. Medication usually leads to a dramatic improvement in the ability to tolerate boredom.

ATTENTION DEFICIT DISORDER

Even when diagnosed by pediatric neurologists and neuropsychologists, identification of an attention deficit disorder is based on behavior exhibited in a variety of settings; reported by parents, teachers, or other firsthand observers; and defined on the basis of one of several rating scales. Since most ADD youngsters are evaluated without taking their learning problems into consideration, the characteristics associated with an attention deficit disorder include a wide range of difficulties outside the academic area. These children usually have many of the attributes described in this chapter, but the traits most commonly associated with their disorder center around concentration, disorganization, hyperactivity, and impulsive behavior.

Children and adults with ADD are almost always restless, wiggly, and easily distracted. Unless involved in some activity in which they are passionately interested, they are quickly bored and easily frustrated. When they do become absorbed in some enterprise, they drift into a deep overfocus that makes them forget meals, bedtime, and other routine events and commitments.

Those with ADD are famous for blunt remarks that hurt feelings or reveal secrets in conversation—blurted answers, ignored directions, and careless errors in class. They never know when to quit talking and often seem to lack the most basic social graces. They speak before they think, grab what they want, interrupt frequently, talk incessantly, and fail to realize that such behavior is offending others.

Snap decisions based on emotion and intuition are typical of those with an attention deficit disorder. Parents and teachers criticize them for acting without thinking. They see themselves as alert, spontaneous, decisive, strong, and brave. Their style of quick thinking leads to outstanding performances on the playing field, courageous actions in emergencies, and heroism on the battlefield. But it is devastating when applied to financial decisions, social situations, and schoolwork.

Individuals with ADD have a tendency to live outside the control of schedules and deadlines. When criticized for their chronic tardiness and told it is inconsiderate of others, they are highly offended and hurt. This is usually a lifelong source of friction with family, friends, teachers, and employers. Procrastination is typically part of the pattern, particularly on tasks that place heavy challenges on areas of weakness. Academic failure often results from their inability to get motivated until the pressure reaches explosive levels. In elementary school, it's book reports; in high school, research papers; in college, term papers, the master's thesis, and the Ph.D. dissertation. (How often does the A.B.D. of "All But Dissertation" really mean ADD?) Whenever it is that they hit the wall, it's likely to be a large written report that stresses their organizational skills beyond capacity.

10. DISORGANIZATION—TYPICAL

The tendency to be disorganized is common to almost all of those who have either a learning disability or an attention deficit disorder. They don't organize their time, their materials, their thoughts, their words. They show very little interest in maintaining a structured environment. Their bike is out in the yard or down at the park for the night, despite repeated warnings about rain, thieves, and punishments. The teacher has a string of zeros after their name for failing to turn in homework. Day after day, they claim they did the assignment but left it on the bus, on the kitchen table, in their locker. Sometimes, it's right there in their notebook, but their papers are in such a mess they can't find the one they need. If left to their own devices, they rarely figure out a logical method for keeping their stuff in order. And they have no desire to do so.

If a parent or teacher makes an attempt to get one of these students organized, the youngster is usually highly resistant to the whole idea. He doesn't want to use memory joggers like the rest of us. One teenager claimed he wasn't using the calendars and assignment sheets in his time-management system because he was philosophically opposed to being so pressured: "If I have so much to do that I have to write it all down just to stay on schedule, then I'm too busy. I don't want to live like that."

When LD or ADD individuals do get organized, they tend to go to extremes by setting up a system that strives for complete control and total order. They don't just hang up their clothes; they create a closet that's a work of art. The short-sleeve shirts go on one type of hanger, each one spaced precisely a quarter of an inch from its neighbor, in a particular section of the closet. The long-sleeve shirts require some other type of hanger and are kept in a neat row between the color-coded jackets and the sweaters. Linen shelves and silverware drawers get arranged with the perfection of a department-store display. Parents, spouses, and roommates find it extremely difficult to maintain the degree of order required to keep every object in its exact place. Whether they are slobs or neat nuts, organization is a lifelong source of difficulty for those with learning disabilities and/or attention deficit disorders. DISCARDED

The ten learning-disability symptoms listed so far are not directly related to school. They can be observed in any setting and can often be seen as warning signals long before a child actually attempts to learn to read and write and spell and do math. It is important to remember that some symptoms (such as mixed dominance and directional confusion) are very meaningful when seen in an older child but are of little or no significance in younger ones. Thus, it is important to avoid the temptation to jump to conclusions. A five-year-old who has directional confusion is not necessarily learning disabled; however, the same symptom should cause suspicion if seen beyond the age of seven. If observed in a ten-year-old, it would definitely be cause for concern.

Children with an attention deficit disorder are often recognized long before they enter school, particularly if they are hyperactive and difficult to manage. Once a youngster is labeled ADD, there is usually no further investigation regardless of the degree of academic success or failure.

Many professionals refuse to test for a learning disability until after a child has entered the first grade. These experts say that a young child with most of the symptoms discussed above is "high risk" and recommend an attitude of "wait and see." They do not believe in beginning therapy until the youngster actually tries to learn—and fails.

Other professionals, equally qualified, hold the opposite view. Research has shown that careful testing can be from 82 percent to more than 95 percent accurate in predicting learning failure in children age five or older. Unfortunately, the evaluation process necessary to make such a forecast is extremely time-consuming and expensive. Based on that fact, many believe in "early intervention" or "preventive measures." They recommend screening all youngsters in four- and five-year-old kindergarten classes, then thoroughly testing those who show signs of potential learning problems. By doing this, the high-risk children are taught their basic skills by alternative methods that are known to be effective for LD and ADD students. Then they may never have to experience failure.

It is very, very difficult to be certain that a child under the age of six is learning disabled. However, no LD child should go beyond the middle of the first grade without being recognized and given appropriate help. On the other hand, those with a severe attention deficit disorder are often recognized long before beginning kindergarten.

The remaining symptoms of learning disabilities and attention deficit disorders cannot be observed until after the child has entered school.

11. TENDENCY TOWARD REVERSALS—TYPICAL

Many people think the learning disabled (or at least those with dyslexia) read backwards. It's not quite that simple. If it were, correcting the problem would be easy.

The person with a learning disability (and a great many with ADD) will read *some* letters backwards or upside down *sometimes*. For instance, the formation of a "stick and ball" can be arranged five different ways to form the letters *b, d, p, g*, and *q*. A child with reversal problems might look at the word *got* and read *pot* or *dot* or *bot*. But this same youngster will sometimes guess the letters correctly and read it as *got*. In reading, certain letters are more commonly reversed than others: *m* and *w, n* and *u,* in addition to *b, d, p, g,* and *q.* In writing, almost any letter may be reversed.

This tendency usually carries over to reading whole words or some of the letters within a word: *was* becomes *saw, pot* may be read as *top, lisp* might be interpreted as *lips* or *slip.* The letters within a word are sometimes totally scrambled: *early* may be read as *really, usually* might be called *casually,* etc. This tendency is especially noticeable in math, where the child will scramble the order of large numbers in either copying a problem from the book or working it: *7200* might become *2700, 17* turns into *71,* etc. Not every number is rearranged. Not even most of them get jumbled. But it happens often enough to make math very difficult. Teachers usually know to watch for this tendency in students with a learning disability. However, students with an attention deficit disorder are prone to such reversals, too. When seen in the written work of those with ADD, it's almost always blamed on carelessness.

Words or phrases within a sentence sometimes become totally rearranged: "Was it really?" might be read "He was really" (or even "He was early"). "He lived in the house under the hill" might become "He lived under the house in the hill."

All young children make some reversals. This is not necessarily a sign of a learning disability unless the child is still doing it after the age of seven or eight. The tendency toward reversals is related to directional confusion. It is very hard for the learning disabled to stick completely within the pattern of reading from left to right. Most of them would just as soon read upside down or backwards.

12. POOR ORAL READING—TYPICAL

The learning disabled are famous for the trouble they have in reading "little words." Teachers find it puzzling that these youngsters seem like they could read if they'd just put their minds to it. Most of their mistakes look like careless errors. This same pattern is very common among children diagnosed as having an attention deficit disorder.

It does seem strange that a person who can read *elephant, shrimp, father, mother, Mississippi*, and *Kellogg's Corn Flakes* cannot read *of, who, from, does, he, in, it*, and the other three- or four-letter words that make up most of our language. But that is the normal pattern for the learning disabled.

> At twenty-two, Bob tested at twelfth-grade level in silent reading. When reading to himself, he definitely read well. Yet when he read aloud, he made so many errors that the material often made no sense at all.
>
> This didn't bother Bob. He'd butcher the passage but still be able to understand it completely! He seemed to have a mental translator that somehow unscrambled the mess.

LD individuals with high intelligence very often become excellent silent readers but never overcome their difficulty with oral reading.

13. POOR HANDWRITING AND DYSGRAPHIA—COMMON

Illegible penmanship is extremely common among males with either a learning disability or attention deficit disorder. In the primary grades, they have trouble developing enough skill at manuscript to make their work even moderately readable. Most of them never switch to cursive. Although they usually claim that they know how to write in the more mature connected form used by their classmates, they almost always insist that they prefer to continue using their messy printing on the grounds that it's faster. Those with artistic talent often develop the exquisitely geometric printing typical of architects and draftsmen, yet they refuse to even consider cursive for anything other than the formality of a signature.

Girls, on the other hand, rarely have such difficulties with dysgraphia. Those who have trouble acquiring skill in reading and spelling may have to struggle to master penmanship. But LD and ADD females who follow the common pattern of academic problems focused in the areas of math and reading comprehension usually have no trouble with the manuscript of the early grades and easily switch to cursive in the fourth or fifth grade. Typically, they develop a style of backhand writing with evenly spaced, chubby, rounded letters.

For students with some degree of dysgraphia, the writing problem encompasses more than the simple matter of not being able to get a pencil to do what is wanted. There's a wide range of other difficulties involved.

When first learning to write, children with dysgraphia have trouble remembering what the different letters look like. A child may know that he needs to make a letter *g* but be unable to recall how a *g* looks. Without therapy, this problem sometimes lasts into or beyond the third grade. And after the student finally gets a picture of each of the letters in his head, he finds he has trouble remembering how to form them with a pencil.

> I always placed a large handwriting chart in the very front of my classroom. My fourth- through eighth-grade students often referred to it. Even with the alphabet written clearly before them, it was not at all unusual for a pupil to ask, "How do you make a *j*? I see it on the chart. I know what it looks like. But I forgot how to make it. Where do you start?"

LD and ADD children find this problem terribly bothersome and embarrassing. In a regular classroom (and often at home), they catch a lot of sarcasm and criticism because of their inability to remember how letters are formed, particularly if they have been diagnosed as ADD but have no awareness of the LD component of their problem. Comments such as the following, often uttered by teachers and parents with a sigh of disgust, are common. "For heaven's sake, you're in the sixth grade. Don't you think it's about time you learned to make your letters?" Or "I just showed you how to make an *f* last week. You can't have forgotten." Or "Okay, I'll show you again. But this is the last time."

Most LD or ADD sixth-graders wouldn't raise their hands to ask for such help in the first place. They're not stupid. In asking for assistance, they'd be revealing dangerous information to their classmates.

Most twelve-year-olds would handle the situation with this logic: "I'll hide the fact that I don't know how to make that letter by writing extra-messy." The other students probably *would* make some very cutting remarks if they ever discovered the problem. Getting into trouble for a messy paper is much less painful.

Even those who master recall and letter formation may not be home free. There is one further problem that is even more horrible than the others. It can be called "stubborn hand." As an example, let's say a child wants to write the word *sat*. He knows he wants to make an *s*, he knows what an *s* looks like, and he knows how to make it. So he gives his hand the command to write an *s*. And out pops an *l* or a *v* or some other unintended letter. It makes the youngster furious. If it happened only once in a while, it wouldn't be so bad. But this happens all the time! The student gets so angry and upset that he wants to jump up and down and scream. He can't even trust his own hand! Sometimes, the frustration gets to be more than a child can bear. Tears, tantrums, thrown pencils, papers ripped to shreds—this problem can produce absolute rage.

No wonder LD and ADD children erase so often. Their handwriting difficulties go far beyond poor penmanship. Their problems with getting words onto paper go far beyond poor spelling.

Dysgraphia is usually just a small part of a larger, more general disability. But chances are that if you ever see an LD or ADD child fall apart completely, the tears and tantrum will come when there's a pencil in a balky hand.

14. INABILITY TO COPY ACCURATELY—TYPICAL

"How do you spell *applesauce*?" an LD or ADD child asks.

The teacher writes it on the board, or his mother jots it down on a piece of paper.

Still, one of the *p*'s gets left out, or the *le* is reversed, or the *c* gets turned into an *s*.

Noticing the error, the adult then spouts the standard lecture: "It's bad enough you can't spell *applesauce* yourself. But when I take the time to write it for you, you still misspell it. All you have to do is open your eyes! Good heavens, *anybody* can copy!"

Anybody but those with an attention deficit disorder or a learning disability.

From the youngest children to adults who read successfully, LD and ADD individuals have a great deal of difficulty copying accurately.

This copying problem doubles a child's chance for errors in math. Even when the calculations are done correctly, problems turn out to be wrong because they were copied from the book inaccurately. For those who dislike math in the first place, this makes it really rough.

It is common for a mother to tell of the awful experiences she has had trying to help her LD or ADD child write a report. After hours of struggling to get it all down on paper and getting the spelling corrected, the youngster is sent off to copy it neatly. For every spelling mistake that has already been found and repaired, the child puts in two new ones by making mistakes in the process of copying. The finished paper may be neat, but it's full of spelling errors again.

Phone numbers, addresses, dates, and times are constant problems for those with a learning disability or an attention deficit disorder. Their inability to copy such information accurately causes them much inconvenience and embarrassment.

15. POOR SPELLING—TYPICAL

Difficulty with spelling is the most sensitive indicator of a learning disability. And almost all those who have an attention deficit disorder have trouble with spelling as well. Many LD and ADD individuals conquer their problems in other areas but never manage to become better-than-adequate spellers—if they become that good. No matter what type of disability they have, almost all LD and ADD people are poor spellers.

Several weaknesses come together to cause this. The inability to remember a sequence in the correct order is one factor. The tendency toward making reversals is another. A "stubborn hand" that can't be trusted to produce the desired letters can make it still tougher. And, as if that weren't enough, LD and ADD children often have a poor visual memory. They can't examine a word they've written and tell whether or not it "looks right."

In reading, there are ways to compensate for these weaknesses; the printed page is full of clues that help the reader figure out difficult words. In spelling, however, the writer is forced to rely on his own resources. Training in phonics and the rules of spelling helps. But only about 80 percent of English words are spelled phonetically. For anyone who is a poor speller by nature, that leaves a lot of room for error.

Becoming a good speller is similar to becoming a good violinist. No amount of instruction and practice can overcome a basic lack of talent. Students need to understand that with real effort they will improve, but that it is highly unlikely they will ever qualify for the Olympic spelling team.

16. TROUBLE GETTING IDEAS ONTO PAPER—COMMON

Most of those with a learning disability or an attention deficit disorder are good at expressing themselves orally. In fact, they often have difficulty in class and in their personal lives because they talk too much. (Among those with an attention deficit disorder, it is considered normal to be overly—even compulsively—talkative.) Whether LD or ADD, the vast majority can carry on an intelligent conversation with no difficulty. Their thoughts flow smoothly, their vocabulary is rich, their pronunciation is clear and precise, and they present their ideas in a way that is interesting and easily understood. But put a pencil in the hand of those same individuals and they can't think of a thing to say. All their ideas dry up. They simply cannot express themselves in writing!

Children who have this problem hate to write. Their constant protest of "I don't know what to say" makes it look as if they're just trying to get out of doing their work. This is only partly true. Indeed, to them there is no torture worse than trying to put a few ideas on paper. But their pitiful pleading about not knowing what to say is also true. It's more than a mental block caused by their hatred of writing. It's a major part of a learning disability, and it's almost always a significant difficulty for those with ADD.

Even on those occasions when they know what they want to say, the idea slips away before it gets recorded on paper. With this kind of expressive disability added to the problems involving handwriting and spelling, it's no wonder LD and ADD children explode with rage while trying to write a small report.

17. BEHAVIOR PROBLEMS—TYPICAL

LD and ADD children who are not given help and understanding tend to become either hostile and aggressive or withdrawn. Their self-esteem crumbles. Which child will turn against the world in anger and which will wither in shame? The type of reaction a youngster displays seems related to the child's basic personality, rather than to the type or severity of the learning or concentrating problem.

The human mind is never idle. Students who cannot do their classwork find something else to do. Whether they make spitballs, wander around the room, draw, pester classmates, or daydream, they find a way to keep themselves occupied. This behavior is *not* the problem. It is the child's way of dealing with the problem.

In young children, such behavior problems almost always go away as a result of successful academic therapy, since frustration and bad behavior haven't continued long enough to become habits. As they overcome their learning weaknesses, they go back to normal behavior. If given help in the first or second grade, they never have a chance to suffer from the anger and pain of failure. They aren't forced deeper and deeper into patterns of poor behavior and psychological problems because they understand themselves and their learning difficulties.

But most learning disabilities are *not* discovered in the first grade. (Many of those with severe ADD are recognized at a young age, but they are rarely offered any help beyond medication.) And the learning difficulties are usually only the beginning of the students' problems.

Parents and teachers are quick to put pressure on the struggling first-grader. They tell the child to try harder, pay attention, sit still, quit fooling around, get down to business. In their frustration, they accuse the youngster of being lazy. The struggling first-grader sees all his classmates learning easily and wonders how they do it. It looks like there must be some secret to their success, but no one will tell what it is. So the child becomes convinced that the failure to learn is his own fault. He feels stupid. From this, two emotions develop: anger and guilt. Every little failure hurts. Each defeat makes the child angry. His failure makes him feel ashamed. With these feelings controlling the child, it becomes difficult for him to get along with others. Very quickly, the lack of success in school affects everything and everybody.

Teachers usually have names for their reading groups: the Bluebirds, the Cardinals, the Robins, the Sparrows, the Buzzards. No matter how careful they are to hide the fact with cute names or numbers, their students know which group is the low one. Being in the low group hurts; being unsuccessful in the low group hurts even more. Classmates tease. They make fun of failing LD students because they just can't seem to do anything right.

Those with an attention deficit disorder don't just fail in reading. They can't sit still and pay attention during *any* of the day's academic activities. Their trouble with disorganization sets them up for failure in almost every area. And teachers spend a lot of time criticizing and punishing them. They're usually not very popular with the other children unless they show real talent on the playground and get chosen first for kickball games and running races. Their classmates get tired of hearing the teacher yell at them. It often ruins her sunny disposition, so no students have as good a day as they would if this out-of-control troublemaker were elsewhere.

Unfortunately, word spreads. It isn't long before LD and ADD youngsters become unpopular around their neighborhood. Somehow, everybody finds out that they can't read the baby books with the big print, spell their name, produce a neat-looking paper, remember to bring their homework. Stories of their disasters in school spread among their friends. The kids on the block laugh at them. Young children with a learning disability or an attention deficit disorder spend a lot of their playtime running home in tears, starting fights, or changing friends (often taking up with younger children who don't know what's going on in school). Or they quit playing with other children altogether.

These troubles quickly ruin two parts of a child's life: school and play. Home is the only hope left. But by the middle of that first school year, the child's mother is in a panic, his father is furious, and his brothers and sisters have started making fun of him. He's already feeling angry and ashamed. From every side, he gets criticism and pressure. No matter where he turns, he can find no help or understanding. So he becomes hostile and aggressive, or he withdraws. He either takes on the whole world as his enemy or slips off to daydream in an imaginary world of his own. His whole life revolves around either fighting or hiding.

The farther such children go in school, the worse the problem becomes. A few years of this does emotional damage, but it can usually be corrected. Four or five years does great psychological damage that can sometimes be overcome, but not always. Seven or more years of this horrible pattern usually leaves scars that can never be totally erased. By junior high school, the learning disability or attention deficit disorder has become so deeply buried under emotional problems that the child is very hard to recognize as disabled, and often cannot be reached.

Adolescents with unrecognized learning disabilities or attention deficit disorders often try to escape through drugs or alcohol. (Doctors and psychologists call this "self-medicating.") When the world is as black as theirs is, anything that will allow a few hours of pleasure is welcomed. Suicide, of course, is the ultimate out. But it's rare. Somehow, most of these teenagers manage to limp along. They wait to turn sixteen and drop out of school. They develop patterns of behavior—often bizarre—that allow them to cope. If diagnosed as LD or ADD during their teens, they often refuse help.

Although these emotional problems make LD and ADD children hard to deal with, they often are the symptoms that lead to diagnosis. Students with behavior problems draw attention to themselves. The child who is obnoxious has a good chance of being sent to the school psychologist for testing. Yet the LD youngster who fails to learn but amuses himself quietly and fades into the woodwork rarely gets help.

A fourth-grade teacher had a strange little boy in her class who was always eating the cuffs of his sweaters and shirts. Alert and bright, Barry was one of her best readers. But he never did his homework. Fed up with his habits, she cornered him in the hall one morning and demanded an explanation. He responded by shrugging his shoulders and piping, "I guess I'm just lazy."

Any child who can so glibly confess to being lazy deserves further investigation. No one expected to find anything of significance, but Barry was given a full evaluation just in case.

The testing quickly confirmed two things: Barry had a high IQ, and his reading skills were well above his grade level. However, much to everybody's surprise, the testing also revealed a definite learning disability. Barry had a severe case of dysgraphia.

If he hadn't been eating his clothes and come out with that one off-the-wall remark, his school problems never would have been understood.

Therapy and counseling started immediately. After four years of a long, uphill fight, Barry received an award for being the most improved student in his school. He was also given a prize for some of his artwork. By the time he was fifteen, he was in great shape.

Barry hopes to go to a top-notch university and become an aeronautical engineer. He'll probably make it.

Ty began LD therapy when he was twelve years old. Very small for his age, a year behind in school, prone to tantrums and other emotional outbursts, the child was having serious difficulties. Ty was so insecure that he still sucked his thumb in front of his sixth-grade classmates.

After working with him one-to-one for nearly a month, Ty's therapist went in for a routine conference with her supervisor. She reported on her progress with the boy, then concluded, "I think he needs a psychiatrist."

The supervisor, who had an extensive background in learning disabilities and a Ph.D. in clinical psychology, replied flatly, "Ty needs to learn to read. He needs LD therapy."

The therapist thought her overseer was wrong but promised to follow orders and just keep teaching the child.

Three months of work on Ty's learning disability proved the psychologist right. With every step of progress he made with his language skills, the boy's behavior in class improved. His therapist did not do any counseling with the youngster. She was open about the fact that she liked him and cared about him, but their time together was devoted strictly to LD therapy.

Ty's emotional problems were not being solved because he was working with those problems themselves. His emotional problems were helped because he was learning at last.

TWO SIDE ISSUES WORTH KNOWING

In addition to the symptoms already discussed, there are two characteristics that seem to be found in most LD and ADD children. One makes their problems all the more difficult to overcome. The other is a quality that is probably their greatest asset.

LEAKS AND LAPSES

Children with a learning disability or an attention deficit disorder seem to have a memory that leaks. They can learn something new in class, practice it until they have it down pat, convince everybody they've got it, then wake up one morning with the whole skill gone. Sometimes, what was learned has leaked out and will not come back until it is relearned. Other times, it's just a lapse of memory and the skill will come back by itself later.

Because of these leaks and lapses, LD and ADD children are "on" one day and "off" the next. The fact that a student cannot do the multiplication tables today does not mean the task was equally impossible yesterday. And there is no telling what skill level will be there tomorrow! Living with this kind of memory is rough. LD and ADD children don't understand it either.

CREATIVENESS

Most of those with a learning disability or an attention deficit disorder are unusually creative. They seem to look at the world in a different way. They are more observant than other people. They approach problems from a unique perspective and come up with surprising solutions. Many researchers have demonstrated that the reason for this is physical. The majority of those with learning disabilities or attention deficit disorders have weaknesses in the verbal, analytical processing style associated with the left hemisphere of the cerebral cortex. These deficiencies in left-brain development are balanced out by an overdevelopment in the right hemisphere. And the right half of the brain is the seat of creativity. Many of the world's greatest creative geniuses had the characteristics we now associate with learning disabilities and attention deficit disorders: da Vinci, Edison, Einstein, Picasso, and Rodin, to name just a few.

> For several years, I taught language arts to seventh- and eighth-graders in a small private school for underachievers, almost all of whom could be classified as LD or ADD or both.
>
> The headmaster and I agreed that the students needed an art program. Though unskilled and untrained, I ended up taking on the project. Armed with a very small supply of paint, chalk, brushes, paste, paper, and various scrounged materials, I began teaching art.
>
> The students were self-conscious and cautious at first. Gradually, they loosened up and began expressing themselves freely. Their work was so amazing that the headmaster began coming in to observe. Halls, corridors, and classrooms were soon covered with some truly fine samples of children's artwork.
>
> In March, my twenty-three art students prepared and submitted more than forty pieces of their work to the Red Cross International Children's Art Festival. Of the works entered in the contest, the judges accepted twenty-four. They became part of a permanent collection that was exhibited all over the world! That's incredible.

> My fifth- and sixth-grade LD class was working on a social studies lesson. Tommy was participating in the discussion from a position behind a room divider made of shelves and cabinets. (He was the hyperactive one who was so restless that he was allowed to roam freely in the back half of the classroom.) During that particular class, he often wanted to ask a question or volunteer an answer. To do so, he would crawl to the edge of the cabinets, poke his head around the corner, and raise his hand. Desks and chairs and legs and feet made it hard for me to see him down there on the floor. Sometimes, he had to wait a long time to get my attention.
>
> Tommy must have gotten tired of waiting so long to be called on. But he gave no sign of being unhappy with the situation. He simply decided to resolve the problem for himself.
>
> At a key point in the lesson, I asked a really tough question.

Several students tried to answer it, but no one seemed to be able to figure it out.

From over the top of the room divider, something caught my eye: a hand—no, a mitten—waving on the end of a long stick. Tommy had his "hand" up.

I nearly burst into laughter right there in front of the class. But Tommy's face was serious. The junk in the cupboards had not been fashioned into a hand as a joke. The mitten on the stick was "for real." Tommy wanted to participate in the discussion, so he created a solution that allowed him to be called on.

When he finally got his chance, he wasn't even grinning. He just gave the right answer.

The creativity of LD and ADD children is a fascinating subject worthy of a whole book in itself. Those who have run LD classes for years learn to rely on their students to solve routine problems. When the janitor is unsuccessful in fixing the pencil sharpener, one of the students is sure to bring in the necessary tools and take care of it. When a window gets broken and the repairman can't get there immediately, some young member of the class will take the initiative to round up some odds and ends from the cupboards and have it patched up in just a few minutes. Time after time, these creative youngsters solve problems around the classroom—usually in ways no adult would ever have thought of. I learned from experience that if an LD or ADD child says, "Why don't you do it this way?" it pays to listen. If any kid in the school can figure it out, build it, rearrange it, put it together, adjust it, fix it, or make it work, the LD or ADD kid can!

Because of their open-ended approach to solving problems, their free-flowing creativity, and their imagination that considers possibilities most of us do not see, LD and ADD children are a constant source of amazement and delight.

3

ADD AND MEDICATION:
What Else Helps?

Some people have trouble controlling their focus of attention. Their minds wander. They're easily distracted. They have a short attention span. Some can't sit still. They're wiggly and restless. Modern medicine has created drugs to adjust the balance of the brain chemicals that control concentration. Many embrace them as an avenue to the rich benefits of academic achievement otherwise unavailable to students having attention deficit disorder. An equal number abhor them as part of the medicine-closet mentality that dominates our drug-crazed culture and its desire for easy answers and instant gratification.

The controversy over medication rages. It will subside. Other answers will emerge. But the problems will remain the same: children who don't pay attention have trouble in school, and adults who have problems with concentration are handicapped in their work as well as their private lives.

With or without medication, those who have difficulty concentrating can learn to direct their focus of attention. The suggestions in this chapter are for those who want to take control.

> Fireball Hurt was a farm boy from Idaho, full of energy and burning with ambition. He equated himself with go-getters like those in Horatio Alger stories. He was smart. He was determined. He thought of his boundless energy as his greatest asset. He died at the age of eighty-four racing to the airport to catch a plane with his fifty-eight-year-old girlfriend. To his grieving ladylove, he left diamonds, furs, a fancy car, and a condo in Florida.
>
> Fireball Hurt considered his life a success. He never slowed down.

In his day, Fireball Hurt was a powerhouse—conscientious, observant, spontaneous, quick, daring, and outspoken. Today, he would be labeled as someone with an attention deficit disorder—hyperactive, compulsive, distractible, impulsive, impatient, impetuous, and rude. The live wire of the 1920s is now described as loud and restless. When judged by the social standards of the 1990s, the human dynamo of the past was a workaholic.

Those with attention deficit disorder have always been with us. They have been described as strong-willed, energetic, quick, alert, fast-paced. We used to make allowances for their artistic temperament. Nonconformists were assumed to be innovators. We had use for the exuberance of adventuresome little rascals. After dipping pigtails in inkwells and sneaking cigarettes behind the barn, they went off to war to become heroes. They got addicted to nicotine and caffeine (and possibly alcohol) and thought of themselves as courageous, honest, hardworking, and strong. We were building a nation and needed their energy, their creativity, their enterprising spirit. We needed their sweat to make our assembly lines hum. There was work for everybody, and success in school was not a requirement for making it to the top. We were a restless nation. We wanted everything bigger and better and faster. Those we now characterize as having an attention deficit disorder embodied our highest ideals. They hurled themselves into creating a great American society that would have no use for the boundless energy they passed on to their children and grandchildren.

In today's schools, the traits that were tolerated and often admired by previous generations are likely to lead to punishment and failure. After over fifty years of research into human behavior, we now have definite limits on what we consider "normal." Children who blurt out answers in class, interrupt, can't wait their turn, never follow directions, rarely seem to listen, shift from one uncompleted task to another, and jump into action without thinking are labeled *impulsive*. In a nation alarmed by increases in crime and violence, impulsivity is *not* acceptable. In addition to providing the traditional academics, educational institutions are expected to teach young people to think before they act. This never was an easy task, but now that it is receiving such emphasis, ADD children seem to be coming out of the woodwork. This could also account for the rapid rise in the number of children on stimulant medication. For youngsters who respond well to medication, even a moderate dosage can vastly improve the ability to control impulsive behavior.

> A woman in her mid-forties was on a panel of ADD adults. When asked to explain how her life had changed since she began to take Ritalin, she talked about increased concentration, decreased hyperactivity, and newly developed organizational skills. In the two years since starting on medication, she had returned to college and completed a degree in accounting. But she believed that academic success was not the most important thing she'd gained through medication.
>
> To this mature woman, the most prized achievement was her new ability to control her impulsive behavior. "Now I have patience," she said, "and it's changed my life." She was delighted with her ability to quietly consider her options before leaping into action. She said she no longer made so many "dumb decisions."
>
> It was surprising how many aspects of her life had changed since she started making carefully thought-out choices rather than snap judgments. There had been a radical change in her relationships with other people. She said, "Now that I don't just blurt out the first thing that pops into my mind, I have friends. I get along better with my children. I'm an entirely different person." Even her financial situation had improved. For years, she'd been an impulse buyer. Although still paying off some of her debts, she was finding it easy to exercise self-control on issues concerning when and where to spend money.

After describing the "knee-jerk decisions" that had kept her in a perpetual state of crisis, she beamed, "Now, I'm in control." With a deep sigh, she surveyed her audience before adding, "And it feels wonderful."

Her new attitude of calm and poise was clearly evident.

For schoolchildren, impulsive behavior combines with hyperactivity and an inability to concentrate to produce some devastating results. Antsy youngsters who don't pay attention to schoolwork tend to amuse themselves with whistling, humming, constant talking. They keep their hands busy with spitballs, paper airplanes, toys, and jabs at neighbors. The ones who are quick-witted take center stage as the class clown. Teachers can't stand it when a student wiggles, talks, taps, bounces, makes noises, fidgets, and roams around the room, keeping everybody else in the class from concentrating. And when restless children don't change their behavior after repeated corrections, classmates and teachers alike resent the offenders' uncooperative attitude and lack of consideration. The ugly confrontations that result keep everyone on edge. In a regular classroom, the behavior that is typical of ADD students makes them extremely unpopular with everyone unfortunate enough to be trapped in the confined space with them. They are repeatedly punished for behavior over which they have no control, and so is everybody else.

Historically, those who have lived successfully with an attention deficit disorder were the ones who learned how to use it. Athletes who train for hours don't find excess energy to be a disadvantage. Entertainers who perform far into the night need sleep patterns that don't match the rest of the world's.

A night watchman at a large hotel was complaining about his son's academic difficulties. The teenager stayed up most of the night tinkering with his car, listening to his stereo, talking on his CB. With the late hours he kept, it was nearly impossible to get him out of bed in time for school. He slept through most of his morning classes. Naturally, his grades were horrible.

When asked about his own sleep habits, the father explained that he found it easiest to stay on the same schedule even on nights he didn't have to work the late shift. He said he hated lying in bed for hours, tossing and turning, unable to drift off to sleep.

The son's pattern sounded very similar to that of his father. The youth insisted that no matter what time he turned in, he couldn't get to sleep until it was almost dawn. He hated lying in bed tossing and turning. Like father, like son.

The schoolboy's sleeplessness caused problems; the father's wakefulness was an asset.

Times have changed, but there are still lots of jobs that take advantage of the unique patterns common among those with ADD.

Writers, artists, inventors, architects, and poets find daydreaming and overfocus particularly useful. They lock themselves away for days or weeks while bringing their ideas into reality. It's said that Handel created the entire *Messiah* in just twenty-three days. In that gigantic three-hour oratorio, the "Hallelujah Chorus" is just one of the *smaller* pieces! Researchers report that Thomas Edison slept only a few hours a day. He believed others wasted a large portion of their lives on needless slumber. Edison was so completely consumed by his work that he slipped away from his own wedding reception to put in a few hours at the lab. Once there, the time warp of superfocus caught him and he forgot about the wedding party entirely. The new Mrs. Edison didn't see her bridegroom until the best man was sent to get him around midnight. When the creative process flashes white-hot with inspiration, the ability to get totally engrossed in a project has tremendous value.

Those with ADD may have trouble with a wandering mind and forget to pick up a few items at the grocery store, return a phone call, or take out the garbage, but when they're "doing their thing," no detail is too insignificant to hold their attention. They may race through everyday life at breakneck speed, but when the work is part of their passion, no amount of pressure can force a faster pace. Methodical to the point of perfectionism, patient to the point of obstinacy, dreamers with the power of superfocus keep going far beyond the point where others would give up. It's said that Thomas Edison made over sixteen hundred prototype light bulbs before he finally got one to work. Surely, some of his friends were saying, "Don't you think maybe it's time to give up?" What we admire now as perseverance and tenacity must have appeared to be muleheaded stubbornness to those who didn't think he would succeed.

> A highly talented artist and illustrator is well known for the slapdash pattern of his daily habits. He has locked himself out of his car so many times that his wife had the locks taken off the doors. His neighbor shudders when he walks into her house because she knows the extent of the destruction his carelessness causes to upholstery and china. Yet when this one-man demolition team sits down at his drawing board, he becomes totally focused and calm. He becomes so absorbed in his work that he loses track of time. The hours usually set aside for meals and sleep come and go unnoticed. His movements become slow and deliberate as he painstakingly draws his exquisitely intricate pen-and-ink illustrations.
>
> This artist thinks his greatest gift is his amazing power of concentration. He has no idea that his ability to sustain attention is really the overfocus associated with an attention deficit disorder.

Living comfortably with ADD is easy for those who have a passionate interest that makes their attention problems into an asset. Dreams that fit their talents provide an overriding purpose into which they can channel their energy. By totally committing themselves to attaining a goal, they develop a clear sense of direction that makes every element of their personality part of the drive toward success.

GOALS

Goal setting is a powerful tool in controlling and directing the scattered energies of those with ADD. Having a dream provides an overriding purpose that makes it much easier to make day-to-day choices. Big dreams focus attention and aim activity into channels leading toward the objective. They make time and energy into valuable commodities that are too precious to be wasted. Those with a clear vision of what they wish to attain develop the insight (and desire) to think before they act. Whims of the moment become less appealing when seen as detours leading away from the path of success. Lofty ambitions create a tolerance for boredom. Even the most tedious tasks can be satisfying when recognized as important steps

toward a desired achievement. Major aspirations create the determination to overcome failure and frustration.

For those with no obvious talent, it takes some searching to find
activities that could develop into areas of special interest. Activities
that allow for personal creativity are the most likely to have appeal.
Some of the ones worth exploring include sports (particularly
individual athletics like swimming, cross-country, track and field,
wrestling, weightlifting, and gymnastics); music; art; drama; dance;
photography (including video); mechanical tinkering and repairing;
racing of all kinds (as participant or spectator); breeding, raising, and
training animals (horses are particularly popular with girls); outdoor
activities like camping, backpacking, sailing, and fishing (especially
adventuresome pastimes such as rock climbing, rafting, surfing, skiing, scuba diving, windsurfing, hang gliding, skydiving and street
sports like in-line skating and skateboarding); games like chess, back-
gammon, and billiards; arts and crafts (girls often have a special fond-
ness for working with fabrics and yarns, while boys show a strong
preference for creating three-dimensional objects in clay, metal, glass,
and wood); drawing, architecture, and interior design; computers;
electronics; aviation; collecting. The list goes on and on. As long as
the activity has a strong physical component and relies on the use of
visual/spatial thinking, it is likely to have great appeal.

Not every activity offers the possibility of developing into a passionate interest. There has to be the promise that success will bring
rewards that make all the effort worth it. Only successes that make
the individual proud of himself are likely to grow into the kind of
overriding dream that can make a person with ADD want to achieve
control.

Although most ADD youngsters seem to prefer individual sports,
athletic teams and school-based activities offer some unique advantages. In addition to providing highly attractive goals, they create a
comfortable environment for easy social interaction and offer rich
rewards in social status.

Youngsters who join a team will change their habits in order to
meet the coach's training requirements or maintain eligibility. They'll
stay away from smoking, drinking, and drugs. They'll give up their

favorite junk foods to follow a power diet designed to build the muscles and stamina needed on the playing field. They'll keep more reasonable hours and get plenty of sleep. They'll override impulsive urges that might get them in trouble. They'll keep up with their homework and avoid classroom conduct that might damage their chance for the good grades needed to stay eligible. They'll use memory joggers and pocket calendars to keep track of practices, games, and school assignments that have to be squeezed in among sports activities. They'll spend hours running off the excess energy that used to keep them from concentrating in class. Whether the motivation is football or basketball or soccer or wrestling or swimming or track, every aspect of their life will benefit from habits adopted to increase the chances of good performance in sports.

Leon's whole life revolved around sports. During his junior year of high school, he was voted the most valuable player in football, basketball, baseball, and track. This youth found athletic success so satisfying that he had no trouble keeping away from activities that could jeopardize his eligibility. While the other teenagers in his neighborhood stayed up half the night hanging around street corners and getting into scrapes with the law, Leon did his homework, worked out, and got eight hours of sleep. He watched his diet and never broke training to try caffeine, tobacco, alcohol, or the street drugs his classmates found so cool. Instead of being thought of as a goody-goody, he had the status of a local celebrity and the respect of everybody in his small hometown.

Leon had an unrecognized learning disability. He was functionally illiterate. He always squeezed by, but his grade point average was never better than barely passing. Although hard work and sheer determination allowed him to get the grades needed for eligibility, his poor reading prevented him from even trying the college boards. No recruiters were waiting on the sidelines offering scholarships, and he was too young for scouts to be interested in drafting him to turn pro. At eighteen, Leon's days as a serious athlete were over.

When his eligibility ran out, Leon lost his motivation. He had attained his goals but had developed no plan to replace them with new ones. With no overriding reason to stay sober and in control, he let his life begin to drift. The allure of drugs caught him. Hanging out became his main pastime. As his grades fell, he dropped out of school. As his drug use turned into addiction, he began supporting his expensive habit with larceny. By the time the small-town hero turned twenty, he was trapped in the vicious cycle of drug addiction and criminal activity that kept him in the state penitentiary for thirteen of the next fifteen years.

Goal-oriented youngsters tend to put their energy into productive activities both in and out of school. Outside activities do not detract from schoolwork; they lead students to organize their lives for peak performance in everything they do.

The first step in getting a grip on ADD is choosing goals that have enough appeal to make obstacles pale into insignificance. To be effective, goals must be intentionally chosen, clearly stated, and deliberately nurtured. It takes more than talent to make a dream come true. Not all objectives are dramatic. They can be very small and very personal. Dreams derive their power from the passionate desire of the individuals who are willing to pay the price to achieve them.

Through goal setting, attitude development, and mental conditioning, parents, teachers, and coaches build drive and enthusiasm in aspiring young athletes, singers, actors, and musicians. A large number of those with ADD have natural gifts in music, art, dance, drama, sports, creative writing. Among history's most highly respected inventors, builders, engineers, architects, and mechanical wizards, the characteristics of an attention deficit disorder were common.

Those who thrive with ADD learn to overcome their weaknesses and develop their talents by harnessing the power of their dreams. What's needed is the determination of an Olympic athlete. A powerful purpose is essential in providing the driving force that makes all sacrifices worth it.

To overcome problems with ADD, build a dream and pursue it.

COACHES, MENTORS, AND EXPECTATIONS

Many researchers have explored the effect of attitude on the outcome of instruction. In medicine, there is the "placebo effect" to explain patient improvement caused by expectations. In education and industry, the same kind of phenomenon is referred to as the

"Hawthorne effect." The term originated at the Hawthorne Works of the Western Electric Company in Cicero, Illinois, where the simple environmental adjustments made by efficiency experts *always* worked. When they increased the lighting, productivity went up. When the lights were later turned back down, productivity increased again! The puzzling results were explained by a theory that says researchers and workers tend to get the results they expect. From this study and many others like it, the worlds of business, industry, and science were forced to acknowledge the influence attitudes and expectations have on the success or failure of scientific experiments and business ventures.

A great many research projects have demonstrated that the Hawthorne effect has a powerful influence on the outcome of coaching and teaching as well. In the Hunter Point studies, students who were deliberately mislabeled succeeded in accordance with their teachers' expectations, rather than their past performance. In study after study, it has been proven that teachers who are told a student is bright tend to expect high achievement from that youngster—and usually get it. When instructors believe a pupil will not succeed, they are almost always correct in their prediction of failure.

A number of recent investigations have demonstrated that children can surmount even the most severe hardships and deprivations when inspired by the strong support of a loving mentor who believes in their ability to overcome the odds against them. Regardless of the type of handicap, youngsters draw tremendous strength from unwavering support given to them by someone they trust. This role can be filled by a parent, an older brother or sister, a grandparent, or a neighbor. In a thirty-year study of Hawaiian children recounted in Emmy E. Werner's *Overcoming the Odds: High Risk Children from Birth to Adulthood*, at-risk youngsters who succeeded in growing into competent, confident adults often gave the credit to a teacher. Coaches and teachers are in a unique position to be the ones who will listen, the ones who will offer compassionate guidance in the face of repeated failure, the ones who will accept the student exactly as is while demonstrating and encouraging a full exploration of the many changes possible.

A former student once wrote me a note of thanks, saying, "By accepting me as I was, you allowed me to become who I *could* be." With the simple eloquence of one who's been there, this appreciative young lady explained the underlying principle that produces the positive results that can be achieved through mentoring. Children who have overcome seemingly insurmountable obstacles almost always had someone who stood by them when the going was rough—someone who believed in them and their power to succeed.

When adopting the role of mentor, parents should watch out for getting too emotionally involved. Their ego is attached to the outcome. They have hopes, dreams. They may find it all but impossible to let go of their own plans and raise a child in the way *he* should grow. When a youngster expresses an interest in harp but the father has always dreamed of "my son, the violinist" or "my daughter, the organist," something more practical is likely to be provided—like piano lessons. Mothers who always yearned for dance lessons often fulfill their own unmet desires by enrolling a tomboy daughter in ballet classes she hates instead of sending her off to a soccer camp she would love.

For effective mentoring, the idea of "molding" has to be replaced by a commitment to help in the process of "unfolding." Truly outstanding coaches act as advisors and cheerleaders, as well as demonstrators and instructors. Teachers who are inspiring show great respect for the natural instincts that lead students to explore, discover, and develop areas of uniqueness and talent.

To continue to believe in a student despite defeats, it is essential to acquire the ability to see beneath the surface. Avoid labeling the child with words that predict failure. The helpful coach learns to suspend judgment for now and trust that even this situation can lead to immense success. Effective mentors have the kind of faith that inspires courage and stability.

An investigative attitude is essential. That's the mind-set that kept Edison going after sixteen hundred experimental light bulbs refused to glow. Once, after a new filament had been tested without success, an associate was disheartened. When asked by Edison what was wrong, the colleague replied that they had experienced another failure. "Oh, no. That's not a failure," said Edison. "We now know over sixteen hundred filaments that won't work. We've narrowed the field down considerably." Thomas Edison was sure he could produce light with electricity. To his way of thinking, it was just a matter of figuring out how to make it happen.

When looking for solutions to the problems caused by a child's attention deficit disorder, stay focused on the fact that all children can concentrate. It's just a matter of experimenting to find the combination that unlocks the secrets of the child's mind.

Lots of homeschoolers have miniature trampolines right in their classrooms, so that when the wiggles of hyperactivity become overwhelming, the lessons can go on while the child bounces off the excess energy. For some students, calling out spelling words or reciting multiplication tables works great when accompanied by the rhythmic movements of dribbling a basketball or jumping rope. But that doesn't help everybody, and it is difficult to utilize in a traditional classroom. Some brains don't focus in response to the steady beat of repetitious physical activity.

When using the exploratory approach, if one possibility doesn't produce the desired results, move on to the next without getting discouraged. ADD youngsters who want to take charge and get control need a strong, persistent, clever, optimistic partner/teacher/coach/guide to join them in their investigations. They're unlikely to achieve success without it.

EXERCISE

Some children are very physical. They're always in motion. For them, "sitting quietly" includes touching, handling, moving, talking. When at their desks, they roam the room with their gaze. Their eyes are constantly exploring, questioning, examining, investigating. Inside their heads, their minds race. These are the youngsters who burst onto the playground like caged animals freed. They run just for the joy of it. They race to embrace the world with exuberance and enthusiasm. Their social interactions are likely to include lots of physical contact and a great deal of rough-and-tumble play. They tend to be tough, fearless, and fast.

These high-energy children are a terrible mismatch with standard American classroom practices. Their boundless curiosity prompts them to dash across the room, dart into the hall, or duck into another classroom without thinking to ask permission. When a notion strikes, action starts immediately.

Parents and teachers criticize them for acting before thinking; psychologists label them *impulsive*; physicians put them on medication. By emphasizing the desire for immediate change in behavior, they make no attempt to develop a long-term plan to teach ADD children to channel their excess energy into productive activity.

The human body is like a steam engine. It burns fuel to create the energy to do work. It's designed to lift and pull and carry. When it's been stoked, it creates steam so it can keep running at top speed for miles. In order for such a powerful engine to sit at the station and not explode, it has to let off steam.

Youngsters who are very physical are frequently well coordinated and strong. They tend to be attracted to sports and strenuous activities that allow them to work up a good sweat. When left to their own devices, they may find unacceptable activities to burn off their excess energy. This applies to teachers and parents as well as children. (Many of these physical types are klutzes whose brains can't keep up with their muscles. They, too, need ways to let off steam. For them, athletic activities not only act as an outlet for excess energy but also provide an opportunity to develop better motor control and improve coordination.)

One homeschooling family has designed a schedule that allows at least two hours a day for the strenuous activity the mother needs. During that time, the children play music, work puzzles, and do art projects while the human-dynamo mom rakes leaves, chops wood, shovels snow, rototills the garden. When bad weather forces this mom to stay inside, she has trouble keeping her mind on the lessons she's teaching.

Stimulant medications typically used to help control ADD make a significant difference in controlling the racing motor of hyperactivity. However, it is unrealistic to expect pills to take care of the problem with no effort on the part of the family, the school, or the child. Those who truly wish to teach youngsters to live comfortably with ADD must provide a carefully coordinated program that includes academic tutoring, study-skills training, organizational training, and behavior management.

With or without medication, the most effective classroom solutions involve environmental changes that allow for movement while thinking, studying, and participating in discussions; instruction that allows for hands-on learning; and prolonged periods of strenuous exercise daily. The children who need recess and physical education the most are the ones most likely to be deprived of it as punishment for incomplete assignments, low grades, and poor behavior. When a student's restlessness and inattentiveness increase, the answer is *more* recess, not less. With appropriate adjustments and compassionate guidance, hyperactive youngsters can be taught to become strong, vigorous, high-spirited adults who use physical activity to burn off excess energy.

Sandy was a mildly hyperactive tenth-grader. Although the pretty teenager was not a particularly good student, she was an excellent swimmer. She always managed to keep her grades high enough to maintain eligibility for her favorite extracurricular activity: swim team.

In the early fall of Sandy's sophomore year, her parents became concerned that her grade point average was not high enough to get her into a good college. They pressured her to put more effort into her studies. At the middle of the first marking period, Sandy's grades showed no improvement, so her parents clamped down by imposing a study schedule that took away all weeknight privileges. To make sure their daughter put maximum effort into the grade-raising program, they set up a goal, a deadline, and a stiff penalty: by the end of the first marking period, Sandy's grades would average at least 2.5 (instead of her usual 2.0) or the time she devoted to swimming would have to be applied to even more studying.

There were loud complaints from the teenager. She particularly resented being deprived of her phone and her television. But basically, the girl cooperated with her parents' schedule by spending her evenings quietly locked away in her room with her books.

When the first report card arrived, Sandy's family was surprised to find no appreciable change in her grades. All extracurricular activities were curtailed until the end of the next marking period. Swim team was dropped. All the time previously devoted to swimming practice was to be applied to schoolwork.

The grounded teen accepted her plight with fewer complaints than expected. She got up in the morning, dressed, put on her makeup, grabbed her books, a banana, and a bagel, and let her mom drop her off at school. At three-thirty, she'd be on the curb waiting for her ride home.

The first hint of trouble came when the school called to check on Sandy's absences. As far as the girl's family knew, she'd had three months of perfect attendance. When the parents made an appointment with the school counselor to clear up the error, the accused truant gave no indication of concern.

At the conference, school records revealed that this college-bound sophomore had not attended any classes in nearly a month! Her parents were appalled as Sandy casually admitted to taking lots of time off in the six weeks since she'd been removed from the swim team. At first, she'd played hooky a day or two a week. (The counselor had her forged notes to prove it.) Since her old crowd was locked away in classes, she had linked up with a network of teenagers who joined her in skipping school. Her new friends amused themselves by smoking marijuana and hanging around the mall. Most of them were just waiting to turn sixteen so they could drop out of school.

As the truth of Sandy's recent pastimes was exposed, it became obvious that money mysteriously missing from wallets and cookie jars had been filched by this drug-using teenager. The girl's parents were devastated.

Rather than let this shattered family go home to work out its own solution, the school counselor suggested that they consider an unusually creative plan of action. She wisely proposed that Sandy be allowed to return to active status on the swim team.

At first, the parents protested that this would be rewarding their daughter for bad behavior. Without blaming or criticizing, the counselor carefully guided the threesome to see that each of them had made a series of bad decisions that could be corrected. The parents needed to let up on the unrealistic pressures and punishments; the girl needed to get back to her commitment to work toward goals that were important to her. When seen in this light, it seemed logical that restitution of money stolen and schoolwork missed would be sufficient as the just rewards for poor behavior.

As soon as all parties came to agreement, the details were arranged. It only took one phone call for the delighted teenager and her coach to work out her return to the swim team's training program and practice schedule. The whole plan was so reasonable that Sandy and her family left the counselor's office with a new sense of commitment and optimism.

One of the most inspired aspects of the counselor's plan was that it made pot smoking and school skipping into side issues. Nobody had to tell Sandy that she needed to change her ways. Serious swimmers don't smoke or drink, they get plenty of rest and keep their grades up. They don't have time to get in trouble, because early practice has them in the water by six every morning. Instead of hanging out at the mall, they spend their afternoons hanging around the pool. Their excess energy gets used up swimming laps, practicing turns, and competing in meets. Athletes who are involved in a serious training program rarely have trouble with hyperactivity.

Oddly, those whose attention deficit disorder includes hypoactivity also find exercise a powerful tool in counteracting problems with concentration. They may not be bursting with the energy found in the hyperactive, but they do have the kind of mind that thinks in short bursts. After fifteen or twenty minutes of focused attention, their brain shuts down. A sustained period of daily physical exercise helps counteract this problem, but they usually need to include regular short breaks of vigorous activity during study sessions as well. Twenty minutes of concentration, then ten minutes of swimming or jumping rope or climbing stairs works well. For some, studying while *on* a stair-climbing machine or a stationary bike is even more effective. By increasing the pulse rate, aerobic exercise clears the cobwebs, increases alertness, and adjusts the attitude. Whatever a "runner's high" is, it's a great state for mental activity that re uires determination, optimism, intelligence, and a sustained focus or full attention.

Those who control classrooms almost always think of physical education as a luxury that is expendable. When students misbehave or fail to get their work completed, depriving them of recess is considered an appropriate punishment. When teachers get behind schedule, they leave out the time set aside for art. When principals run out of space, they give up the music room. When administrators cut back on the size of the faculty, drama and intramural sports are among the first programs to be eliminated. When legislators determine budgets, they fund the basics and eliminate the "frills."

We've got it backwards. Children who have trouble concentrating need *more* physical activity, not less. By systematically removing right-brain activities from our schools, we create the very problems we're hoping to solve.

INSIGHT THROUGH EDUCATION

Knowing and understanding the truth about how one's mind works gives an individual the power to take control. And if there's one thing those with ADD yearn for, it's to take charge of their rampaging minds and fidgeting bodies. Anyone who can lead them to the self-knowledge that makes this possible is likely to get full cooperation, if not downright adoration.

Throughout the last half of the twentieth century, there has been great interest in exploring the human brain and determining how it functions. Equipment of ever-increasing sophistication has made it possible to analyze and quantify even the tiniest anatomical structures and the most subtle of processes. Each new discovery leads to questions worthy of further investigation. We now know more about the human mind than ever in history. But our understanding of learning disabilities and attention deficit disorder is frustratingly skimpy. Still, patterns are emerging.

Although problems with learning and attention are not new, the terminology came into existence only recently. Dyslexia and reading deficiencies have been under scrutiny since the 1930s, but the term *learning disability* only came into use in the late 1960s. Hyperkinesis and hyperactivity were recognized in the 1950s and 1960s. With the increased popularity of the stimulant medication methylphenidate (more commonly referred to by its brand name, Ritalin) in the 1970s, a whole new concept of distractibility, impulsivity, and hyperactivity emerged. In the 1980 edition of the *Diagnostic and Statistical Manual of Mental Disorders*, the terms *attention deficit disorder with hyperactivity* and *ADD without hyperactivity* were introduced. Studies conducted in the early 1990s indicate that learning disabilities and attention deficit disorder represent the most common problems seen by child neu-rologists, developmental pediatricians, and neuropsychologists. Up to 70 percent of their patients are referred because of a suspicion of these two disorders! Learning disabilities and attention deficit disorder are also seen in close to 80 percent of the children referred to mental health practitioners and in a *very* high percentage of the prison population.

BRAIN TRAINING

LD and ADD kids are everywhere. It's time we figured out what to do. It's time we shared with them what we *do* know about their styles of thinking and behaving so we can be a partner in helping them get themselves under control.

One way to do this is through a program of "brain training" that introduces them to the work of researchers who have discovered information they can apply to the situations that come up repeatedly in their everyday lives. By leading them to understand the findings of those who have meticulously studied the brain, learning, memory, attention, hyperactivity, and so forth, we can give them facts they need to think about their own thinking. The knowledge and insights gained through this educational process can then be put to use in a systematic training program that includes instruction in study skills, organizational systems, time-management techniques, behavior control methods, and appropriate academic therapy.

Those who examine their own learning style in the manner of Drs. Kenneth and Rita Dunn (see appendix) can gain insights that allow them to take control of their learning. By developing an awareness of their work habits, they can adjust their environment for maximum study efficiency. By exploring their psychological makeup, they can seek instructional relationships that increase their learning. By analyzing the emotional aspect of their attitude toward learning, they can take advantage of their basic temperament so it works for them, rather than against them. By figuring out their bodies' perceptual preferences and limitations, they can personalize their study techniques so that new information is taken in through the sensory

channels that work best. By observing the physical components of
their personal habits and major successes, they can revise their classroom activities to be more in line with their preferences. With just a
small amount of brain training, students of all ages can learn to take
responsibility for managing the modifications that will make academic success possible in any setting.

Even the most superficial study of learning styles includes an
introduction to the two halves of the human brain. Once LD and
ADD students see the charts and hear explanations of the characteristics, they are quick to recognize themselves as right-brain, or "global," learners. Traits they had never considered begin to stand out as
talents that balance the weaknesses that make certain types of academic activities a chore.

THE LEFT BRAIN	THE RIGHT BRAIN
■ is "verbal." It takes in and processes messages coded in language. It thinks by talking to itself as it manipulates words and numbers.	■ is "nonverbal." It thinks with pictures and feelings. It deals directly with concrete reality.
■ has a keen and constant awareness of time. Much of its evaluating and organizing is done in reference to time sequences and an inner clock.	■ has no awareness of, or interest in, time.
■ has no sense of space.	■ has a highly developed awareness of patterns, colors, shapes, and spatial relationships. A great deal of its thinking is done by manipulating concrete or imaginary objects in space.

THE LEFT BRAIN	THE RIGHT BRAIN
■ breaks information into small, manageable pieces.	■ takes in data as whole units.
■ organizes material by putting its component parts into a specific order. Sequence is a vitally important element in most of its processing. It works with step-by-step logic.	■ organizes information by seeking relationships and recognizing similarities between wholes. It works in analogical leaps of sudden knowing.
■ focuses attention by concentrating very narrowly on small pieces and component parts.	■ expands the focus of attention to take in the whole scene all at once and deal with large, whole units.
■ specializes in analyzing. It notes differences between parts so they can be labeled, evaluated, compared, and categorized.	■ specializes in seeing the big picture and thinking globally. By making analogies, it seeks to build, synthesize, alter, create.
■ prepares factual information for storage in well-organized, easily accessible memory.	■ produces sudden insights that are steppingstones to still bigger revelations.
■ reasons its way to a conclusion without feelings or emotions. It figures things out by being factual, systematic, and detached.	■ feels its way to conclusions by hunches or trial and error. It knows intuitively by being sensitive, imaginative, and whimsical.

Among educators and researchers, students with ADD are sometimes referred to as "right-brain thinkers." This is a gross oversimplification, but it is also a helpful description when seeking insight into attention deficit disorder. Because of the way the brain is structured, it makes sense that the two separate halves work in very different manners and that some people strongly prefer to use one side's type of thinking, rather than the other's.

A number of experts divide students into two categories based on which side of the brain they use more successfully.

Dr. Sandra Witelson, an educational researcher, has focused her investigations on measuring brain hemisphere activity during various kinds of thought processing. Her studies provide such overwhelming evidence of a strong preference for right-brain processing among those with learning disabilities and attention deficit disorder that one of her research papers is entitled, "Two Right Hemispheres and None Left."

As part of the process of determining a student's learning style, Drs. Kenneth and Rita Dunn classify students as either "global learners" (right-brain preference) or "analytical learners" (left-brain preference). The traits they use to describe global thinkers are very similar to those commonly used to describe people with learning disabilities and attention deficit disorder. In addition to having problems sustaining a narrow focus of concentration, global learners usually have difficulty with other tasks mediated by the left brain, such as organization, memory, and the concept of time. Punctuality is often a lifelong problem. Sequencing techniques that put items in alphabetical or chronological order give them trouble, and they almost always have difficulty with the verbal skills needed for spelling, writing, and memorization of math facts. In seeing these weaknesses as associated with the left brain, it's logical to look to the right side to explore for natural gifts and talents.

According to the research of Drs. Roger Sperry, Jerry Levy, Michael Gazzaniga, and a host of others, the right hemisphere uses a wide focus of attention in order to do global thinking. That's the kind of processing needed to take in the whole picture and keep track of many details all at once. It's the mode of thinking that keeps us safe when driving a car. To get a three-thousand-pound mass of steel to merge onto an expressway, it's necessary to keep an eye on the vehicles approaching down the ramp from behind, the auto speeding along in front, the flow of traffic in the lane to be entered, road conditions far ahead, traffic signs announcing speed limits or reasons for caution. At the same time, it is also important to monitor the speedometer, the gas gauge, the oil-pressure indicator, the engine temperature, the sound of the motor, and the comfort level inside the passenger area, where adjustments in temperature, ventilation, radio volume, seat position, and rearview mirror are frequently required. In addition to all this constant surveillance, attention has to be devoted to controlling the car: pushing the gas pedal, braking, steering. Dealing with the whole scene and its many details at the same time is a job the right brain does with ease. The left brain could never do this. Its analytical style of processing must be done step by step. It deals sequentially with one piece at a time. Only the right half of the cerebral cortex does global, or holistic, thinking.

In a classroom, the right brain's tendency to notice everything is called "distractibility." A talent for spatial thinking leads to "daydreaming." Constant monitoring of the environment is referred to as "short attention span." These characteristics are not helpful in doing schoolwork. Reading the book and filling in the worksheet requires a narrow focus of left-brain concentration to tune out the activity in the room, the noises from the playground, the voices and footsteps in the hall. Paying no attention to the thousands of interesting things going on in the immediate environment and focusing on just one abstract, verbal, reasoning task—only the left brain can do that. But in the real world, holistic thinking has many advantages. It's unfortunate it has so little value in school.

GLOBAL THINKERS

Once LD and ADD students see themselves as the global thinkers they are—and not the analytical learners they've spent so long trying to be—their whole attitude changes. Suddenly, the pattern of their strengths and weaknesses makes sense. Their talents are in spatial areas like drawing or building with Legos. Or they have gifts in music or sports. Their brains are designed for fast decisions in tough situations where creative solutions are needed. Their difficulties with punctuality are merely an indication that they are not left-brain people and have no reliable inner clock. Since they don't feel the minutes ticking by, the time to do something is *now*. They are emotional and sensitive, not reasonable and practical. They're usually not cut out to be bankers or bookkeepers or secretaries. They're equipped to be poets and artists and musicians and athletes and dancers and inventors and salespeople and architects and engineers. *Smart* is a word often applied to analytical thinkers. Right-brain learners are better described by words like *talented, creative, clever*. Years ago, these youngsters would have been told they had an "artistic temperament." Such a description points out their differences while still acknowledging that they are part of the plan. It sounds so much more natural than terms that refer to disabilities and disorders!

GETTING A GRIP ON IMPULSIVE BEHAVIOR

The human brain is the center for both reasoning and emotion. Those with ADD usually make decisions with their emotions, rather than with their reasoning abilities. They feel comfortable trusting the hunches and feelings associated with the processing style of the right side of the brain. They see their tendency to act quickly as being flexible and spontaneous. Others believe they let impulsive behavior lead them to foolish choices. The admonition to "think before you act" has very little appeal to those with ADD. They see careful deliberation as indecisive, overcautious, stifling, boring, and perfectionistic. They rarely have the patience to use the slower analytical reasoning associated with the left half of the cerebral cortex.

As brain training teaches students to think about their thinking, those with ADD begin to recognize their ability to get control of the impulsive tendencies that urge them to ignore tomorrow and jump after the pleasure available today. As they learn to exert their analytical side to veto sudden "hot ideas" proposed by the impulsive global side, they find that taking control over their actions gives them the satisfaction of achieving important goals. Regularly saving a small amount of a weekly allowance creates the opportunity for the surge of pleasure available through an occasional big splurge. Postponing play until after homework sets the stage for a delightful celebration of academic achievement. Planning ahead to get schoolwork completed by an established deadline helps stop parental hysteria and keeps the home front peaceful. Just as rambunctious children need a mature supervisor to protect them from the dangers caused by their own recklessness, the spontaneous, intuitive, fun-seeking side of the mind needs loving supervision from the analytical mind. Once introduced to their brain's ability to provide that guidance, those with ADD can begin to apply some of the left hemisphere's reasoning skills to the decision-making process.

To develop this balanced approach to making decisions, it's necessary to create a working relationship between the reasoning side of the mind and its emotion-driven counterpart. It helps to think of these apparently opposing forces as "the professor" and "the little kid." By establishing an attitude of mutual respect and cooperation, these two can learn to work together as partners instead of opponents.

When this relationship is first developing, the powerful intellectual side tends to try to take charge completely. The nonverbal right side can't explain all the logical reasons why its needs should be considered—but just like a little kid, it will resist. There will be whining and sulking and foot dragging and sneaking. When global thinkers make sweeping promises to behave in ways totally contrary to their basic nature, a resentful attitude will build up and sabotage even the most carefully designed plans. "I'm going to change my ways entirely." "I'm going to get organized if it kills me." "Never again will I be late." These are all admirable intentions, but none of them can bring about a real change in behavior until they are compatible with the operating style of the little kid, who represents the right hemisphere's method of processing.

In establishing a healthy relationship where both parts of the brain get to participate in the making of decisions, the professor's intellectual abilities and organizational skills must be put to use for the highest good of the partnership. The goal is not dominance but balance. To function at full capacity, the duo needs the little kid's spontaneity, intuition, energy, imagination, sensitivity, love of beauty, sense of humor, and desire for fun. These traits of the emotional side of the brain need to be controlled, not obliterated.

The easiest way to get started is to select an area where both sides of the mind agree on the need for some simple, straightforward solution to a problem.

Nancy always ran out of money before the end of the month. She was a shopkeeper's dream—an impulse buyer. She knew she needed to be on a budget and had tried several, but she couldn't force herself to stick with them. In addition to always being broke, she had chronic guilt feelings about her financial irresponsibility. Nancy's uncontrollable extravagance was undermining her self-confidence and seriously damaging her self-respect.

The answer to this young woman's problem came from an unexpected source. A televised series on the brain got her to analyze her own strengths and weaknesses in terms of the two hemispheres of the brain. With a simple worksheet, Nancy got a new perspective on the inner conflict behind her problem with money.

Every time she tried to get control of her impulse spending, she used her professor-like left brain to draw up complex systems of recordkeeping. By emphasizing long lists of strict rules that did not allow for any flexibility, she felt like her financial management programs were designed by the money police. Protests from the carefree little kid part of her nature were swept aside with, "Nonsense. Other people do this. You can do it, too."

For a while, her fun-loving right brain would try to live up to the new rules by entering figures in expense ledgers and making detailed shopping lists. But after she obediently monitored even the tiniest expenditures for a few days, a carefully saved receipt would disappear, or she'd forget to take her list with her to the store. Failing to follow through on something so simple would make her feel stupid, and she'd begin to hate all the organized plans she'd talked herself into. After a couple of weeks, something would come up and the Sunday-afternoon bookkeeping session would get postponed. Then it would get skipped with promises to pull all the records together at the end of the month. By that time, the whole project had dissolved into a pointless jumble.

These nonproductive crusades had been going on periodically for years. The results were always the same: shame and guilt for Nancy, with no change in her reckless spending.

As soon as she recognized her problem as a conflict between the reasoning side of her mind and its more emotional counterpart, Nancy came up with an entirely new approach. Instead of letting the judgmental, rule-bound side of her brain take full charge of devising a plan, as she had done in the past, Nancy looked to her logical side just to give her ideas. Without thinking of them as "rules," she recorded several dozen *simple* suggestions on a legal pad. After further consideration, some of these *might* be accepted as guidelines.

With her new understanding of herself as a global thinker, Nancy knew that the strong right-brain part of her nature would never cooperate with most of the rules she had listed. In order to give consideration to that part of herself that preferred to act like a little kid, she decided to trust her feelings. Slowly and deliberately, she read through the list. Most of the monetary ideas struck her as ridiculous. She didn't try to talk herself into anything. The list got pared down to those few rules she thought she could cheerfully abide by. It took some adjustments in the language to make them palatable enough to be accepted as guidelines.

Finally, Nancy devised an experiment. She decided to live by the following rules for one month: (1) pay off the plastic; (2) observe a two-dollar limit on junk; (3) think twice if an item cost more than two hours' wages.

Nancy scrawled the guidelines on the back of an old envelope and stuck it on the refrigerator door with a magnet. She had let the professor side of her mind establish some budgetary restrictions, so she took the little kid part of her nature out for ice cream (two-dollar limit). It seemed an appropriate way to celebrate the new plan.

With this balanced recognition of her tendencies, Nancy learned to keep her spending under control.

As the success of the money-management rules became obvious, Nancy began consulting the reasoning side of her mind in regard to other decisions. At first, she used it to provide information and offer suggestions *when asked*. Any ideas that were harsh or critical were met with a raised eyebrow, a stony silence, and a reminder that bullying would not be tolerated. Gradually, this inner source of good judgment became more cooperative. After several successes with joint decisions, the analytical professor and the global little kid developed an attitude of mutual respect. As they grew to trust each other, Nancy found that she could think through choices by consulting her analyzing ability *and* her feelings. The two sides of her thinking became so attuned to each other that *both* of them got veto power. Today, Nancy relies on her left brain's sharp business sense for practical matters but counts on the right hemisphere's whimsical ideas when it's time to have fun.

Those who establish communication between the two sides of their brain quickly discover some sharp contrasts in the way they work out the solution to a problem.

The professor, our representation of the verbal left brain, is a talker. He relies on facts, figures, and inner dialogue. Inside the head, his voice can be heard chattering away as he measures, weighs, analyzes, compares, labels, categorizes, and organizes information. He takes no action until he has thought the entire situation through carefully and figured out the right answer. He is a planner—a talker and a thinker—characterized by caution and patience.

The imaginary character who represents the right hemisphere prefers an experimental approach. The little kid has no desire for analysis or advance planning, preferring to take action immediately with the hope that a good solution will develop through trial and error. She's a doer, characterized by boldness and ingenuity.

As students become better acquainted with the two ways of thinking, they begin noticing the same thinking patterns in others. Once it is understood that the left brain must do all its thinking with words and numbers, it makes sense that the professor insists on precision and accuracy. The job of reasoning and problem solving relies on information that is precisely described, thoroughly analyzed, carefully categorized, intelligently evaluated, and meticulously stored for easy retrieval. This kind of work *has* to be done methodically. It requires an orderly, well-organized environment where a high value is placed on neatness, punctuality, and discipline.

The habits needed for left-brain processing are not usually very appealing to those right-brain thinkers labeled as ADD—unless they go into overfocus or the superneat practices of the compulsively organized. Their minds tend to flit from one object of interest to another, observing, building, experimenting. They much prefer the excitement of exploration and sudden insight typical of the processing style of the action-oriented right half of the brain. They thrive on the drama of inventing and creating.

Youngsters with ADD often show a preference for the forms of nonverbal thinking processed in the right brain. Talent with visual and spatial processing is common. Those with this ability frequently slip off into that inner world of visual thinking called daydreaming. At every opportunity, they draw or paint or color. Athletic skill is extremely common among those with ADD. Some use their gift for tactile/kinesthetic thinking in playing sports. Others direct their talent for movement into dance and drama. Musical thinking is another form of nonverbal right-brain processing. When rhythm and melody are produced spontaneously, left-brain activity is not necessary. When "reading" musical notes, language processing is required of the left hemisphere. Thus, right-brain thinkers may have a strong preference for composing and improvisation. Sculptors, woodcarvers, plumbers, carpenters, builders, and mechanics say there is no inner discussion going on as they carry out their activities. They do their thinking with their eyes (visual/spatial) and their hands (tactile/kinesthetic). Many of them have a learning disability or an attention deficit disorder, but when involved in hands-on activities, they have no trouble with concentration or impulsive behavior.

SEVEN FORMS OF INTELLIGENCE

Another researcher whose ideas throw a whole new light on learning disabilities and attention deficit disorder is Dr. Howard Gardner of Harvard University. After a great deal of investigation, Gardner has concluded that our traditional ways of looking at human intelligence are inaccurate and unrealistic. We typically think of individuals as having intelligence that falls somewhere in a continuum from "smart" to "stupid"—with no consideration of abilities outside the skill areas valued in the classroom. Even the sophisticated IQ tests done individually by psychologists examine only a portion of two aspects of mental ability: verbal and performance. Gardner thinks we should move away from intelligence tests designed to predict success or failure in school and take a look at the full spectrum of the human brain's thinking capacity.

According to Gardner's studies, there are seven distinct and separate areas of intelligence: verbal/linguistic, mathematical/logical, visual/spatial, body/kinesthetic, musical, interpersonal, and intrapersonal. A person who is a whiz at math might have no skill whatsoever in the interpersonal skills of reading social signals and understanding what other people are thinking. A verbally talented individual might possess a great deal of the intrapersonal intelligence necessary to analyze and understand his own thoughts and feelings but be totally lacking in musical aptitude and only moderately capable in visual/spatial thinking.

Schools are mainly interested in two of the seven areas of intelligence: verbal thinking and mathematical thinking. The athlete can use his kinesthetic gifts only after achieving success in the two basic academic areas that determine eligibility. The artist can't graduate until he passes algebra. Five of the seven aspects of human intelligence are treated as frills! And those with an attention deficit disorder and/or a learning disability almost always have their main strengths in several of those five areas—and weaknesses in one or both of the areas that count for everything!

When students learn to understand their own pattern of strengths and weaknesses in each of the seven types of intelligence, they gain the power to use strength in one area to compensate for weakness in another. Visual/spatial learners can improve their concentration by adding color and illustrations to their note-taking technique. They can develop a better understanding of difficult subject matter by drawing out information and concepts with flow charts, graphs, and diagrams. Kinesthetic thinkers can do their homework in areas that allow for movement. They can carry something in their book bag to keep their hands busy when they're not actively involved in writing. They can ask permission to sit in the back of the classroom, where their need to move and stretch won't disturb others. Once LD and ADD students see that they're not defective, that it's not *wrong* to be the way they are, they find ways to use their talents to make boring classes interesting.

Teaching young people to think about their thinking can transform unmotivated potential dropouts into eager learners. It gives students an understanding of themselves and a chance to take control.

DIETS

Two basic types of diets have been proposed to alleviate ADD: additive-free and sugar-free. Since medical doctors utilize research to identify therapies to help the majority of people with a particular problem, they rarely suggest using dietary changes to control ADD. Studies have shown that only a small portion of those with an attention deficit disorder find their situation improved by eliminating additives or simple sugars from their daily intake. In other words, for any given individual, a special diet might help, but then again, it might not. However, for those who are really serious about getting control of ADD, they're worth a try. Some people have found them extremely helpful.

The additive-free diet is based on the work of Dr. Benjamin Feingold. The basic Feingold diet is not hard to understand and remember; it requires eliminating all food that contains preservatives and additives for coloring or flavoring. (Sometimes, foods containing salicylates are removed as well.) The person who does the family's shopping has to read labels carefully. Very few breads, cereals, salad dressings, crackers, soups, and candies will qualify. All processed products like frozen dinners, lunchmeat, sauces, sausages, gravies, and baked goods have long lists of additives on their labels. Junk food has to be eliminated almost entirely. Home-popped popcorn and nuts can be substituted for pretzels, chips, and nachos. Fruit juices and some of the flavored soda waters can replace the chemical-laden soft drinks found in vending machines. Cakes, pies, and cookies have to be homemade. It's a tough diet to live by. But when it works, it's worth it.

A family in Texas had explored a long list of remedies in its attempt to help its two LD/ADD sons overcome the problems that made them the terrors of their school. They'd flown all over the country trying the various treatments and cures so often touted on afternoon talk shows. They'd also tried standard medications, classroom adjustments, and special schools. Some things helped more than others, but there seemed to be no answer.

The parents and the children had all but given up when a friend told them of a special diet that had made a huge difference in her hyperactive nephews. It seemed unlikely that anything so simple as eliminating all artificial flavorings, colorings, and preservatives from the boys' diet would make any difference. It seemed even more unlikely that two unmanageable teenagers would stay away from junk food for more than a few days. But all four family members agreed to give the diet a thirty-day trial.

By the end of the first week, some surprising changes began taking place. It was summertime, so there were no teachers to comment, but around the house, there was a new attitude of cooperation and an unexpected atmosphere of calm. The parents were reluctant to credit it to the adjusted menu and assumed that their wild offspring stuffed themselves with forbidden foods every time they got away from watchful parental eyes.

In midsummer, the older son had a nasty bout with allergies and swimmer's ear. When he curtailed his activities and began using eardrops and antihistamines, his attitude turned surly. Everyone in the family tiptoed around the house, hoping not to provoke any outbursts.

One morning, the mother overheard the tail end of a conversation her two boys were having over their breakfast cereal. "I gotta get off these drugs," the fourteen-year-old was telling his younger brother.

The mother stopped in her tracks as a wave of panic clutched at her chest. Before she could decide how to react, her first-born child continued, "I *hate* being out of control."

As the mother raced into the dining room to confront her son, a small object flew past her head and shattered against the wall. Dozens of brightly colored antihistamine pills scattered over the floor.

"I can't live like this, Mom. *I can't!*" the out-of-control youth raged. "*I don't care if my ears fall off. I am not taking one more of those pills.*"

The mother was so relieved to see what drugs were being rejected that she almost laughed as her seething teenager pounded the table for dramatic emphasis. The boy was so startled by the look of relief and amusement on his mother's face that he lowered his voice and calmed down immediately. "They are making me crazy, Mom. Those pills are making me crazy. They really are."

The boy confessed that until the ear troubles, he had been following his diet faithfully. Even at fast-food restaurants with friends, he'd stuck to foods he knew he could trust to be free of additives. "I've eaten a lot of French fries!" he chuckled.

"And milk," his brother added.

Both boys burst out laughing. As they compared notes, it turned out that they had developed the same tricks. And they had both been sticking to the diet.

Whatever the diet was doing for them, they obviously thought it worth the price. They liked being in control.

Once the antihistamine pills were replaced by a coloring-free prescription, it took two weeks for the house to simmer back down to the peaceful levels established since the diet.

From then on, whenever the boys referred to the amazing change in their behavior, they spoke of *BD* and *AD*—before diet and after diet.

A second type of diet involves reducing the intake of sweets. Table sugar, junk food, candy, and products with various sugars listed among the first few ingredients provide the body with concentrated "simple sugars." For many people, simple sugars put their blood sugar on a roller coaster. If they skip meals or go too long without food, they'll get a headache or become irritable and lose the ability to think clearly. A jolt of sugar and caffeine will get them reenergized but make them jittery and restless. A snack that's loaded with simple sugars will get them going again but drop them back down in two or three hours. Children who get depressed or have tantrums are the ones most likely to benefit from the kind of diet that will smooth out wild up-and-down swings in blood-sugar levels.

Controlling blood sugar so that it stays at steady levels is best accomplished by shifting to a diet that limits simple sugars and is high in protein and complex carbohydrates. A diet based on "real foods" such as fruits, grains, meats, dairy products, and complex carbohydrates (as found in rice, beans, pasta, potatoes, and vegetables) provides a stable program which will smooth out the blood-sugar roller coaster. Frequent snacks are strongly encouraged. Junk food is acceptable as long as it contains no simple sugars. This type of diet requires some label reading, especially when selecting processed foods like cereals and frozen dinners. If a form of sugar (including dextrose, corn syrup, maltose, fructose, honey, maple syrup) is listed in the first five or six ingredients, the product should be avoided. It sounds brutal and takes some getting used to. Fortunately, if reducing concentrated sweets is going to be beneficial, it will make a noticeable difference in less than a week. The biggest changes are usually in attitude and behavior. For those who find such a diet helpful, it doesn't take much discipline to stay on it. Once a person who has always been out of control has the experience of not being crazy anymore, stability is a bargain at any price.

School had always been hard for Edna. She found it difficult to pay attention in class and had problems understanding and remembering new concepts and information. Through high school and college, she compensated for her difficulties by giving up her social life and working harder than her classmates.

When Edna got to graduate school, the work load was more than she could handle. It didn't matter how much determination and effort she put into her studies, she simply could not get all of her work done. As she fell farther and farther behind, she got discouraged. As her grades plunged, she consoled herself with chocolate. Failure was not something this high achiever had experienced before, and it made her depressed. More and more, she relied on sweets to lift her spirits. By the end of the first semester, she'd gained fifteen pounds and was an emotional wreck.

Edna flunked most of her first-semester courses. As panic and paralysis set in, she sought the help of a counselor. A month into the second semester, it was determined that the desperately struggling student had an attention deficit disorder. She was given stimulant medication and encouraged to develop more effective study techniques. But increased study efficiency and improved concentration didn't make a noticeable difference in her grades. As the second semester raced toward disaster, Edna tumbled deeper into depression and despair. Sleeplessness, anxiety attacks, and another ten pounds were added to her problems. The doctor increased her stimulant medication and added an antidepressant. It was suggested that she use the summer vacation to get control of her anxiety level and take a study-skills course, then come back in the fall for another try at the first year of her graduate program. She felt lucky that the university was compassionate enough to give her a second chance.

Throughout the summer and early fall, Edna worked with her counselor and a study-skills specialist. As she explored the types of changes that could help her overcome her attention problems, she decided to go into training like an athlete. Motivated by a resolve to succeed in graduate school, Edna put herself on a sugar-controlled, high-protein diet and began working out two to three hours a day. By the middle of the fall semester, her new study skills and training routine were paying off. Her grades were not fabulous but were definitely acceptable. The pounds were melting off and, best of all, she was beginning to feel confident, optimistic, and under control.

Edna passed all her courses in the fall semester and started the new year with great enthusiasm. Things started getting a little tough in February. She missed a couple of days of classes due to a bout with the flu, then found it difficult to make up the work she'd missed.

As midterms loomed, the pressure got so high that she sought solace in a bag of chocolate chip cookies. Within twenty-four hours, Edna was right back to the panic-stricken frenzy of the previous year. Just that small amount of concentrated simple sugar, and all the new study techniques she'd learned over the past six months abandoned her. She stared at her mountains of outlines and lecture notes but couldn't figure out a way to get any of the information into her memory. She couldn't concentrate, and her antidepressant and stimulant medication didn't help. It never occurred to her that the bag of cookies from the day before had put her back on the blood-sugar roller coaster.

The next day, in an effort to make herself feel better and get in the mood for serious studying, Edna treated herself to a big chunk of angel food cake topped with ice cream and smothered with chocolate sauce. But the bribe did not have the intended effect. After her snack, the amount of material she had to review looked so gigantic that it was overwhelming. She knew she needed to study for her exams. But her anxiety level had gotten so high that she couldn't sit still. She knew something was terribly wrong and was fighting to hold down the panic. To calm herself, she puttered around her apartment doing housework and bathing her cat. She went to bed at midnight without ever touching her books!

The next day, Edna met with her study-skills coach. She was irritable, jittery, and unusually talkative. When explaining her unsuccessful attempts to stick to her study schedule, she tried to assure her coach that there was no need to worry. But her optimism quickly faded, and she admitted that she was so frightened by her runaway emotions that she was afraid to be alone.

It was obvious that Edna was not thinking clearly and had no notion of what was wrong. "Have you been sticking to your diet?" her study coach asked.

Edna's nervous chatter stopped instantly, and she looked down as though studying her shoes. "Well, I cheated a little yesterday." Her first midterm was two days off, and she had completely abandoned her diet and training program! Her blood sugar was back in its pattern of wild up-and-down swings. As the truth came out, it became clear that this bright, highly motivated young woman did not realize what benefits she gained by staying away from concentrated sweets. She had been thinking of waistline, weight, and calories—not brains, mood, and concentration.

It was a tough lesson, but Edna pulled her grades out of the fire. They weren't anywhere near what they should have been, but she did pass all her midterms. With renewed determination and a new appreciation of why she should avoid simple sugars, she hoped to regain lost ground in the second half of the semester.

Sugar-controlled diets don't always help. But when they do, they make a dramatic difference.

TOTAL FOCUS THROUGH ADVENTURE

Many of those with ADD take great delight in being adventurers, explorers, and daredevils. Living on the edge provides them with the opportunity for sustained periods of the crystal clarity of overfocus. In a TV special on "extreme skiing," one of the sport's champions described the dangers of hurtling over rocky cliffs and streaking through thick powder on the steep pitches of mountain peaks. When asked what kind of mind-set made it possible to succeed at something so dangerous, he said, "Focus. Total concentration." He shook his head and shrugged his shoulders, as if explaining something obvious: "If you fall, you die."

From the footage shown on the program, that was no exaggeration. To ski such rugged terrain, young men race wide open in a state of totally expanded global focus. To survive, they must notice everything all at once—and do it quickly. Performing under such conditions absorbs their full attention. It is so physically demanding that it requires the complete involvement of every fiber of their bodies. Their exertion is so complete and the danger so imminent that the feat produces a huge rush of adrenalin. Extreme skiers are sometimes referred to as "adrenalin junkies." That description could also be applied to racecar drivers, sky divers, and members of any other group who repeatedly put themselves in death-defying situations for prolonged periods.

Among those with ADD, the daredevil instinct is strong. As toddlers, they climb. Their spirit of adventure knows no bounds. Parents often tell of death-defying escapades on ledges, walls, and rooftops. Throughout childhood, ADD youngsters terrify their families.

Amid such elevated explorations, these global adventurers remain calm. For them, fear seems to be replaced by focus. As they mature, they grow to love and seek that type of concentration. Their minds are clear when at fully expanded attention. If there is real danger, the release of adrenalin enhances the pleasure. The experience is addicting. Situations that paralyze the rest of us move right-brain thinkers into clarity. Their minds and bodies blend into perfectly coordinated units. They feel like they have been freed to become the ideal human they were designed to be.

There seems to be no limit to this expanding capacity. Astronauts who have done spacewalks describe the experience as a powerful feeling of being part of the entire universe. Such peak experiences usually occur only once or twice in a lifetime. Daredevils learn how to create that same expanded focus every weekend.

For those equipped for it, life on the edge is as natural as walking and talking. Their jobs are often as dangerous as their pastimes. They clamber over I-beams to construct great towers or swing from wind-swept scaffolds to keep windows clean. Those with the capacity for right-brain expanded global focus are made from a different mold than the rest of us. They can "think on their feet." It's easy for them to make snap decisions. In classrooms, they struggle with subjects they seem to find unintelligible. They can't do much with grammar or spelling or long division, but all their classmates envy the solid *thwack* they can give a kickball. And when a kite or a kitten gets stuck in a tree, all the other kids watch in wonder at their agility as they shinny up to rescue it.

These are our rescuers—our emergency-room attendants, our ambulance drivers. Their competence increases with the desperation of the situation. The more dangerous the circumstance, the greater their ability to cope with it. Although everyone hates to encourage young people to engage in dangerous activities, global thinkers are equipped to handle essential jobs that the rest of us wouldn't even consider attempting.

> As a medical student, Allison's learning disability and attention deficit disorder made the academic side of her training extremely difficult. Even with medication, she had a strong desire to be on her feet and moving around. It was impossible for her to sit still for prolonged periods. In preparing to choose a specialty, this young woman wanted to be sure that she selected a field where her hyperactivity and her style of concentration would work for her as assets.
>
> Allison felt drawn to crisis situations. She thrived on drama and excitement. She did her best thinking when in motion. To her, the intense atmosphere of the emergency room was very stimulating. She wanted a career that would keep her busy with activities that were both important and exciting.
>
> Allison's learning disability and attention deficit disorder gave her the advantage of being very inventive. She was well equipped to be an autonomous problem solver. She was eager to develop her skills to the point where her competence as a doctor would give her the sound judgment needed to make critical decisions under pressure. For this aspiring physician, the ideal career would take the global focus of extreme skiers and apply it to medicine.

Years ago, teachers used fear as a method of classroom control. Paddling, rapping knuckles, and making students stand in the corner or stay after school were popular punishments. Such physical demonstrations of disapproval spoke very clearly to certain types of children. For many, it was a highly effective method of maintaining a quiet, disciplined atmosphere. Many global thinkers flourish in such harsh environments. If the rules are precise and strictly enforced, if you have to be tough just to survive, if there is one clearly established authority figure backed by a system of powerful rule enforcers, if there is a "right way" to do everything, if punishment is certain, swift, and unpleasant, then global thinkers are able to use their heightened alertness to their advantage.

They make great marines. Those who have learned to use their superfocus find it a tremendous asset on the battlefield, where it's a matter of staying totally alert or dying. (The various branches of the armed forces will not accept applicants who are on stimulant medication.) Between skirmishes, all the drilling, training, and strictly enforced discipline help the troops burn off excess energy and stay out of trouble.

> While he was in the army, Tony's attention deficit disorder kept him alive. His ability to remain alert and highly energetic was extremely valuable when he went out on patrol in Vietnam. It wasn't until he got out of the military and into college that having an attention deficit disorder became a problem.
>
> The first semester on campus was a painful transition for Tony. He found it impossible to concentrate when his daily routine included nothing but sedentary activities like classes, labs, and studying. He needed much more physical activity than academic life provided.
>
> Through a process of experimentation, Tony developed a workout schedule that allowed him to keep his attention focused through an entire day of scholarly pursuits. His day started at four in the morning with an hour of karate and weightlifting. He was at the YMCA when the doors opened at five. For one solid hour, he swam laps. He showered and shaved in the locker room, then returned home for breakfast. Before leaving for his eight o'clock class, he got in twenty minutes of meditation. Around four in the afternoon, when his restlessness was growing and his focus was fading, he'd run for an hour and do another twenty minutes of meditation. That was usually enough to give him control of his concentration so that he could comfortably settle into an evening of reading and study.
>
> As long as Tony stuck to his routine, he could control his attention deficit disorder enough to be a successful student.

Since global thinkers tend to have trouble organizing their lives, many of them thrive in an atmosphere where structure is imposed on them from the outside. Sylvester Stallone often refers to his lifelong struggle with ADD. He hates schedules and the restrictions of a routine; however, in order to be productive, he has to force himself to be extremely disciplined. He finds that when he lets himself follow his preferences, he not only gets nothing accomplished but also makes dumb decisions that he later regrets.

The rigorous discipline of early-twentieth-century classrooms kept most ADD youngsters in line. Fireball Hurt forever remembered the teacher who ran the one-room schoolhouse of his Idaho childhood. She wore a thimble on one finger and used it to give unruly youngsters a sharp rap on the head to draw their attention back to their studies. Spirited mischief-makers learned to maintain a high level of vigilance in order to keep an eye on this dangerously armed schoolmarm.

All through his life, Hurt claimed that it was in that little country schoolhouse that he learned the people-reading skills that made him successful in business. He totally rejected any suggestion that he was a right-brain thinker gifted with a high degree of intuition. He insisted that he had deliberately developed his ability to predict human behavior by keeping close watch on a teacher who loved to swoop down to administer a quick flick with that thimble.

He must have been good at it. He was the teacher's pet. As an adult, he was extremely hyperactive, yet as a schoolboy, he managed to keep all that energy under check. It's possible that the motivation was fear.

Teacher trainer Susan Kovalik often refers to her childhood experiences in a Catholic school. She makes it sound funny when she tells how scary it was to know that the least little slip-up might prompt an angry nun to sweep over to administer some horrible punishment. She and her grade-school classmates lived in terror. Despite being in huge classes of fifty or sixty, the students kept their work neat, their lines straight, and their mouths shut. They knew that no offense went unnoticed by the black-robed sisters, who were rumored to have eyes in the backs of their heads underneath all those veils. By today's standards, it was a brutal environment. Where were the ADD youngsters in those old-style parochial-school classrooms? (Many of those who were unmanageable were thrown out. And no one tried to discourage them if they switched to a vocational school or dropped out to stay home and work on the farm.) Of the ADD children who chose to stay in school, what was it that enabled them to function without medication?

With our current attitudes and practices, we create classrooms that make it all but impossible for global thinkers to concentrate. Strict rules are neither encouraged by the community nor supported by the administration. Physical punishment is unpopular. Unrealistic expectations are imposed on young children under the pretext that they are being prepared for high school or college or "the real world." Criticism and confrontation are avoided for fear of damaging young egos, inciting a riot, or incurring a lawsuit.

The most active, interesting, and dangerous aspects of the environment attract and hold the attention of global thinkers. In classrooms where the subject matter and the teacher happen to fit that description, ADD youngsters get involved with their schoolwork and thrive. When the real show is the antics of ill-mannered classmates, the surly throng in the halls, and the threat of violence on the grounds, then right-brain learners get their minds riveted on the activities of other students.

Unfortunately, the exciting action in today's schools is rarely the teaching.

IMPULSE CONTROL THROUGH UNDERSTANDING

Those who live successfully with ADD learn to say no to the constant demands of the impulsive four-year-old within. "I want a candy bar." "Let's have another drink." "I want that new stereo." "I don't want to go to bed now." The little begging voice is always alert to opportunities for immediate pleasure. It is very persistent. It isn't easily brushed aside. Those who develop self-control do so with firm but loving management of the fun-seeker inside their head.

By making a commitment to an important goal, individuals create a reason to stand up against temptations that would lead to foolish decisions. By understanding the nature of the child within, they find the strength to consider every momentary whim in terms of how the outcome would effect the overall plan. With this understanding, the reasoning self is brought to bear as a balancing factor. When it goes to work, a process of deliberate decision making overrides the tendency to jump into impulsive actions. Children can be taught to put the power where the wisdom is.

Jerry had lots of problems with the kids in his eighth-grade class. They stole his hat, made crude comments about his constant tapping and rocking, and called him "retard" every time he demonstrated his inability to read cursive writing. School was not pleasant for Jerry.

Years of counseling and medication had not helped. Nobody could stand to be around him. He was just *too* hyperactive. Even the most compassionate teachers found that the only way to keep peace in their classroom was to put Jerry out in the hall.

It was not a healthy situation. In the middle of the eighth grade, the boy's self-esteem sank to an all-time low. Although he had no desire to improve his grades, he desperately wanted to get his classmates to quit picking on him.

Jerry begged his mother to shift to homeschooling. Since his parents felt that such a change would avoid the problem rather than solve it, they refused.

In exploring his options, this fourteen-year-old with severe attention deficit disorder realized the cost of being weird had gotten too high. He told his parents and his counselor, "I'm desperate. I'll do anything." He was ready to do whatever was necessary to change the conduct that made him such an outcast.

Jerry chose two goals: he would stop the bouncing (and wiggling and tapping and jiggling and rocking) and master cursive handwriting. The youth's family found a tiny private school that agreed to help him get a grip on his hyperactive behavior. An LD therapist started teaching him cursive handwriting. For the first time in his life, Jerry was highly motivated. He became a full partner in the project and began monitoring his own actions. His progress was so rapid, it was startling.

Motivated by the strong desire to stop looking "weird," Jerry got control over his excessive movement patterns in less than a week. Within a few months, he was trying out his growing social skills at school events. Being comfortably accepted by the other students was a great sign of success. Jerry's big moment came in the graduation program, when he carried off two different solo parts with poise and dignity. For his teary-eyed mother, the fact that he remembered his lines and spoke up clearly was just a bonus. The big thrill was that, for the first time, Jerry successfully participated in a school production and looked just like all the other children. His family was very proud of him. He'd made the decision to overcome a major problem, and he'd succeeded.

Students who get a new view of themselves can choose to take command of urges that have become habits. Those who learn to see themselves from a clear, unbiased perspective gain the ability to face their weaknesses in open, honest confrontation. By helping children develop an understanding of the undisciplined voice within, educators and psychologists teach youngsters to know how their mind makes decisions. When trained to think about their thinking, individuals become aware of, and can take charge of, the mental processing going on within.

When those with ADD see themselves as right-brain thinkers, they gain a perspective on their actions that allows an honest appraisal of strengths and weaknesses. They learn to recognize the pleasure-seeking voice of "the little kid" and guard against the impulsive behavior the emotion-driven side of their brain is constantly suggesting. They realize that wise decisions call for the use of reasoning to balance the tremendous appeal of hunches. They deliberately apply the organizational skills of the left brain to plan activities that will lead to the achievement of specific goals. They trust the inner "professor" to sound the alarm and override dumb choices that will lead to certain trouble. Growth in understanding takes place as this new knowledge is demonstrated in daily life.

The basis for self-control is a thorough but compassionate understanding of the self.

4

ON BEING DIFFERENT:

A Label or a Failure—Which is Worse?

Once a child has been identified as having a learning disability or an attention deficit disorder, parents are faced with several important decisions.

First, they must decide whether or not to believe the diagnosis. Occasionally, parents feel that a particular expert's judgment cannot be trusted. In such a case, a second opinion is needed. Sometimes, parents are unable to deal with the news that their child is learning disabled but are open to the idea that their youngster has an attention deficit disorder. (Since there are pills but no special classes for students with ADD, it usually has less stigma attached to it.) Some families refuse to allow their offspring to be given any kind of label. They don't want their child to be considered defective. Until the parents accept the fact that their child does indeed have the traits associated with such unpleasant (and inappropriate) labels as *disabled* and *disorder*, nothing much can be done to help. (In school systems where a policy of "inclusion" keeps special education children in regular classes, some classroom adjustments might be made despite the lack of formal permission from the parents.) Therapy cannot begin at school or in a clinic. Necessary adjustments cannot be made in the home. Gaining a thorough understanding of a child and his particular learning disability is crucial. Parents who have a clear picture of what the problem is rarely have trouble accepting it.

Even those who are homeschooling need to accept whatever current terminology most accurately fits their child. Curriculum guides and book catalogs are full of helpful suggestions on successfully teaching LD and ADD students. For those who are educating their child at home, being able to pinpoint the type of difficulty their youngster is experiencing makes it possible to choose appropriate instructional techniques and materials. Those who refuse to explore which categories of difficulty apply to their youngster deprive themselves of knowing where to look for the crucial information that can make the difference between success and failure.

The second step involves a question: "My child has a learning disability or an attention deficit disorder or both. What do I *do* about it?" The choices are all but unlimited. Some parents try to keep the problem a secret or pretend it does not exist; others decide to ignore it and hope it will go away. At the opposite extreme are those parents who make such a production of the matter that the learning disability becomes the focal point of the child's entire life. So the issue is whether or not to take action. The decision must be made.

Often, parents make the mistake of basing their decision on the question, "Should we single out our child and make him different, or would it be better just to leave him alone?" (They are really asking themselves, "Which is worse, freak or failure?")

But that is a nonsense question. LD and ADD children already *are* different. They already stand out. They will have a learning disability or an attention deficit disorder whether or not they are given that label. They can be taught by special methods that allow them to learn, or they can be left to their own devices to struggle with social rejection and academic frustration. The fact that they are disabled cannot be changed. Parents can choose only between helping them to succeed and allowing them to fail.

Failure, frustration, and ridicule are destructive. Learning disabilities and attention deficit disorders are not destructive.

Parents are often reluctant to put their LD child in a special class. They hate to send him to a therapist even when the special instruction he needs is provided free of cost, right within the school. They're afraid he will be miserable.

"More miserable than he already is?" the specialists ask. "What do you think goes on in his head when his classmates laugh at him and treat him like a freak? How do you think it feels to be teased and not have any friends? How do you think he feels about being called 'dummy' and bringing home a report card full of F's?"

Yes, it would be preferable to have every child succeed in a regular class. But when parents face the fact that they can't change whether or not their child has a learning disability or an attention deficit disorder, they are left with the question of what to do about it. They do have the ability to change the pattern of school failure into one of success.

Under federal law (PL 94–142), it used to be mandatory to provide appropriate services for LD students while mainstreaming them in the "least restrictive environment." In every area where the LD child could succeed with regular classwork in a normal classroom, he was supposed to be allowed and encouraged to do so. In areas where he had difficulty, he was supposed to receive special instruction from a trained LD teacher. It sounds like a perfect solution to a thorny problem, but in actual practice, it didn't work very well. LD classes and resource rooms became the dumping ground for troublemakers and misfits. Children who had serious learning disabilities failed to meet constantly changing guidelines and fell through the cracks. The paperwork imposed on teachers and administrators was staggering. And the number of students officially diagnosed and labeled far outstripped the schools' capacity to supply (or afford) services.

The trend of the 1990s is called "inclusion." This style of program has special ed students diagnosed and labeled, but all their instruction is provided within the regular classroom. It is highly unlikely that inclusion will prove to be the cure-all that so many long for. Regular classroom teachers do not have the time or expertise to design modified, individualized instruction for the 15 to 25 percent of each class that need it. Teachers' workshops and staff development rarely provide the training necessary to give inclusion a real chance for success. Budgetary limitations may make it essential that every child be included within the regular classroom, but it is unrealistic to pretend that this is in the best interest of any of the categories of exceptional students who cannot thrive without highly specialized instruction tailored to their needs.

Parents of LD and ADD youngsters tend to like the idea of having their children avoid the stigma of being labeled and being sent out of the room for special classes. However, when these children are included in regular classes without the benefit of any kind of meaningful special help, parents are forced to accept some heavy responsibilities and make some tough choices.

Regardless of their opinion of inclusion or mainstreaming or any other program the school systems adopt, it is up to the parents to monitor their child's progress and make sure successful learning is taking place. If it isn't, it is up to the parents to see to it that the situation is changed to one in which the child can and does succeed. The family also needs to be sure the youngster is well adjusted and content within the classroom arrangement provided. If the answer is no (and it usually is), it is up to the parents to see to it that the situation is changed.

In a regular classroom, with or without an inclusion program, LD children are usually teased and picked on by the other students. They are not accepted. As their frustrations mount, their behavior problems increase. In addition to being treated as dummies, they become known as troublemakers, crybabies, and bullies. By the time they are in the fifth or sixth grade, they have often built a reputation as petty thieves, liars, foul-mouthed screamers, loners, weirdos, or worse. Frequently, they are more than unpopular; they are outcasts. Occasionally, youngsters become so despised by classmates that teachers worry about keeping them safe from deliberate attacks in bathrooms, in halls, or on the playground. When LD children say, "They're picking on me," that is likely to be a true description of the situation.

Yet when they are told that they are going to be put into a

special school or program or sent somewhere for therapy, they shriek that they don't want to go. They want to be left just as they are in a regular class.

These protests should be ignored. Any child who spends a large part of the school day fighting, crying, or pretending he doesn't care does not know what happiness is. Not by any stretch of the imagination could he be said to be "happy" in a regular class. He just thinks he would be even *more* miserable in some special situation designed to help overcome the problems associated with his learning disability.

Just as parents have to accept the fact that their child has a learning disability or an attention deficit disorder, the child must come to terms with that fact. As long as the youngster is in a regular class where no help or therapy is provided, he can pretend he is just like everybody else. Adjusting schoolwork, providing therapy, or offering placement in a special school or class makes his disability public knowledge. The child already is different and knows it. But any kind of real action forces the youngster to admit his differentness to himself and others.

This is a very difficult step to take. But it is vitally important. LD and ADD children need a great deal of help accepting the fact that, whether they like it on not, they *are* different. Encouraging them to hide from the truth about themselves is *not* in their best interest. The first step in helping them overcome their difficulties involves guiding them to accept the fact that they have a specific, identifiable problem.

> Tony had received more than two years of intensive LD therapy at a private clinic. But it was unsuccessful. He could not do any of the regular work in his fifth-grade class. For all practical purposes, Tony was a nonreader.
>
> There were no special LD services available in Tony's school. He had been given all the therapy he could stand. There did not seem to be a good solution.
>
> Tony's therapist joined the parents in a conference with the youngster's teachers and the principal of the school. In the meeting, they all agreed that the boy truly was happy and well adjusted. He was liked and accepted by his classmates. He un-

derstood his learning problem and felt no anger or shame. His attitude was good; he was cooperative and willing to try. Except for the fact that his parents (by agreement with the school) did his homework with him, his home life was normal and satisfying in every way.

There was no class where Tony could learn more successfully. He was getting along so well in his regular class that he really enjoyed school. It would have been foolish to deprive him of the pleasure he found in being part of a class where he was understood, accepted, and liked. Moving the boy to a different school and a new class would have done more harm than good. He had very little to gain and a lot to lose.

Tony's teachers loved him. With the principal's permission, they designed a special program that would allow the boy to learn as much as possible while staying in the regular class.

At the end of the conference, the principal made a very unusual statement. As he shook hands with the family and the therapist, he emphatically said, "I personally guarantee that as long as Tony is in my school, I'll see to it that he gets the special treatment he needs. I have a very fine faculty that I know I can count on. They will back me. Until the end of the sixth grade, Tony is ours—and we'll take good care of him." (There are many fine public-school principals like this man. But it is rare that one will risk making such a firm commitment on behalf of a particular student. If there were more dedicated, courageous administrators of this type, inclusion would certainly work.)

For Tony, this was the best possible solution. But the key was that he was happy and well adjusted in his regular classroom. Except for the fact that he could not read, he was fine.

Unfortunately, that is rarely the case.

As a fifth-grader, Cal was one of the wildest boys in his private school. Between his midnight adventures riding minibikes on the country-club golf course and stealing hubcaps with high-school dropouts nearly twice his age, he was rough and tough, streetwise, and headed for serious trouble.

In school, Cal's behavior was awful. He was constantly disrupting his class, always starting trouble. His impulsive behavior and boisterous mannerisms made the other students stay clear of him as much as possible.

Cal's learning disability was not particularly severe. However, he was so hyperactive that he could work only one-to-one. (As is the case with most ADD youngsters, he spent all his time even in a very small group trying to impress the others by clowning and showing off.)

Cal's parents hired a therapist to go to his school and work with him privately three times a week. The boy was honest about the fact that it embarrassed him to be pulled out of his regular class for his special lessons. His teacher made sure none of his classmates made comments to add to his discomfort. His departures for therapy got to be so routine that nobody in the classroom paid any attention when Cal left his desk to go across the hall for his private lessons.

The therapy progressed very well. Cal was cooperative and cheerful. He worked hard, his attitude was excellent, and he was proud of his progress.

About eight weeks after the private therapy began, Cal's mother had second thoughts about singling her son out and leaving him open to ridicule. She said, "It's just too embarrassing for him to have to leave his regular class," and stopped his special lessons.

The therapist and the school told her she was making a serious mistake. But she would not listen.

The following year, Cal began hanging around with a rough gang of teenagers. They amused themselves with drugs, alcohol, and activities such as stealing sirens off police cars. Although Cal did not get arrested, he had several brushes with the law by the end of the sixth grade. His behavior in school became so uncontrollable that his parents were asked to put him elsewhere for the seventh grade.

Cal did not live to reach twenty-one. In his late teens, he and a group of friends died in a horrible crash. Drugs, alcohol, and extremely poor judgment were involved. It's painful to know that he might not have come to such a tragic end if his parents had had the courage to give him the help he needed.

"DON'T LABEL THAT CHILD"

Educators and writers for women's magazines shout with passion, "Don't single him out. Don't make him different!" But a child with a learning disability already *is* different. A youngster with an attention deficit disorder already stands out. He isn't learning, he's hard to get along with. He's disorganized, forgetful, chronically tardy, and socially unacceptable. He feels inferior, and he's very unhappy.

The child has a problem. The problem is a learning disability and/or an attention deficit disorder. Help is available from many sources. By using the appropriate term for the problem, it is possible to identify the difficulty and point the way to where to look for help.

I HAVE MET THE ENEMY AND HE ISN'T ME

There is one thing that helps LD and ADD students more than any other: knowing that the problem is *not* their fault.

LD and ADD individuals almost always feel guilty about their failure to learn. They grab the blame, accept the guilt, and suffer the burden alone. (Parents usually blame the school, a particular teacher, each other, or some outside event, such as an illness the child had or a change of schools due to a move. Sometimes, they blame the child.) In later life, LD and ADD adults almost always believe they could have done better in school if only they had tried harder. They see their failure as all their own fault!

When children are not learning, everyone around them searches frantically to find *who* is the cause of the problem. That approach is absolutely useless. The question must be, "*What* is the cause of the problem?" In looking for someone to blame, a person must be pointed out as the culprit. But in seeking *what* to blame, the learning disability or attention deficit disorder can be recognized as "the enemy."

As one explains to a child that he is LD or ADD, the amazed question almost always comes out, "You mean it's not all my own fault?" It usually takes time for the fact to sink in. Once the student realizes that his problem is caused by something over which he has no control, he is tremendously relieved. He's still ashamed of his failure, but he doesn't have to feel guilty anymore. He isn't stupid or lazy or bad, as he's always feared. There are others like him, so he isn't the freak he thought he was. The adults in his life understand and are going to help. He can trust them now that they see what's going on and really do understand. Knowing the name and nature of his enemy gives the LD child a whole new outlook. Because he can now take an active interest in his progress, he has a chance to overcome his difficulties and find real success.

LD and ADD children cannot be helped until they can look their parents and teachers in the eye and openly join in the battle cry.

"I have a learning disability. I am not the adversary; my learning disability is."

"My problem is called attention deficit disorder. I am not the enemy; ADD is. Along with anyone who will help me, I will fight it."

5

ISN'T ANYBODY WATCHING?

Why Public Schools Don't Recognize LD/ADD Children

Most teachers are not trained to recognize symptoms of learning disabilities and attention deficit disorders. Even at colleges with outstanding special ed programs and LD clinics, the regular education majors are not necessarily taught about LD and ADD youngsters.

Principals and administrators come through the same universities and the same programs. They're not taught anything about learning disabilities either.

Unfortunately, the few teachers who are taught about learning disabilities are usually given instruction that is not practical for use in a classroom.

> The English teachers at George Washington Junior High School were unusually well informed about learning disabilities. All of them had participated in two courses of in-service training. They knew the statistics. They knew the symptoms. And most of all, they cared. They were a fine group of dedicated professionals.
>
> These teachers wanted to help their LD and ADD students. But they openly admitted that they didn't know how. Only two

of the school's six hundred students had been identified as learning disabled. The teachers had no idea even how to find the other LD children in their school. They wanted guidance.

When asked, "Which of your students do you suspect might be LD?" all five members of the English department gave the same answer: "In all of my classes, I don't have any students that look learning disabled." They had many doing poor work and a lot who weren't paying attention, but in each case, the cause appeared to be something other than a learning disability or attention deficit disorder.

While experts use various figures, it is generally agreed that from 5 to 25 percent of all schoolchildren are LD and/or ADD. Based on even the low figure of 5 percent, Washington Junior High had at least twenty-eight unidentified LD/ADD children. These five English teachers came in contact with every child in the school. Yet only two students had been recognized as learning disabled! Where were all the others? Why couldn't anybody spot them?

Most teachers have some understanding of ADD and are quick to ask that hyperactive youngsters and those with behavior problems be taken to the doctor for medication. Few classroom teachers have much knowledge about learning disabilities. Among those who have had an introduction to the topic, most can't apply their knowledge to real children. They may have taken a course or a workshop or an in-service training class. But they were merely taught lists of symptoms and told inspiring stories about famous men who were successful despite their learning problems. It's very rare that teachers are taught anything they can use!

For example, teachers are rarely shown samples of work by LD children and told what to notice. And if they are, they're shown samples from extreme cases unlike anything they're likely to see in an entire career, or they're given samples of work by children vastly different in age from the ones they teach. (Seeing the types of mistakes LD students make on high-school themes is not very helpful to second-grade teachers.) The flood of jargon characteristic of courses in learning disabilities is another problem teachers must overcome. ("Innate tendencies toward proximodistal movement" means little to the average teacher.) And the techniques teachers are encouraged to use with these children are seldom practical. Either the techniques demand that students work independently in an environment where their distractibility and short attention span are major problems, or the techniques are so complicated that only a trained specialist would be able to employ them, or they require more time than any classroom teacher can spare. ("Give him fifteen minutes one-to-one every day," experts chirp. "When?" the teacher screams. She's got thirty-four other students, at least three LD children, and a very limited amount of time. She doesn't *have* forty-five minutes to devote to just three children. What's she supposed to do with the rest of the class while she's dabbling with LD therapy?)

Parents, LD consultants, school psychologists, and administrators often think this plea is a cop-out. It's not.

Look at a typical school day. Elementary schools usually run a six-hour day from, say, eight-thirty to three, with a half-hour for lunch. Most elementary schools have "self-contained" classes; except during periods when art, music, and physical education are taught, the child is with one teacher all day. There are at least thirty children in each class (often more nearly forty). The children range in ability from slow learners to geniuses. They may all be in the same grade, but they're working at many different levels.

> One year, I taught a regular fourth-grade class in a city public school. Of my thirty-six students, six excellent readers were reading at or above sixth-grade level; eight good readers were working at about fifth-grade level; ten average readers were at grade level; seven poor readers were a year or two behind; and five very poor readers were reading preprimers or other books designed for first-graders. I had to have five reading groups in order to come even close to meeting their needs.
>
> For an hour and a half each day, I juggled my time among those five reading groups. While one had my attention, the other four did independent work—silent reading, answering questions, looking up vocabulary words, etc. I spread myself so thin I could barely stand the strain. Every night, I carried home mountains of papers to grade. We never had time to do any of the creative, fun-type activities that are usually included in good reading programs. Some important areas had to be dropped: the top group never got to read aloud, the second group got to read orally only once a week, and only those in the bottom group got to check their work with me. To work in five groups, we had to

stay bound by a schedule. The fun and the personal touch were gone.

The bottom group got most of my attention.

If I had been able to find some extra time, I'd have used it for enrichment with the two neglected top groups. Had some outside expert come in and told me to give just ten minutes a day to each of my five extremely poor readers, I'd have been rude, if not hysterical.

I was young, energetic, and idealistic. I cared very much, and I wanted to help every one of my students. But I was already pushing myself to the limits of my strength.

Having five reading groups in one class is almost unheard of. But having children reading on so many different levels is typical. In almost all classrooms, the pupils are at various levels of readiness, achievement, and ability.

The classroom teacher is trying to teach six subjects to thirty children in a six-hour day. Can it be done? On the days when she doesn't have bus duty, lunchroom duty, hall duty, playground duty, reports to fill out, or some committee meeting, she gets her class started right at the opening bell. Into this day, she's going to try to squeeze the following:

15 minutes—attendance, lunch count, announcements, collecting money for various good causes, filling out forms, etc.

1 hour—reading

1 hour—English

1 hour—math

30 minutes—spelling

30 minutes—lunch

30 minutes—physical education (often required by state law)

45 minutes—science or health

45 minutes—social studies

45 minutes—art, music, library, etc.

15 minutes—clean room; assign homework; hand out notices for various civic, charitable, PTA, and government groups; and dismiss

That totals seven hours and fifteen minutes. Getting more than seven hours of work into a six-hour day requires a lot of careful planning and very tight scheduling. The teacher is already cutting corners. She's already standing on her head to fit so much into so little time. She usually doesn't even get to go to the bathroom until after the children have gone home for the day!

And then some out-of-town LD expert breezes in to tell her, "If you'll spend just fifteen minutes a day with that LD child doing what I tell you . . ." So the teacher tunes her out. She doesn't have fifteen minutes a day. (And she doesn't have just one LD child, either.) Such sessions would probably not be in the LD child's best interest anyway. Fifteen minutes of work a day would make for very slow progress even if carried on by a specialist over a long period. Any therapy that is not successful acts to further convince the child that his case is hopeless. A botched job is worse than no therapy at all!

INCOMPETENCE AT HIGH LEVELS

Principals, supervisors, administrators, and the machinery of the system often prevent teachers from helping learning-disabled children.

Although a teacher may not suspect that a failing student is learning disabled, she usually tries to do something to help. The reading coordinator is often the first person she sees in her search for assistance. This expert is right there in the school, ready to help with special problems. However, reading coordinators rarely know much about learning disabilities. When asked for ideas that might work with a fifth-grader reading at second-grade level, a reading coordinator usually pulls out a few easy books with big print and lots of pictures, along with an armful of old workbooks. Handing them to the teacher, she expresses her opinion with a comment like, "That Joe Woods could read if he wanted to. He's just too busy being a smart aleck. Just look at his eyes—that boy's smart. What he needs is somebody standing over him with a stick." At this point, some government-funded program might be suggested. The end result is that the teacher goes away feeling that only a fool would waste time trying to help that sorry Woods child.

A lot of teachers would give up then, if not earlier. But this discussion will follow one of the few who refuses to quit trying.

By Thanksgiving, the special material supplied by the reading coordinator proves useless. Joe Woods is still not learning to read. Again, the teacher searches for a source of help.

The next step is to discuss the child's problem with the reading supervisor when she comes around for her next monthly visit. Within school systems, supervisors are powerful people. They run whole programs and have the authority to hire and fire. They are supposed to be experts in the area over which they have command. But even when they do have the training and credentials, they frequently lack meaningful experience in dealing with the type of children they are supposed to know about.

Reading supervisors are usually old classroom teachers who have moved into their specialized area as a result of recent training or degrees. They tend to use jargon and a knowledge of trends in the field to support their very conservative views. They usually hold firmly to the one-room-school theory (currently known as "inclusion"): if the child is *your* student, *you* should handle all his problems. Reading supervisors rarely know much about learning disabilities, and if they do, they are likely to think the whole idea is merely an excuse for poor discipline or poor teaching.

The supervisor makes many suggestions for helping Joe. Being well informed about the newest materials and latest trends, she offers to order some teaching aid that is new on the market. From her experience as a classroom teacher, she tells of some game or puzzle that once produced wonderful results in one of her own pupils. The conference almost always ends the same way. The reading supervisor says, "I'll send those books over to you first thing tomorrow. And remember, any teacher worth her salt can help that child right there in her own classroom." Sometimes, she merely encourages the teacher to handle Joe's problems herself; sometimes, she insists on it. Either way, the teacher must follow her supervisor's recommendations; it's part of the process required by state guidelines. It'll be at least January before the teacher can pass this hurdle and move on to look for help for Joe elsewhere.

At this point, any further action involves a great deal of red tape. If the teacher goes to her principal, he'll tell her one of three things: (1) "There's nothing wrong with that child that you can't handle yourself" (or that a good swift kick in the pants won't cure, or that any of his past teachers noticed, or that can be helped at all); (2) "Fill out this eight-page request in quadruplicate and we'll get the school psychologist to look into it"; (3) "Fill out this twenty-three-page form and we'll call a meeting of the school-based committee to discuss it."

The names and procedures vary from one school to another, but the functions of these committees are basically the same. A school-based committee is called together to discuss one particular child who is having major problems in that school. The committee always includes the principal and the teacher responsible for the child. It usually has two or three permanent members chosen by the principal. In some states, it must have at least one member of the same race as the child in question, plus one member of a minority group. Special ed teachers, counselors, and social workers attend lots of school-based committee meetings.

To get a child's case brought before the school-based committee, his teacher must first convince the principal that the child is in critical need of such attention. (Sometimes, the teacher fails to do this and the whole matter is dropped there.) After he sees the need, the principal calls a meeting of the committee. It often takes more than a month to find a time when six busy teachers can squeeze this added responsibility into their schedules. Getting a child's case before a school-based committee can be a major production.

At the meeting itself, the student's teacher carefully describes the child's difficulties and discusses them with the others. Then the committee decides what should be done about the problem. (Sometimes, the teacher fails to convince the committee members that her pupil needs special help and the whole matter is dropped.)

One of the topics that almost always comes up is medication. Whether a learning disability is suspected or not, children who are having trouble with behavior, schoolwork, or paying attention are prime candidates for stimulant medication. Educators and doctors usually take the attitude, "It's worth a try." To get the ball rolling, the youngster's key teachers fill out a questionnaire designed to determine how much of the difficulty fits into the patterns seen in children with ADD. The family is given a set of the survey questions to answer as well. Once the paperwork is in order, the parents are called in for a conference, at which the teacher suggests that the evaluation forms be taken to the family doctor as evidence that a trial period on medication is appropriate. If the drugs help, the child is labeled as having an attention deficit disorder, and that's pretty much the end of it. If the medication doesn't help, a full psychological evaluation is possible.

Most schools have an overworked psychologist who visits each campus for half a day once a week. When the teacher does catch the psychologist, she hears, "Sounds like something we ought to look into. Fill out the request forms, get the parents' permission slips signed, and I'll try to work him in for testing sometime this spring."

Although the teacher probably does not suspect that poor Joe is learning disabled, if an LD specialist is available, she may turn to her in desperation. From her, she gets, "Sorry, I can't help you. Unless a child has been through the school-based committee and the placement committee, I'm not allowed to touch him."

Typically, there is only one placement committee for an entire school system. The group is usually made up of one principal, one regular classroom teacher, one special education teacher, a psychologist, an assortment of supervisors and department heads, and an assistant superintendent or two. Sometimes, there is no LD specialist on the placement committee. This group meets regularly to decide what the schools will do to help special students who have already been diagnosed. The placement committee must classify a child as learning disabled before the school system's LD specialists become involved.

Getting the child tested may take months; getting his case before the placement committee sometimes takes longer. It is often extremely difficult to convince the various committees that something really is so wrong as to require attention. The fact that Joe Woods has entered the machinery of "the system" does not guarantee that he will get the help he needs.

In a city school system of forty-six thousand students (where we *know* at least 5 percent, or twenty-three hundred children, are learning disabled), it's possible to have fewer than two hundred pupils receiving therapy from the staff of LD teachers. In order to get help, the child has to be a real basket case.

Sometimes, a whole school gets excited about learning disabilities. But school systems can often stop an entire faculty from accomplishing anything.

At Washington Junior High School, the principal and his entire faculty were determined to do everything in their power to find and help their LD students.

A consultant worked with them to develop a plan of attack. The law clearly forbade individual testing and precise diagnosis without parental permission and strong proof of need. It was not practical to ask the school psychologist to test the entire student body. But through careful screening, it would be possible to narrow down the field, then request testing for only those students who looked as if they might be learning disabled.

The five English teachers had contact with every student in the school. They agreed to give tests to screen the student body. Every child was to be given a silent reading test, a special vocabulary test taken both orally and silently, a spelling test, and several smaller tests that required a demonstration of skill with sequencing. Such a screening could not pick out the LD students, but it would provide a good set of clues as to who they might be. The entire faculty agreed to score and analyze the six hundred tests. This amazing group of teachers agreed to take on this huge project in order to find and help their previously unrecognized LD students.

They had high hopes. They expected that by mid-November, they'd be fighting on behalf of LD students in meetings of the school-based committee; that by the end of January, classroom teachers would be exploring creative ways to help the newly identified LD students within their regular classes; that by spring, they'd have between fifteen and twenty LD students officially diagnosed and placed; and that with the many pupils already identified, they'd probably be able to get a specialist assigned to the school for the following year. It was going to be a tough road, but they knew they could do it.

In mid-October, before the first test had been given, the project was stopped dead in its tracks. The assistant superintendent in charge of special education decided that the screening program was illegal. His official opinion was that the Washington Junior High project could be interpreted as "identifying," and that's against the law! By his orders, the LD screening was abandoned.

Most teachers give up their fight for an LD child long before they get to an assistant superintendent. Teachers who have been around a while know that "you can't beat the system."

Most teachers truly do care. They fail to get help for LD children for three basic reasons: (1) they are not trained to recognize learning disabilities; (2) they don't have the time or energy to devote themselves to the needs of just one child; (3) they know that to help one particular child, they will have to wade hip deep into red tape and might have to take on the whole system.

IT TAKES AN ACT OF CONGRESS TO GET HELP FOR AN LD CHILD

In reading the dismal stories in this chapter, one wonders that any of the learning disabled are ever helped. It is obvious that parents cannot rely on the schools to identify these children and provide them with the special instruction they need. But in the 1970s, the federal government passed two forms of legislation designed to help LD and ADD students get the special services they must have in order to succeed.

The first one, section 504 of the Americans with Disabilities Act of 1973, gives both LD and ADD students grounds for demanding adjustments in classroom environment, equipment and materials, and support services. It is particularly useful to older students who need modifications such as private rooms, extended time limits, and revised formats on tests like the SAT and MCAT. Under section 504, it is even possible for some learning-disabled candidates to take college and graduate entrance exams with either a reader or a tape recording of test material. By working closely with a school's 504 coordinator, those who have an official diagnosis of ADD, ADHD, or LD can insist that appropriate modifications be made to accommodate their special needs. It is up to the student to take the initiative, and when schools are not in compliance, it is the student's responsibility to bring in lawyers and outside experts to exert pressure. For those who are persistent, the law is clearly on the side of the student.

Public Law 94-142 was passed by Congress in 1977. It states that, nationwide, public schools must meet *all* the educational needs of *all* their pupils free of cost. The blind, the deaf, the mentally retarded, the emotionally disturbed, the learning disabled—for exceptional children as well as "normal" ones, a free and appropriate education *must* be provided under the law.

When the law first went into effect, *mainstreaming* became the buzzword. Public Law 94-142 states that students must be provided special services within the "least restrictive" environment. Most school systems interpreted this to mean that self-contained classes and one-to-one instruction should be avoided. Many "pullout" models were designed based on the resource room model; these programs were designed to pull the student out of the regular classroom to spend several hours a week in a small group taught by an LD teacher. And the Individual Educational Plan (IEP) came into being to keep records on the hordes of children working to overcome specific academic deficits.

Public Law 94-142 helped in that it led regular classroom teachers to see that LD youngsters can be taught effectively when provided proper instruction in an appropriate environment. But by creating whole new categories of specialists, it led teachers to believe that exceptional children can only make academic gains when taught by experts. Many teachers felt no responsibility for special-needs youngsters beyond referring them for evaluation and hoping they got placed in a special ed class.

Some school systems designed LD programs that lived up to the spirit of Public Law 94-142 by providing excellent alternative instruction for learning-disabled youngsters. But most schools never figured out what was really needed by these nontraditional learners. In some ways, this well-intended legislation may have done more harm than good. Schools poured more and more students into already overcrowded LD classes taught by poorly trained special ed teachers. These programs were frequently supplied with totally inappropriate materials—or no materials at all. Many schools claimed that they were providing appropriate instruction simply because an LD child had occasional contact with a certified LD teacher. And the law applied only to those diagnosed as LD; students who were labeled as ADD or ADHD did not qualify for special services.

Four conditions are necessary for a class to be appropriate for learning-disabled children. It must have (1) a specially trained teacher, (2) special methods of instruction, (3) special books and materials, and (4) a small number of students—ideally, between six and ten. Many school systems pretend that methods, materials, and class size are not important. They are wrong. If *any* of the four factors is missing, an appropriate class for LD students is *not* being provided—and the law is being violated.

In the late 1980s, school budgets started getting tight. At the same time, the educational pendulum started swinging away from pullout programs. The new buzzword became *inclusion*. The general idea sounds wonderful: special education children will be much happier (and thus more successful) if none of them has to suffer the stigma and embarrassment of being singled out as defective and sent off to some special room for the dummies. And "normal" children will have their lives enriched by being exposed to the full variety of types that make up the real world.

The arguments in support of inclusion are glowing and very persuasive. However, when applying this trend to children with learning disabilities and attention deficit disorders, there is one fact that is never mentioned: the vast majority of LD and ADD/ADHD youngsters are extremely distractible. And the thing that is *most* distracting to them is groups of their fellow students. If there is any disruptive behavior going on, they'll be watching it, participating in it, or causing it. In normal-size classes of twenty or more, they are so busy monitoring the environment and horsing around that they get very little schoolwork done. And their constant disturbances prevent their classmates from concentrating as well. Even when thoroughly medicated and taught by an experienced specialist, students with attention problems *cannot* keep their minds on their work when surrounded by more than eight or ten of their peers. Inclusion might work for some types of special ed students, but children who have trouble paying attention are probably going to find themselves among the disruptive students who spend lots of time in the office.

A DEGREE DOES NOT AN EXPERT MAKE

There are so many out-and-out quacks in the field of learning disabilities that parents and teachers don't know whom to believe. And among experts who *do* know what they're talking about, there are so many different approaches and theories that the specialists can't believe each other. They don't even agree as to what a learning disability is! It has gotten to the point that one just doesn't know who can be trusted. A string of degrees is no guarantee.

> There is a state superintendent of special education who has a Ph.D. in psychology. He is said to be an expert in testing and diagnosis. He's in charge of all the LD programs in his state. Yet he has never taught a single LD child! If he were locked in a small room and told to teach one of these youngsters to read, he wouldn't have the faintest idea what to do. This man is not qualified to set policies and guide LD teachers.

> A young woman had a shiny new Ph.D. in learning disabilities from an outstanding university. Unfortunately, the emphasis in her training was on research. She knew how to set up a study, evaluate a program, analyze the statistical findings of large studies. She knew how to read a set of test scores (though she was not qualified to do the testing herself) and prescribe therapy for disabled children.
> But she had never taught an LD child. She had many ideas— she called it the "eclectic" approach—but had never tried out a single one of them on a real student.
> This lady was unusual. She had sense enough to realize that her degree was not enough. If she got a job in her field, she'd be faking it. She needed someone to teach her how to teach.

> A mother at a Cub Scout picnic proudly announced, "My son was diagnosed as learning disabled at the age of three." It turned out that the family's pediatrician was a self-proclaimed ex-

pert on learning disabilities. He prided himself on recognizing all his little LD patients long before they reached school age.

She felt that this doctor had positively saved her son from certain doom.

It would be nice if her doctor really was the miracle worker she believed, but it seems unlikely.

A highly respected doctor came to a CHADD (Children with Attention Deficit Disorder) meeting to explain the appropriate uses and possible benefits of stimulant medication for students with attention deficit disorder. At the end of his presentation, he said that he believed all four- and five-year-olds should be screened for ADD.

And how would he do that? This physician wanted to give all preschoolers a thirty-day trial on stimulant medication. If it made no noticeable difference, they didn't have an attention deficit disorder. If it improved their behavior and increased their concentration, they would stay on it because they obviously needed it!

Every LD expert has a pet theory about treatment. Diets, color-coded alphabets, exercises, eyeglasses, perceptual/motor training, eye-movement patterning, medication—a huge variety of possible cures has been proposed. A tremendous amount of research is being done. And a lot of it looks very promising. Someday, someone may discover *the cure.* To the best of my knowledge, it has not been found yet.

6

WHAT TO DO WHEN PROFESSIONAL HELP IS NOT AVAILABLE:

Adaptive Techniques

In spite of the laws, many LD children do not get the help they need. For bright youngsters, their high intelligence helps them to compensate for their learning problems. Such children rarely qualify for public-school LD programs because they seldom fall two years below grade level; most public-school programs are limited to those who are two or more years behind. Small private and church-related schools will probably never design programs to provide special services for their LD students. Children with less common learning disabilities will probably continue to be ignored; they don't fit into programs aimed at those with the common types of specific language disabilities centered on problems with reading and spelling. And as always, some LD children either will not be recognized at all (as with many of those labeled as ADD or ADHD but not recognized as LD) or will be turned down by placement committees. No matter what the reasons, there will always be LD children who cannot get professional help. In such cases, parents and regular classroom teachers need guidance. In fact, all parents of LD children need advice. Those whose youngsters are getting professional help should look to their child's therapist as a source of information. Part of good LD therapy includes counseling parents.

THE "OFFICIAL" DIAGNOSIS

Those who wish to take advantage of the special services available through school systems and government agencies must have a complete evaluation done by a medical doctor or a psychologist. No matter how remote the area or how poor the school district, competent psychologists are available to test children at no cost to the parents. Even though the interpretation of test results may be inaccurate (many of them are), the testing will provide one key piece of information. Through use of either the Stanford-Binet Intelligence Scale or the Wechsler Intelligence Scale for Children-III, the evaluator can get a reliable IQ score. (See chapter 8 for explanation concerning the meaning of such scores.)

In addition to the testing available through the local schools, most counties have some type of public clinic where a psychological evaluation can be obtained at low cost. Such clinics usually have well-trained psychologists who are experienced in testing children. While specialists at local clinics often know little about learning disabilities, they *can* tell if a child is either mentally retarded or emotionally disturbed. So the information they provide is almost always quite valuable.

Many colleges, universities, and hospitals have clinics that specialize in learning disabilities. Sometimes, getting a child tested at one of these clinics is expensive, but not always. Many have a sliding scale for fees. Often, family health insurance will cover most of the cost. Through the family doctor or pediatrician, through the public-school psychologist or social worker, through local mental health agencies, or through organizations like the Learning Disabilities Association, the Orton Dyslexia Society, and CHADD, parents can find guidance in their search for such clinics in their area.

In seeking a good diagnosis, it is important to remember that many people will want to help the child, but most won't know how.

WHAT ABOUT TEACHING YOUR OWN CHILD?

Many children who desperately need specialized instruction will never qualify for it through their school. Private learning-disability therapy is very expensive. Television talk shows and advertisements offer some slick-sounding home-remedy kits that suggest that just twenty minutes a night with some family-fun phonics game can teach any child to read.

Buyer beware! These materials will *not* work for the majority of LD and ADD children. They might be helpful to some youngsters, but those with a learning disability need to be taught by techniques that are radically different from the ones used in products offered to the mass market. And usually, the children who are forced to participate in these wonder home courses do so with the same kind of awful attitude they display when doing homework.

After a hard day at the office or the shop, parents are not likely to find tutoring activities pleasant or successful. In order to help a child, his teacher must be calm, patient, confident, and understanding. Many are capable of maintaining this attitude with someone else's kids; not all adults can be unemotional with their own children. Parents should not ruin their role as parents by trying to squeeze in a little LD therapy on the side. Rather, they should love, care, try to understand, sympathize, and help their children adapt. Youngsters with a learning disability or an attention deficit disorder need a home with fun and laughter and kiteflying and fishing trips and picnics in the park. They need help in finding activities outside of school that give strong feelings of success and pleasure. More than anything else, LD children need a place where they can feel good about themselves whether they spell well or not. Anyone who is around an LD/ADD child can help him feel accepted and loved just as he is—but parents can do this best.

There are situations, however, where the only LD therapy is what the family can provide within the home. In such cases, it is vital that the parents get guidance and training in the instructional methods appropriate for their youngsters. It is also crucial that they acquire specially designed materials. It often takes six months to a year of reading, studying, coursework, and training to prepare a family member to supervise a home-based LD program. It can be done. And when done properly, it can be very effective.

Those who take the time and trouble to learn to teach an LD youngster often find that the best way to apply those skills is in homeschooling. Not every parent has the time or temperament to homeschool an LD child, but for those who choose to try it, the results are often very, very good. When these children are removed from classrooms where every breath from a classmate is a distraction, they find a new interest in learning.

ASSUMING RESPONSIBILITY

When professional LD therapy is not available, the parents of a learning-disabled child must be *totally* responsible for two things: (1) they must see to it that their child does not become emotionally damaged, and (2) they must see to it that their child gets an education despite the learning disability. Even when therapy is available, these responsibilities still belong to the parents.

PREVENTING EMOTIONAL DAMAGE

In leading an LD child to an honest acceptance and understanding of his disability, parents must be sure that they never do or say anything to make him feel guilty about or ashamed of something for which he is not to blame. The youngster's home should be the one place in the world where he can count on finding understanding and encouragement. Unless parents work toward this goal, the child will develop strong feelings of guilt and worthlessness.

> Bob was an attractive and intelligent young man. He stayed in high school until he was twenty-one, but his learning disability was so severe that he could not pass enough courses to graduate. Shortly after he dropped out, he was diagnosed as LD. Never having met a single person who understood his problem, he felt that he was a worthless failure and that it was all his own fault.

Bob loved to travel. He had hitchhiked all over the country, but he had never stayed in any one place for more than a few days. He once explained, "I was afraid that if I stayed long enough for people to get to know me, they wouldn't like me."

Bob was a gentle, loving person. Yet he had been a loner for years. It wasn't that he didn't like people. He was afraid to let anybody get close to him. He was afraid of being rejected. He believed that anyone who learned about his poor spelling and reading would see him in the same way he saw himself—as a worthless bum.

In order to accept and like himself, Bob had to come to understand his learning disability. After he recognized some of the beauty in himself, he opened up to let others see it, too.

Convincing an LD child that he is not stupid is always a long process. It cannot be accomplished by one speech that is never repeated. Day by day, things will happen to make the youngster feel dumb: he'll spend three hours studying for a test, then flunk it; he'll misread *ask* as *ass* in front of the whole class and turn flame-red with embarrassment; he'll get thrown out of art class because he's so clumsy with a ruler and scissors that the teacher thinks he's not trying; he'll be suspended from high school because he ripped up his Shakespeare book and threw it at his English teacher's feet. As such situations arise, the child will need help getting over the hurt feelings, anger, and embarrassment. He will often need to have someone calmly lead him to figure out which of his LD characteristics caused the problem, how that particular problem is different from general stupidity, and how to avoid letting the problem get him into another bad situation in the future.

A student teacher was giving dictation to my LD class of ten-to twelve-year-olds. She was reading sentences, which the students were writing on their papers. I was observing.

Sam, an older boy with a quick temper and a severe disability, was having trouble keeping up. Wanting Miss Long to slow down, he raised his hand once to get her attention, but she didn't notice. Struggling with his spelling and his handwriting, he tried to catch up. Finally, he slammed his pencil on his desk, folded his arms across his chest with a "Humph!" and gave up. The color rose in his neck and face as he glared straight ahead to fight back the tears. Sam was very near exploding.

Still, Miss Long didn't notice.

Several of the boys glanced at him with sympathy. They understood his frustration and would have offered help if they could. But they had problems enough of their own—the dictation was still going on.

There were only five more minutes until break. I decided that as long as Sam didn't explode, I would not interfere. Those five minutes seemed to last for hours.

Finally, Miss Long collected the papers. When she took Sam's from his desk, she commented, "You've only got the first part. Why didn't you finish?"

"I didn't *want* to," he snarled.

Miss Long didn't push it. She dismissed the boys for break.

I caught Sam's attention and motioned toward the door. "I'd like to speak to you in private."

In heavy silence, he followed me into the hall.

The rest of the students moved freely around us on their way to the drinking fountain and bathroom. The area just outside our door was recognized as the place where pupils could talk with me in private despite the hordes of children streaming by.

I put an arm around Sam's shoulder. He stared at the floor. I tried not to be too gentle—that would have made him cry and embarrassed him further. "I want to compliment you for the way you handled that situation," I began.

He didn't answer by even a nod.

I went on, "Miss Long didn't notice that you got stuck— and I'll speak to her about that. For your part, you handled your anger well. You didn't throw anything or shout anything nasty." I paused to let him think about how much his behavior had improved over the past six months. "Your learning disability makes spelling really tough. For you, and some of the other guys, too, these dictations are really murder."

Sam nodded his head in agreement. He was winning his battle over the welling tears but still didn't dare look at me.

"You *were* rude to Miss Long. But considering how upset you were, what you said was not all that bad." I gave his shoulder a squeeze, then concluded, "You go on in the bathroom, then get yourself a drink, walk around the building for a few minutes, and cool off."

Sam was pretty well back together. I gave him a pat on the rear and he ambled down the hall.

When I explained the situation to Miss Long, she was surprised and ashamed. "But why didn't he raise his hand?" she asked.

"He did raise his hand—once. But you were dictating and didn't notice."

She shook her head. Now my student teacher was on the verge of tears.

I tried to calm her while also making her understand. "I know you don't have eyes in the back of your head. When a kid puts his hand up one time for three seconds, you won't always notice. That's not where you blew it."

Miss Long stared at me.

As gently as I could, I laid it on the line. "A 'normal' kid will flap his hand around in the air all day and insist that you wait while he catches up. But Sam's LD. He hates dictations. For him, they're hard. He's ashamed of just how hard—and besides, if there's any possible way around it, he'd rather not do them at all. If getting hit in the head with a two-by-four would get him out of doing a dictation, he'd take the two-by-four."

A small smile fluttered at the corners of Miss Long's mouth. She was beginning to get the idea.

"It's a wonder he gave you a chance by raising his hand even once, but he did. And you missed it. Okay, so now what do you do?"

"Yes, really," Miss Long nodded. "What do I do?"

"First of all, you get to know your kids. No matter what you're doing, you need to know in advance which ones are going to have trouble with it. Dictations are tough. They all hate them. But four or five of the guys have a *special* hate for dictations."

"Sam, and Bobby, and Ted." She paused, then added two more.

"Right." She had selected the same ones I would have picked. "So during dictation, keep a sharp eye on those five. Don't let them bog down. Don't let them get lost. Don't wait for them to get into trouble or fall apart. Cruise that room. Watch those papers. Tune in to those pencils. You can't teach LD kids standing up in front of the room like a post. Move around. Watch. Get close."

We discussed it for a few minutes, then Miss Long asked, "What do I do about Sam? Do you think I should apologize?"

I advised, "An apology would be nice, if it's genuine. It would help him know that teachers make mistakes, too. But the main thing is for you and Sam to work out a way so it won't happen again. Help him see that it's his learning disability that makes dictations so hard for him. Then find a way where you and he can *both* take responsibility for his keeping up in the future."

She nodded and started back into the room.

I tapped her on the shoulder. "Then take him in the back of the room and give him the dictation."

Miss Long seemed stunned. She didn't complain, but her

face plainly showed that she thought I was being too tough a taskmaster on Sam.

"It's like the law of gravity," I explained. "No matter what happens, the students get their work done. *Nothing*—bad behavior, tantrums, misunderstandings, apple-polishing—*nothing* can get one of these kids out of doing his work."

"Right." She smiled with real understanding.

Miss Long took Sam to a table at the back of the room. They talked comfortably for quite a while, then did the dictation. They both had learned something important about themselves.

In the above incident, Sam was helped to understand his learning disability. He was also helped to deal with his anger.

LD and ADD youngsters feel a lot of anger. They must be taught to deal with it.

Many adults make the terrible mistake of denying LD and ADD children the right to feel angry. These children have a problem. Their problem embarrasses them, makes them look stupid, and prevents them from doing many of the things they want to do. They don't *want* to be LD and/or ADD. But they are—and most of them hate it.

Of course they get angry.

The anger itself is not bad. It's what they do with it that causes trouble and terrifies others.

When an LD child (or any child, for that matter) is furious about something, it is wrong to tell him that he should not feel angry. That doesn't stop the anger; it just adds guilt to it. He already *is* angry. He needs someone to help figure out what to do to get rid of it.

The way to get rid of anger is to express it in some way that does no harm. This is something children must be taught.

There are two ways to express anger that seem to work best: physically and vocally. An angry child needs to release a burst of energy by ripping, throwing, smashing, jumping, kicking, running, crushing, pounding, stomping, hitting, squeezing—or by screaming, yelling, shrieking, cursing, bellowing, shouting, swearing. One or the other or both, directed at something that will not be damaged and won't fight back, will use up all the anger.

The boys in my class were always getting into fistfights during their touch football games. If a play didn't work out right, one of them would get angry and throw the ball at somebody—hard. A fight was almost always the result.

We solved the problem by agreeing that anger does make a person want to throw something. That method of releasing anger would be allowed, provided two rules were observed: (1) nothing would be thrown *at* another person, and (2) the one who hurled the ball halfway across the field would be the one to go and get it.

Throwing the ball didn't appeal to everybody, though. Some of my students were more prone to shouting and cursing at others when they got angry. A few simple swearwords almost always led to real filth, followed by references to "your mama." And then the fur would fly.

We resolved this problem by agreeing that anger does make a person want to scream. Anyone overwhelmed by this need would be allowed to go over by the woods and shout anything he felt like shouting. Anything the rest of us overheard was ignored. As soon as the anger was spent, the screamer would be taken back into the game with no questions or comments. (The screaming never lasted more than three minutes.)

Those rules saved the guys from a lot of fights.

Fifth-graders Ted, Bobby, and Ken hated math. Though their problems were different, all were struggling to learn second-grade arithmetic. I would work with them closely, then leave them to work alone for five or ten minutes. It never failed—each of them would ask permission to go to the bathroom during the time when they were supposed to work a row or two of problems on their own.

One day, one of them slipped and asked, "May I go in the bathroom and punch the can?"

These three had discovered that when they got upset over their math, they could get rid of their anger by punching and banging on the trash can in the boys' bathroom. They would work as long as they could stand it, take out their fury on the beat-up old trash barrel, and return to finish their math. (We later got permission from a very understanding principal to use the trash can as our official punching bag.)

Sometimes, Bobby would shuffle over to me from some game or work assignment muttering through clenched teeth, "I'm about to explode. Can I go kick the fence?"

No matter where or when, as long as he planned to come back and face the situation again, my answer was always something like, "You sure may. You may shout some, too, if you want."

"I'll be back in a minute," he'd say, and stomp off to have his private, harmless tantrum. Every time, Bobby would be back at work or play within two minutes as though nothing had happened. But something important had occurred in those two minutes: he had gotten rid of his anger.

In most cases, the parents of LD and ADD children cannot control the way other people treat their kids. These youngsters often need to be defended from friends, relatives, neighbors, and playmates who do not understand their disability. Despite the best efforts to protect them, however, there will be many times when they get hurt or embarrassed by their learning problem and the way outsiders react to it.

But within the home, such pain and embarrassment should not be permitted. Brothers and sisters are going to disagree and fight. Parents, however, must see to it that their children fight fair. The LD/ADD child's disability must never be allowed to become a special target for insults.

Below are five situations that are typical of the difficulties that arise between siblings. With each are two statements that an angry child might direct toward an LD or ADD youngster. One is an example of what parents must not allow; the other would be fair in an argument.

1. *Situation:* **The LD/ADD child wants to borrow his older brother's bicycle.**

> *Foul:* "No, you can't borrow my bicycle. I wouldn't trust anyone as dumb as you with my new bike!"
>
> *Fair:* "No, you can't use my bike. The last time you took it, you left it in the park!"

2. *Situation:* **The LD/ADD child and an older sister disagree on whose turn it is to do the dishes.**

> *Foul:* "I do the dishes on Monday, Wednesday, and Friday. Today is Thursday. You can't even tell the days of the week, you idiot!"

Fair: "I remember I did the dishes last night because we had spaghetti and *I* had to clean that yucky pot. Tonight's your turn and you're not going to get out of it."

3. *Situation:* **The LD/ADD child and a brother who shares a room with him are arguing over cleaning up.**

Foul: "All of this mess in here is yours. Your homework papers, your schoolwork—you make a mess out of everything you touch!"

Fair: "I refuse to clean up this mess. It's all yours. All this junk scattered all over the floor is yours, not mine."

4. Situation: The LD/ADD child spills milk at the dinner table.

Foul: "Can't you do anything right? Go get a rag and clean that up."

Fair: "Look at the mess. Go get a rag and clean it up."

5. *Situation:* **A second-grade sister shows an A-plus spelling paper to her sixth-grade LD/ADD brother.**

Foul: "I got an A-plus on my spelling. Take a good look at it. Looking at *my* papers is the only way *you'll* ever see an A-plus!"

Fair: "I got an A-plus on my spelling paper. I'm the best speller in my class."

Sometimes, the tone of voice is as telling as the words used. In the last situation above, the fair statement would become foul if it sounded like this: "*I* got an A-plus on *my* spelling paper. *I'm* the *best* speller in *my* class."

The four ways in which parents must guard against emotional damage to their LD/ADD child bear repeating. No matter what the school is or is not doing to help the child, it is the responsibility of the *parents* (1) to help him understand that his learning disability and/or attention deficit disorder is not his fault and is no cause for guilt or shame; (2) to teach him that he is LD and/or ADD and *not* stupid; (3) to teach him to deal with his anger; and (4) to protect him from his brothers and sisters so that his home can be a place where he feels loved and accepted no matter what's going on in school.

SEE THAT THE CHILD GETS AN EDUCATION

Many LD and ADD students never acquire the information needed for successful living. It isn't that they can't learn and understand history, science, health, and other subjects, it's that they're not able to read and write about them. LD and ADD children are limited in how they learn; parents need to see to it that they are not also limited in what they learn.

Parents seem to think it's cheating if someone reads a social studies or science book to a student. If an assignment is for reading class, yes, the pupil should be the one to do the reading. But if an assignment is for science class, *who* reads it is unimportant. Children are not being taught to read about science; they are being taught the ideas and information of science.

> My first LD student was a boy I worked with while I was still in high school. Jack was a bright ninth-grader who was a total nonreader.
>
> With the school's permission, Jack's parents paid me to come to their house every night and act as their son's secretary. I read him all his assignments, asked him the required questions, and recorded his answers. If he had to write a report, I read the material to him, then he dictated his report to me.
>
> In school, Jack was treated as though he were blind. He was never asked to read or write. He *was* expected to participate actively in all other class activities and to learn the material being taught. His tests were given to him orally but were exactly the same as the ones his classmates did in writing.
>
> Jack was a good student and made good grades. He learned everything taught in his courses despite the fact that he could neither read nor write.

At that time and place, no one was able to teach Jack to read. Yet his parents made sure he got as much as he could out of the education offered him in their local public schools. When Jack graduated from high school, he was *illiterate* but not *uneducated*. And there is a huge difference.

Parents must see to it that their child learns in spite of his learning disability and/or attention deficit disorder.

ADJUSTMENTS IN THE HOME

It is amazing how many parents allow life at home to be ruined by an LD or ADD child. The process starts out slowly and gradually builds. As a first-grader, the youngster is helped with reading homework for perhaps half an hour a night. In the second grade, the youngster requires an hour or so of help with reading, spelling, and math. By fourth or fifth grade, the parents are spending almost four hours a day hunched over schoolbooks at the kitchen table. The pattern is always deadly.

LD and ADD children hate it. They have no self-confidence and can't learn anything by themselves. They've learned to depend on those at home to teach them. Instead of fighting their books for hours, they want to play and watch TV like other youngsters their age. They hate the entire mess but don't know how to change it. Their whole day, their whole life, centers around their problems at school. They become hard to get along with as their unhappiness grows. More and more of their time is spent screaming and fighting in rage or crying and sobbing with hurt feelings and shame.

Brothers and sisters hate it. Their home is turned into a study hall to help this one sibling. It doesn't seem fair. The LD/ADD child gets all the parents' attention. He's always busy doing his schoolwork (or having tantrums about not wanting to do it), so he gets out of doing household chores. His brothers and sisters think he's a spoiled brat who gets away with murder. They are jealous of the special care he gets. They resent the way his problem deprives them of a normal, happy home life. They take these feelings out by teasing and picking on their LD/ADD sibling and complaining to and fuming at their parents. In their anger and frustration, they, too, become hard to get along with. The brothers and sisters don't have the power to straighten out their messed-up home life. But they do have the power to make the situation worse—much worse. And that's what they usually do.

The parents hate the situation, too. After a hard day at work, they'd like to spend a quiet evening in front of the TV or a pleasant few hours at the bowling alley. They can't hire a baby-sitter and go out for dinner and a movie. They can't leave the children and go next door for a visit with a neighbor. If they did, who would help the LD/ADD child with his homework?

The parents feel trapped. They believe it is their duty to spend night after night working with their learning-disabled offspring. "With both of us helping him, it takes at least three hours a night for him to get his homework done," they tell their friends. That one child has become their purpose in life. In making sacrifices for him, they believe they are doing what is right.

Their motive has become fear. They are afraid their child will fail in school if they don't help him and that he will blame them for his failure. They are afraid he will grow to hate them. They are afraid he will give up and drop out, or run away, or turn to drugs, or have a nervous breakdown.

Fear and anger and guilt keep the parents going. They are angry that the LD/ADD child won't cooperate and doesn't even seem to try. They are angry that they have to give up so much for this one youngster, and angry that their other children make the situation worse. Their anger turns to guilt, which is then added to the guilt they already feel for bringing such a child into the world.

The vicious circle continues because the parents are afraid that if they break it, something might happen to make them feel even more guilty and afraid.

Instead of one suffering LD/ADD child, there is now a whole miserable, suffering family. Everybody is angry; everybody feels guilty; everybody is afraid. The parents quarrel with each other and with their children. The children argue among themselves. The normal pleasures found in a home cannot exist in such an atmosphere.

The problem is not the LD/ADD child, and it is not his disability. The problem is the way the parents are handling the disability when the child is at home. There is a better way.

AVOIDING THE TRAP: RULES FOR PARENTS

1. As much as possible, avoid sitting down to do homework with the LD/ADD child.

Some children do best when a study place is set up in their room or some other quiet part of the house where they won't be disturbed. If they need help with a question or a difficult word, they can go to someone for assistance, then return to their room to work alone. Other children are more comfortable working in an area with people around. They feel isolated and insecure when sent off to their room by themselves. Whether at the kitchen table, the dining-room table, a coffee table in the living room, or on the floor, their bed, or the couch, most children have a favorite spot where they do their best thinking. As long as it's a place where they won't be drawn into conversation or distracted by family activities, the choice is best left up to them.

For youngsters who have severe problems with school assignments, it works well if their study place allows them to get help without having to get up or have someone come to them. Working at the kitchen table while dinner is being prepared allows students to get help when needed while working alone most of the time. And even more important, those who are assisting can do so without being kept from their own activities.

When it is necessary to sit down to help children with homework, set exact limits before starting: "You have ten pages to read. Okay, I'll read the first three pages to you, then you read the rest aloud to me while I peel the potatoes." Or, "You have to write a book report? You get it all planned and written down and I'll give you half an hour right after dinner to help you correct your spelling." Or, "We'll read your social studies book together for twenty minutes tonight at bedtime." Stick to the limits you set. If the child has a fit when you have done what was promised, too bad. Leave the room and go about your business.

2. Set time limits on homework.

Young children in the first or second grade should not spend more than an hour a day on homework. By themselves, with some help, or with a lot of assistance, youngsters under eight years old who have really worked for one hour should be told to quit whether they have finished or not. (When children are unable to finish their homework in the one-hour limit, the matter should be taken up with their teacher.)

Older students need time limits, too. These limits provide a good rule of thumb: third- through sixth-graders, an hour and a half to two hours; seventh- through ninth-graders, two to three hours; tenth- through twelfth-graders, three to four hours.

It should be kept in mind that these limits apply to time actually spent working. Time off for daydreaming, tantrums, trips to the refrigerator, etc., does *not* count. It is hoped that no student will study the full limit every night. These are to be thought of as cutoff points for doing regular homework assignments. If the student can't get daily assignments completed within these limits, something is wrong. (Special projects, term papers, reports, and studying for exams might require extra time. Usually, they should not.)

These time limits are for the *child*. The parents should not spend nearly this much time on homework.

3. Limit the amount of time given to helping children with their homework.

As a general rule, parents need to make themselves available to assist their LD/ADD child with no more than half the nightly homework.

> For example, consider a third-grader with a disability in reading and spelling who could do an arithmetic worksheet alone. This would take about fifteen or twenty minutes. Someone could then provide forty-five minutes of help: fifteen minutes to read a social studies assignment together and thirty minutes to help find information for a special science project. His remaining time would be spent working alone on the project. (Notice that nobody checks over the completed arithmetic.)
>
> Or consider a sixth-grader with a writing disability who could read social studies and prepare the answers to chapter questions without help. Someone could then be available for forty-

five minutes to help with writing out the answers to the questions. If there was time left over, this person would copy half of
the math problems out of the book for the student. The youngster would then use the rest of the two-hour limit to finish the
math assignment alone.

No matter how old the child is or how much homework he
has, parents should seldom devote more than an hour and a half a
night to helping with homework. Severely disabled high-school and
college students sometimes need more assistance than this allows. In
such cases, the parents should make arrangements for their child to
get the help needed outside the home. (See rule 5 below.)

It is important that children know exactly how much help they
can count on, from whom it will come, and when it will be available. Clear understanding encourages youngsters to use their helper
wisely. They know that when the time is up, their assistant will quit
and leave them to finish their work on their own.

It is usually best to get students to do their part of the homework first. Save the assistance until they have done as much as possible on their own. This practice eliminates the chance that children
will get the opportunity to trap you with threats like, "If you won't
stay here and help me, then I won't do it." Do not put children in
the position where they can punish you for not assisting. Try to
make them feel that they are given some help as a reward for doing
the best they can on their own.

4. Limit the type of help given.

Be sure the student needs the help that is being given. Parents
often continue to assist a youngster with a subject he once found
difficult even though he has reached the point where he can do it
alone. Helping with that subject has become a habit.

Children who needed help with math in the fourth grade will
not necessarily need such help in the eighth grade. Give them a
chance to succeed on their own. They can outgrow their need for
assistance only if parents will let them.

If a child is capable of reading and understanding social studies
without assistance, let him take the hour necessary to do it, rather

than pitching in so it can get finished faster. If it's a day when mountains of homework have to be pressed into a small amount of time, yes, assistance is needed. But do not let meeting that occasional need become a habit.

If students with a math disability need help working the problems, they can copy them from the book for themselves. If children with a writing disability need help writing their math problems, let them work the problems unaided. Students who cannot read at all need someone to read *to* them; youngsters who can read to some extent need someone to read *with* them. Offer assistance only with those tasks that the child cannot do alone.

Be sure children get their help from a "secretary," not a teacher. Secretaries do the reading and writing, not the teaching or thinking. If the student does not completely understand the material being read, that is not the helper's problem. If the youngster gives an incorrect answer to a study question, it is not up to his assistant to change it. The other students in the child's class read the assignment and answer the questions by themselves. Almost all of them will get at least a few of their answers wrong. The LD child may not be able to read and write his work all by himself. But he must be allowed to do his own thinking—which is to say, he must be given the chance to make his own mistakes.

5. The helper does not have to be one of the child's parents.
In choosing the best person to assist the child with homework, three qualifications must be considered:

> **a.** Most important, the helper must be able to work peacefully with the youngster. Sarcasm, harsh criticism, arguing, sulking, tears, or shouting mean that the wrong person has been chosen.

> **b.** College degrees or high-school diplomas are not necessary. The helper does not have to be terrific at reading, writing, spelling, or the other skills the student may be studying. The assistant merely needs to be more skillful than the

child. An average student in junior high school could easily help a second- or third-grader.

c. The helper should be a volunteer. Anyone forced into the job is likely to have the wrong attitude. An aunt, an uncle, a special neighbor or friend—almost anyone can prove to be the ideal person. (*Caution:* Never insist that an older brother or sister take on the job. If one of them wants to pitch in, great. If not, look elsewhere. Other children in the family do not owe their LD/ADD brother or sister this kind of help.)

Finding a person who works well with the child is the trick!

Parents tend to feel guilty if they don't help their child themselves. They don't seem to realize that parents and children often find it difficult to work peacefully together on homework. There are also many parents who simply do not have the time, energy, or patience to become directly involved with their youngster's studies. Most LD/ADD children definitely need some kind of assistance with their homework. It *is* the responsibility of parents to see that they get it. But there is no reason that this help must come from a parent, family member, neighbor, or friend. Often, the best solution involves finding someone outside the home. An older child who needs more than an hour and a half of help a day *should* get this assistance elsewhere.

Professional therapy and tutoring are usually very expensive. But getting someone to help an LD/ADD child with homework does not necessarily have to cost anything. Churches, community centers, civic associations, clubs and fraternities on college campuses, service groups—many organizations are looking for opportunities to volunteer the time and energy of their members for helping others.

A sixth-grade boy had a young college student assigned to him through the program called "Big Brother." As the two became friends, the "big brother" saw that the LD child had some special needs. They spent many happy evenings together doing homework. After the two had been together for a year, the college student got his "little brother" into a special summer program at a private LD clinic.

As part of a church project, a family "adopted" a widow who lived in a local home for the elderly. They wanted to share some of the joys of their family life with a lonely older person. The lady they befriended took a special liking to their little LD daughter and found it a great pleasure to help the child with her homework. The girl and the old woman were soon working together regularly. Not only did the homework get done, but both experienced the joy of a loving and caring relationship.

ADJUSTMENTS IN THE SCHOOL

The parents of LD and ADD children must keep in close touch with their child's teacher. Through good communication, many of the horrible things that happen to these youngsters can be avoided. Parents should make the first move in establishing communication. This can easily be done by having a conference with the teacher in early September.

Everybody assumes that the teacher knows all about her new class when school opens in the fall. After all, she has files full of records.

Don't believe it!

It is true that schools keep a permanent folder on each of their students. But half the time, the child's file can't be found, or is full of stuff that gives no hint of a learning disability, or is simply never seen. Worse still, test scores and psychologists' reports on LD students are often locked away in a "confidential" file somewhere in the basement. These confidential reports are sometimes kept so secret that even the child's teacher never gets to see them.

If your child is learning disabled or has an attention deficit disorder, do *not* assume that the teacher knows it. Make an appointment at the very beginning of the school year and *tell* her. You can and should assume that she cares and wants to do everything in her power to help. But do not assume that she already knows.

In that first conference, parents need to share the important knowledge they have about their LD child. (Parents means mother *and* father, if at all possible.) Once the teacher knows the purpose of the visit, she can be expected to ask many questions. She will probably want to know about the youngster's past performance in school, his home life, his strengths and weaknesses, his interests and hobbies, and so on. Learning all she can about him will make life easier for her and her student. Parents will usually find their child's teacher interested and cooperative.

During this first conference, the subject of homework, including how the youngster's assignments must be adjusted, should be discussed thoroughly. The teacher needs to know what kind of help the student will get at home. She needs to understand the parents' rules on how long the child may work and how much help will be provided. Once she knows what assistance she can count on from the home, she will be able to adjust accordingly.

The most important object of the first conference is to establish communication. The parents want the teacher to know that they will work with her. They want her to feel free to call on them anytime there is a question or problem. They want her to know what she can expect from them.

But it is too soon to tell her what they expect from *her*. Suggestions of things that have worked well in the past, questions about how the teacher will be running her class, and talk of possible adjustments that might be needed are appropriate. However, parents should not ask for, or expect to be given, a detailed plan of how the teacher intends to work with their LD/ADD child. For students who have been officially diagnosed, the Individual Educational Plan (IEP) will include many of these details, but in early September, the teacher cannot yet know her new class well enough to make firm commitments about the methods that will be used with any one student. At this point, it is important for parents simply to expect the best from the teacher and to indicate to her a willingness to be reasonable and cooperative.

It takes at least a month for a good teacher to develop an adequate understanding of a child's needs and abilities. During that time, she establishes a relationship with the youngster and decides how she can best work with him. The parents are sometimes allowed to take part in the process. Many teachers like to communicate with parents through regular notes or phone calls in that first crucial month. Others prefer not to be influenced during that period. In either case, the parents should make an appointment for a second conference before they conclude the first one. A strategy meeting should be scheduled for early October. Before they leave the first conference, the parents should also get the teacher's home phone number, so they can reach her in case a serious problem arises in the meantime.

By the first of October, the teacher can be expected to be ready to make definite commitments about how she will teach the youngster. Everyone needs to understand exactly what the instructor will and will not do on behalf of the LD/ADD child. That information is what the parents should gain from the second conference.

ADJUSTMENTS IN SCHOOLWORK

Children with a learning disability and/or an attention deficit disorder need their schoolwork adjusted in order to increase their learning and decrease their frustration. These goals can be accomplished in ways that would be helpful to the students but also an impossible burden on the teacher. Just as parents are not going to spend three hours a night working with their child, a teacher can't be asked to spend three hours a night preparing special assignments for him.

However, there are many adjustments that the teacher can realistically be expected to make. The problem is that parents often don't know which possible solutions to their child's problems are workable and which are not. The guidelines below should help parents in making reasonable requests of their child's teacher.

ADJUSTMENTS INSIDE THE CLASSROOM

LD and ADD youngsters need special consideration inside the classroom. Although the parents won't be directly involved in carrying out the required adjustments, it is their responsibility to see that they are made. Parents must be careful that they expect only actions that are both necessary for their child and reasonably practical for the teacher. Basically, it is a matter of rights. LD and ADD students have a right to be treated with the respect that a human being deserves. Teachers have a right to allocate their time in the way they feel would be most beneficial to the entire class.

1. *Expect:* The child will not be criticized, shamed, scolded, or made to feel embarrassed or guilty about his learning and attention difficulties. The teacher will not tell the youngster that he is lazy, stupid, stubborn, or worthless.

   Hope for: The youngster will be encouraged to work around his learning problem while facing it honestly. The teacher will protect him from other children who tease him or try to make him feel inferior.

   Don't ask: In addition to helping the child deal effectively with his learning difficulties, the teacher will lead the entire class to be understanding of the LD/ADD student's special problems and needs.

2. *Expect:* The child will never be asked to do work he is incapable of doing.

   Hope for: The child will be asked to do as much of the regular classwork as possible. When necessary, he will be given smaller amounts of the regular work or special materials that teach the same concepts at a level he can handle.

   Don't ask: All the students' classwork will be adjusted to the LD/ADD child's needs and ability.

3. *Expect:* In reading, spelling, and math, the youngster will be given instruction appropriate to his level of skill. (No child reading at a second-grade level will be asked to work from a fifth-grade reading book, for example.)

   Hope for: In the basic subject areas, the teacher will choose materials and make assignments in accordance with the student's level of skill *and* his individual strengths and weaknesses. (For instance, in describing a scene from a story, the rest of the children might be required to write a paragraph, while the LD or ADD child might be asked to draw an illustration.)

Don't ask: For reading, spelling, and math, the child will be placed in a small group in which the materials, assignments, and methods of instruction are carefully tailored to fit his level of skill, personal learning style, interests, and needs. (Teachers must have special training in learning styles and modification management before they can effectively use alternative teaching techniques. Many schools are moving in this direction, but few are ready to be held responsible for such totally appropriate methods of instruction.)

4. *Expect:* The child will be part of the regular program in such subjects as science, social studies, health, art, music, physical education, and drama, but he will not be expected to use skills he has not yet developed and will not be expected to read the books for himself.

   Hope for: The teacher will help the youngster succeed within the regular school program in such subjects as science and social studies. She will encourage parents to read his homework assignments with him or to him. Classwork will be adjusted so that he can do it alone, or a partner will be selected to assist him with reading, writing, and other areas of weakness.

   Don't ask: The regular programs in science, social studies, and other subjects will be taught in such a way that the child's learning problems will be no real handicap. (Some schools are meeting this need by offering a parallel curriculum in which the courses are more hands-on and less book-oriented.)

5. *Expect:* The teacher will allow the child to take tests aloud. She will either make arrangements to have someone read tests to him or allow the parents to provide that service either in the home or in the classroom.

   Hope for: The teacher will make all arrangements to have the child's tests given orally.

   Don't ask: All tests will be given orally, one-to-one, or in some other way that allows the student to show what he knows about the subject without having to read or spell or use other areas of serious weakness. (For children who have been officially diagnosed, labeled, and placed, this adjustment can easily be included in the IEP.)

6. **Expect:** The child will not be prevented from taking part in activities outside the classroom as punishment for poor performance on schoolwork. Art, music, physical education, recess, or field trips will not be withheld on the grounds that he did not get his work done or failed at some particular class assignment. Of course, those activities might be withheld as punishment for bad behavior.

   Hope for: The student will be encouraged to take part in all activities outside the classroom. Movies, filmstrips, demonstrations, field trips, special projects, art, music, drama, physical education, etc., will be treated as worthwhile activities through which the child may find pleasure and success.

   Don't ask: The teacher will help the child discover outlets in which he can find pleasure and success. The child will be guided in exploring various activities outside the regular classroom. His natural creativity will be prized, encouraged, and developed. (This is the type of self-understanding that private teachers and therapists can help a student develop.)

7. **Expect:** The child will not be allowed to become a bully. In demanding reasonable behavior, the teacher will not tolerate temper tantrums, lack of respect, rudeness, foul language, physical injury to other children, or damage to property. The diagnosis of LD and/or ADD will not be accepted as an excuse for inappropriate behavior.

   Hope for: The child will not be allowed to develop behavior problems. The teacher will encourage him to express his anger and frustration in ways that do no harm to himself, to others, or to property.

   Don't ask: The child will be taught to understand himself and all aspects of his learning and attention problems. In addition to being taught to deal with anger and frustration, he will be praised and rewarded for his successes, so that he will learn to find satisfaction in good behavior. (This kind of instruction is often an aspect of the training provided by LD therapists.)

8. **Expect:** The teacher will cooperate with the parents.

   Hope for: The teacher will take the lead in seeing that the school and the family are working together in the best interest of the child. She will make it a point to keep the parents informed about the student's progress and will remain open to questions and suggestions.

   Don't ask: The teacher will coordinate the efforts of parents, psychologist, social worker, LD consultant, and others in their joint effort to help the youngster.

ADJUSTMENTS IN HOMEWORK

Making it possible for LD and ADD youngsters to complete homework successfully requires *very* careful coordination between home and school. It is the parents' responsibility to see that there is a clear understanding between them and the teacher concerning types and sizes of assignments, time to be allowed, and help that will be provided. An attitude of trust and cooperation is essential. By establishing a mutually agreeable set of guidelines, most disasters can be avoided before they arise. (For students who have been officially diagnosed and placed, these guidelines can be part of the IEP.) Again, on the issue of homework, parents must be sure that what they ask of the teacher is reasonable and practical.

1. **Expect:** The teacher will allow the parents to help the child with regular homework.

   Hope for: By adjusting the work required to complete assignments done at home, the teacher will make it possible for the LD/ADD youngster to do much of his studying without outside assistance. She will inform the parents about general subjects or particular assignments on which their help will be needed.

Don't ask: The teacher will design all the child's homework so that he is capable of completing it by himself. (This is a perfectly reasonable request for students who have been officially diagnosed and placed in a program that demands an IEP to describe special modifications needed.)

2. *Expect:* When an assignment cannot be completed within the time limit the parents allow, the youngster will not be penalized for failing to finish it.

   Hope for: The teacher will see to it that the youngster has no more homework than can be completed within the time his parents allow.

   Don't ask: The teacher will design special homework for the student that can be completed within the time his parents allow. (Children who have been officially diagnosed and placed can have this commitment included in their IEP.)

3. *Expect:* The teacher will allow another student to see that the LD/ADD youngster has copied the homework assignment correctly into memory jogger or notepad.

   Hope for: The teacher will personally check to see that the child has copied down all homework assignments correctly. (This can easily by arranged through the IEP.)

   Don't ask: The teacher will write out homework assignments *for* the child. (Teachers often agree to provide such assistance and commit to it in the IEP.)

4. *Expect:* The teacher will cheerfully explain a homework assignment to the parents if they can't figure it out and have to call her at home.

   Hope for: The teacher will provide examples and carefully explain homework assignments to the child and will encourage him to call her at home if trouble arises.

   Don't ask: The teacher will see to it that the student understands every homework assignment so completely that advice and help are never needed.

5. **Expect:** The teacher will accept work that the parents write for the youngster because he is not capable of writing it himself, *provided* the child does the thinking and the work is in his own words.

   Hope for: The teacher will help the student find ways to do written homework without assistance. She will let him answer questions with one or two words instead of whole sentences; she will accept one or two good sentences instead of a whole paragraph; she will accept a cassette tape recording in place of a long written report. Also, she will encourage him to express his ideas through projects and oral reports, rather than through the usual written reports.

   Don't ask: The student will not be assigned any written work that he cannot complete successfully without assistance. Worksheets will be provided so that questions can be answered by filling in blanks or circling words, rather than writing sentences or paragraphs. Math will be done in workbooks, so the problems won't need to be copied. Answers to questions in science, social studies, etc., will either be presented orally or recorded on a cassette tape and handed in. All written reports will be done *in* school under the direct supervision of the teacher. A cassette tape recording can always be used to meet the requirements of any written homework assignment. (All these are reasonable requests commonly included in an IEP.)

6. **Expect:** Either the teacher will not count off for poor spelling outside spelling class, or the parents will be allowed to proofread and correct spelling errors for the child.

   Hope for: In order to encourage the child to work as independently as possible, the teacher will overlook poor spelling in all work done outside spelling class. When a word is such a jumble that the reader can't figure it out, the teacher will ask the child what was intended, then supply him with the correct spelling. (Students who have been officially diagnosed often have this arrangement agreed upon in their IEP.)

   Don't ask: The student's work will be designed so that poor spelling will not be a problem. When necessary, the teacher will help the youngster proofread work for spelling errors.

GENERAL GUIDELINES

In finding ways to adapt regular schoolwork so that students with learning disabilities and attention deficit disorders can learn, three basic rules need to be remembered:

1. The home should not be turned into a classroom or study hall (unless the family is homeschooling).

2. Adjustments should be made only in areas where the student is not capable of doing the work in the normal way.

3. The teacher should make some adjustments, too (many special adjustments are available to youngsters who have been officially placed in public-school programs that require an IEP).

The object of these rules is simple but important: to help LD and ADD students achieve more learning with less frustration.

7

WHAT LD THERAPY CAN REALLY ACCOMPLISH:
Do You Believe in Miracles?

Therapy for children with learning disabilities and attention deficit disorder is a highly specialized kind of instruction. It is different from regular classroom teaching in four basic ways:

1. LD and ADD therapies are designed to meet the special needs of a particular child. They are not balanced programs that attempt to teach all subjects and improve all skills. For example, a child with a writing disability might use a therapy session to work on eye/hand coordination, pencil control, handwriting, and copying. He would be taught to write sentences, paragraphs, stories, reports, and answers to questions. Drawing and making maps and charts might also be included. The writing and copying skills involved in math would probably be covered. The student would almost always spend the entire session with a pencil in his hand, working on the area of disability. Problems with attention and concentration are always addressed as part of academic therapy.

For youngsters whose main difficulty is with behavior related to

ADD, a counselor or psychologist might be the one providing the therapy. Such a program would focus on training aimed at developing social skills, controlling impulsive tendencies, overcoming hyperactivity, and improving concentration.

2. A program of LD and/or ADD therapy is based on a thorough diagnosis. A quick appraisal does not give the type of precise information that a therapist needs in order to create a plan for teaching the student. Testing establishes the nature and extent of the difficulty, so that a program of therapy can be custom-designed.

3. LD and ADD therapy help students overcome basic problems that affect their ability to succeed in most areas of education.

> Lucida was a lovely sixth-grade girl with a puzzling disability. She had a good attitude, normal intelligence, and adequate skills in reading, writing, spelling, and math. No one was able to figure out how she could work so hard yet continue to fail so miserably.
>
> It was finally discovered that Lucida had a problem with certain kinds of reasoning. She couldn't understand words that were broad enough to include different kinds of things. She didn't understand the relationship between cause and effect. She was unable to take a set of facts and draw a generalization from them.
>
> Her entire school program had to be adjusted. Every one of her teachers had to come up with special methods that would allow her to learn.
>
> Lucida's LD therapy consisted of only one thing: teaching the girl to reason. Her therapist had to invent ways to do this. She would give the child a banana, an apple, and a pear and then ask, "What have you got?" She would show her a picture of a man wrapped in bandages and then ask, "What happened?" She would take her student outside under a tree and then ask, "What season is this?" After getting the correct answer, she'd ask, "Can you prove it?"
>
> Using anything she could think of, the therapist worked toward one goal: helping Lucida develop logical thinking processes.

4. Therapy designed for those with learning disabilities and attention deficit disorder must be done individually or in very small groups. These children are easily distracted. The least little noise or movement will break their concentration. Even in an ideal situation, their attention span tends to be quite short. The normal activity in a room of thirty students is more than they can handle. They simply cannot tune out the many small distractions created by a large class. They need the kind of controlled, quiet atmosphere possible only in a small, highly structured class.

LD classes are usually full of boys. And boys will be boys—LD, ADD, or otherwise. Little boys tend to be wiggly, loud, rough, and playful. Youngsters with ADD are even louder, rougher, and more wiggly. Many of them are hyperactive. Some are very hot-tempered as well.

LD and ADD students (especially those past the age of ten) often have a long history of behavior problems. Behavior disorders, as well as defiant or oppositional behavior, are often seen in this group. Temper tantrums, tears, fistfights, sulking, destruction of property— all are common. Many LD and ADD children are full of anger. And they are quick to show it. A classroom full of such students puts terror into the hearts of all but the bravest teachers. Six are a handful. Ten can usually be kept under control by an experienced professional. Fifteen or more are physically dangerous to the teacher, the building, and each other.

> My fifth- and sixth-graders were cleaning up after an art lesson. Each of the ten boys had a particular task. Moving furniture back into place, putting away glue and scissors—everyone was doing his job. Except Ted.
>
> Ted was supposed to be gathering up leftover tissue paper that was good enough to save for future use. Instead, he stood around while everyone else worked.
>
> At first, I ignored his loafing on the theory that he'd get started on his own. When that didn't work, I tried a few gentle hints.
>
> Ted was in a rotten mood. He snatched up the bag he was supposed to be using and stomped over to one of the big tables. Instead of starting in a spot where no one else was working, he walked right into Tommy. Ted was a big boy. The smaller ones were all afraid of him. But Tommy was big and tough. He stood his ground. Ted grabbed him by the shoulders, shoved him aside, and shouted right in his face, "Move over!"

Surprisingly, Tommy didn't come out slugging. He clenched his fists for just a second, then calmly moved to another part of the table.

I tapped Ted on the shoulder. When he looked at me, I said firmly, "That was rude."

He slammed his bag on the table, folded his arms across his chest with a "Humph," and stared at me with fire in his eyes.

Two of the younger children sized up the situation and acted immediately—one reaching for Ted's bag, one starting to gather up the scraps of paper.

I waved them off. "Don't touch a single piece of that paper. Ted will be picking it up."

"No I won't!" Ted snapped, then walked angrily over to his desk and plopped down.

I gave him a minute to cool off, then went over to him. It seemed stupid to make an issue over a few pieces of tissue paper, but Ted was so hard to handle that he couldn't be allowed to get away with *anything*. I simply told him, "The bus will be here in ten minutes."

He stuck out his jaw, narrowed his eyes, and glowered at me in silence. He knew that nobody was ever kept after school. He figured he had the advantage.

A few minutes later, I gave it one more try. I was calm when I said, "The bus leaves in seven minutes. If you intend to be on it, you'll have the tissue paper picked up."

He sat straight as a ramrod and snarled through clenched teeth, "I ain't pickin' up no paper."

There was no question about it—if I pushed him any farther, he would explode. He looked as if he was ready to smash some furniture or take a swing at me. Any violence would stir at least five other boys into action. It might develop into a free-for-all. With nine other children in the class, anything might happen. And if something happened, I could not control it. I was not about to let Ted get away with such behavior; I had to stand my ground. But I couldn't risk standing up to him alone.

Letting Ted think he had won, I announced to everyone, "Five minutes until the bus gets here. Anybody who expects to be on it will be in his seat with his job done, coat on, and homework in hand."

The boys knew the end-of-the-day system. Everything was calm. Ted was still sitting rigidly, but he was quiet. I slipped out of the room.

When I got to the office, our principal was at his desk. (We were fortunate in having an exceptional principal who was usually available and always cooperative.) Without exchanging even a hello, I told Mr. Northrup, "I need you to come up to my room to get Ted." He got up immediately. As we walked back to my classroom, I briefly filled him in on the situation.

When we got there, the boys were all in their seats, talking quietly among themselves. Mr. Northrup walked over to Ted's desk and told the boy, "I need to see you in the office."

Had Ted gotten up and gone with the principal at that point, no one would even have noticed. Instead, he muttered, "I didn't do nothin'."

Without raising his voice or adding any explanation, Mr. Northrup repeated his original statement.

Ted looked at his lap as he replied through pouting lips, "I ain't comin' and you can't make me."

Mr. Northrup was not a large man. Facing that out-of-control twelve-year-old, he looked small and helpless. Yet his words and attitude were completely firm and calm. "Yes, Ted. I *can* make you. Now come along with me."

Ted shouted more refusals.

The rest of the class sat watching the scene in stunned silence.

Around and around they went. Mr. Northrup stuck to the one issue as Ted kept refusing to go.

"My bus is gonna be here in a minute. You ain't gonna make me miss my bus."

"I need you in the office."

"You can't keep me after school."

"We need to go to the office."

"It's time for me to go home and there's nothin' you can do to stop me."

"Ted, I'm not very big. By myself, I probably couldn't stop you. But I have the authority. I can get others to help me get you to the office."

Although he was still boldly shouting in his fury, Ted suddenly seemed to realize that he had lost. "Okay. I'll pick up the paper."

"No, you'll come with me to the office." Mr. Northrup was superb. Arguing with him seemed about as pointless as fighting the law of gravity. Ted finally realized that and went off peaceably with the principal.

It is impossible for a teacher to maintain control over a large group of LD and ADD children. If an adult does not have complete control, a child like Ted can be very dangerous—and among LD/ADD youngsters, there are many like Ted. For the safety of everyone concerned, LD classes must be kept small.

Also, students with an attention deficit disorder and/or a learning disability need to work in close contact with their teacher. In a roomful of children, their learning difficulties make it impossible for them to work independently for more than five or ten minutes. (Young children cannot work alone for even that long.) If left on their own, their attention drifts off, their minds wander, and they slip into daydreaming or horsing around.

The academic therapy for LD/ADD youngsters is designed individually or for small groups. One of the reasons for this is that no two students have exactly the same set of problems. For example, a youngster who has difficulty with visual memory needs remedial work that is different from that needed by a child who has trouble with auditory memory. If the two children are plopped into the same class, things don't work out very well.

> Brad had an unusually weak auditory memory. He could not remember even a simple four-word sentence unless it was repeated several times. As part of a group of seven sixth-graders, he had a horrible time with dictations.
> If I dictated a ten-word sentence by reading it twice, the rest of the group could carry the whole thing in their heads and write it down from memory. But Brad was lucky if he could remember the first three words.
> There was no way to adjust to Brad's needs without either embarrassing him or distracting his classmates. He should have had the intense special help possible through one-to-one therapy.

Due to their low tolerance for frustration, students with attention deficit disorder and learning disabilities need to work in close contact with their teacher. When they get stuck on a word or question, they need help right away. Their frustration builds quickly to the boiling point. If it takes the teacher a few minutes to get there with help, they become too angry and discouraged to get back to work. Given the right group, a sharp, energetic specialist can maintain the necessary level of close contact with as many as ten students. With classes of more than ten, the chances for maintaining a healthy learning environment are slim. In a regular classroom, it takes an extremely alert teacher to keep these youngsters on task. If anybody can make a shambles out of "inclusion," it's the LD and ADD students. With or without medication, they do not function well in large groups.

ACADEMIC THERAPY

To achieve good results, learning-disabilities therapy must be done systematically and consistently. Whether working with groups or individuals, the LD teacher needs to spend between three and five hours a week with each student. That time should be divided into equal sessions of no more than an hour and a half each. Sometimes, however, it's necessary to squeeze all the instruction into one large lesson per week. That can work, but it has serious disadvantages. And except in a few special situations, if therapy is done for less than a total of two hours per week, it can do more harm than good.

When a good therapist works regularly with an LD child at least two or three times a week, progress should be seen within six months.

The first improvement almost always comes in the area of attitude. Parents often report with delight, "He's happier than we've ever seen him," or "Things are so much better at home. She doesn't have tantrums anymore," or "He's started doing his homework. We don't have the fights we used to have every night trying to get him to do his schoolwork."

Academic therapy usually includes the kind of training that helps a student understand himself, but it rarely includes any work directly related to counseling. Yet as a result of therapy, students usually become more cooperative at home, more confident of themselves in dealing with others, and more interested in the world and the people around them. A new basic contentment begins to emerge.

If that improved attitude is not seen in the first six months of therapy, then something is wrong. Sometimes, the therapist is not suited to the particular child, or her methods may not be appropriate for the child's problems. Or it may be that the child is so severely damaged emotionally that it will take as long as a year to get the youngster to put forth any real effort. That is often the case with older children.

Good therapy does sometimes produce miracles. But those miracles take time. They rarely happen in less than forty or fifty hours of work. Most of them take considerably longer.

By the end of the first semester of work, there should also be a definite improvement in the areas of the child's disability. He should reach important goals in improving his skills in reading, writing, spelling, math, or whatever. But those improved skills will probably not carry over into the rest of his schoolwork until later. After one semester of therapy, his regular classwork may be better because of his improved attitude and renewed interest, but the weekly spelling test will still be a horror, the social studies book will remain unreadable, and the grades on the report card will be basically the same. Gradually, through the second semester of therapy (and into the third and fourth semesters, if needed), the regular schoolwork should begin to improve. If at the end of two years of intensive LD therapy the child is still unable to function successfully in the regular classroom, it's time to change tactics.

Two years of academic therapy are enough for one child with one teacher using one method. After that, it's time either to back off and let the child try it on his own or to find new alternatives. Those alternatives might include a different type of class or school or therapist, a different set of adjustments within the regular class, a new opinion from another professional, or just a pause to take a breather.

For older children, the results of therapy are much harder to predict. An eager teenager can make incredible progress in one month; an unmotivated youth of the same age might make no progress at all in an entire year. Among junior- and senior-high students, great miracles and dismal failures are both common.

So, to state a general rule, students should not be expected to show progress from LD therapy in less than six months, and in most cases, therapy should not be continued for more than two years.

ONCE AROUND ISN'T ALWAYS ENOUGH

LD students learn well while they're having therapy. Since they do not learn effectively by regular classroom methods, their learning takes place in spurts. When they're not in therapy, they tend to coast until they fall behind.

Youngsters who have had successful therapy will read at about grade level, and often above. When therapy is stopped, they get along fine with the help of a few adjustments. But since they don't learn in the same way other children do, their skills don't improve with those of the rest of the class. They gradually slip behind. For one year, they may be terrific; the following year, they'll start to struggle; and by the third year, they will begin to bog down. The basic skills have already been mastered. Instruction in more advanced skills is what's needed. It's not that the child can't read; it's a matter of needing to catch back up.

For some children, that involves another long, tough, two-year fight. For most, it does not. Usually, the desired gains can be made in forty or fifty hours during a summer session, or in three hours of work a week for one or two semesters. In some cases, one hour a week for a year may even be enough.

Children who had successful LD instruction when younger should definitely head back to the same therapist for the catch-up course. If it's not possible to work with the same person, every effort should be made to find a therapist who uses the method that worked before. Once you've found an approach that works for a particular child, stick with it!

Some students need as many as three or four rounds of therapy between grades one and twelve; a few get by with having therapy just once. The younger the child is when the first program of therapy begins, the better the chances are that specialized training will not need to be repeated.

LD children who have successfully completed their therapy should be tested every year or so to be sure they're not falling behind.

HOW GOOD IS GOOD ENOUGH?

Some children take a break from therapy even though they're not yet learning as well as they should be. Others are able to reach the point where they are working at a level in keeping with their mental capacity. When a third-grader of average ability is doing average third-grade work in the area of disability, he's had enough therapy.

Scores on intelligence and achievement tests aren't always the best way to decide if it's time to quit therapy. When a child is happy with his skills, when he finds his level of achievement satisfying, that's enough. The grades on his report card are not the true test.

When the LD child gets to the point that he has more successes than failures, can do most of his schoolwork without assistance, lives comfortably with his weaknesses, feels good about himself, and is leading a normal, happy life, then he's in great shape!

SOME PARENTS ARE NEVER SATISFIED

Brenda was a mildly LD child of average intelligence. But everyone else in her family was unusually smart. Her older brothers and sisters were honor students. Her father was a brilliant doctor. When compared with the rest of her family, this sweet, attractive, hardworking little girl didn't measure up. After a year of therapy, Brenda was getting average grades in a high-powered private-school program. By public-school standards, she was working above grade level. It would have been unfair to expect more from any child of average mental ability.

Brenda's teachers agreed that the girl was no longer handicapped by her mild learning disability. It was time to stop therapy. They believed that her work was absolutely the best that could be expected from a child of her ability.

When told the news, Brenda's father became furious. The doctor insisted that his daughter needed to have more therapy. "Anybody can make C's," he protested. "With a little more effort, she could make B's." All his pressure for better grades was making a nervous wreck out of Brenda. She chewed her nails, worried, and was not able to relax. She rarely enjoyed herself as the other children did. Her dad claimed he would ease off on the pressure when she brought home mostly B's!

The headmistress, the teacher, and the LD specialist spent two hours trying to convince this man that his attitude was causing problems. They insisted heatedly that since Brenda was already a slave to her schoolwork, the pressure to get B's—even if she could manage it—would be too great.

The pleas had no effect. This brilliant man could not see the damage he was doing.

Parents often have great difficulty accepting the truth about their youngsters. Children are given different amounts of mental horsepower. Mothers and fathers don't want any of their offspring to have below-average intelligence. Many can't even be content with average mental ability. But parents damage their children when they fail to accept them as they are.

LD experts occasionally see children who have been dragged from one specialist to another for repeated testing. Conversations with the parents quickly reveal that the test results have always been basically the same—and always unacceptable to the parents. Rather than dealing with the possibility of mental retardation or emotional disturbance, the family continues to seek a diagnosis that labels their child in a way they find acceptable. (Most parents are more comfortable with a diagnosis of ADD than they are with the label *LD*. And while the idea of a learning disability is tough to accept, it is almost always more palatable than the idea that their child is autistic, retarded, or brain-damaged.)

Parents who cannot face the real cause of their child's learning problems tend to push the youngster to achieve the impossible. And in their panic, they spend dollar upon dollar trying to find someone or something to help—tutors, therapists, special schools, mail-order teaching materials, exercises, strange diets, and all kinds of pills. These approaches merely put more pressure on the child.

Great emotional damage is done when children feel that even their best is not good enough.

HOW TO TELL IF YOU'RE GETTING ANYWHERE

LD and ADD children are starved for success and praise. Good therapy helps them recognize and take pride in the real gains they are making. But students respond to the progress they make in different ways. Some children rush home to tell about a new skill they've mastered; some don't.

If the child's attitude and behavior are improved, if he seems happier and more confident, it is safe to assume that successful learning is taking place whether the details are shared or not. Don't pressure the student to tell you what he has learned. Ask his therapist. And don't settle for vague non-answers such as, "We've been working to improve auditory discrimination." Get the details about exact skills being mastered: "He's learned to write the cursive letters from *A* through *M*," or "He's learned to find the main idea in a simple paragraph," or "He can now write one good complete sentence with a capital letter and correct punctuation." Be careful to recognize the difference between important skills and therapeutic techniques. The therapist may show parents some papers and explain, "We're working to improve pencil control. See how much better he's gotten at making nice, round circles and straight, even-slanted lines? Notice how he can now trace these patterns without going out of the lines." Parents should realize that such exercises are important in helping the child overcome problems. But the crucial question to ask is, "How's the handwriting coming?" If the specialist says the student can now tell a triangle from a trapezoid, everyone should rejoice. But more important is, "Can he now tell an *N* from an *M*?"

LD therapy goes very slowly. There are many, many small objectives that must be reached before the major goal is attained. Be sure the child is having success reaching these small objectives. If that's being accomplished, then you know that progress is being made.

PREDICTING PROGRESS

Doctors, mechanics, psychologists, plumbers, LD specialists—people in the repair business who are paid to fix either things or people—are always being asked to predict how successful their work will be, how much it will cost, and how long it will take. All fix-it people are experts at avoiding giving answers to such questions. "There are so many intangible factors involved," they say. "Until we actually open it up and take a look, we can't be certain what we're dealing with." In flowing phrases, they refuse to answer the questions of frightened patients, customers, clients, and parents.

That is a cop-out!

No one is asking for a mystical seeing into the future; everyone knows that precise predictions are impossible to make. But any professional who is experienced in the field knows what results can be expected. A surgeon might tell a patient that if all goes as planned, the operation will take two or three hours, hospitalization will be necessary for three to five days, rest and recovery at home will take three or four weeks, and normal life will be possible again in seven weeks or so. That does not guarantee that the patient will not die on the operating table. Nor does it overlook the possibility of a miraculous healing. It is simply a statement of what will probably happen.

Teaching LD and ADD children is not quite so cut-and-dried as repairing a carburetor or removing a gallbladder. But psychologists and LD specialists can and should share that same type of prediction with the parents of their students. After testing a child and working with him for a month, the therapist knows what she hopes to accomplish with him in a year. She knows the areas in which her teaching methods will be a great help to the youngster, and she also knows the problems that she will not be able to help him overcome. (There is, of course, no way to predict absences, health, moving, and other factors that can interrupt progress or stop work entirely.)

LD specialists *do* believe in miracles. There is always the hope that each new student will have the kind of incredible success that happens to two or three children out of every hundred. However, therapists are also realistic enough to know that a pupil will rarely improve as much as hoped. In all cases, the parents need to be told what gains can be reasonably expected from therapy.

There are many different approaches in therapy for learning disabilities and attention deficit disorders. No two are exactly alike. No two can be expected to produce identical results. For instance, a group in Florida is doing some interesting research in the area of sequencing problems. With its new methods, it is having some success in helping LD/ADD youngsters overcome those problems. But most other experts do not expect to remedy the sequencing difficulties so often found in these children. They believe that students will have to live with it into adulthood. In response to the question, "Will my child ever overcome his sequencing problems?" the Florida group would say yes. Until the results of its research are more widely accepted, most LD specialists would say, "No, but we'll teach him to spell in spite of it."

Thus, it must be remembered that the progress one can expect to see in an LD youngster depends greatly on the method used by the child's therapist. There is no one method that always works miracles. There are many methods that never accomplish much at all.

With that in mind, parents can use the "predictions" below as a guide in measuring what they should and should not hope for and expect from their LD/ADD child's therapy.

1. Parents should hope and expect that the youngster will learn to read.

To be considered literate, a person must be able to read as well as the average child who has successfully finished the third grade. If an individual reads at or above that level, he should be able at least to read ballots, road signs, applications and forms, letters, parts of the newspaper, and a few magazines. This modest level of skill would equip most people to "get by."

Of all the LD children I've taught, there are only three that I honestly believe will never be literate. No teacher, no method, no amount of time or money is going to teach those boys to read. It does happen; a few children have a learning disability so severe that they are doomed to be nonreaders forever. But with the right kind of therapy, almost all LD children can be expected eventually to read at least as well as the average fourth-grader.

To predict how far beyond mere literacy an LD student will progress, one must consider the child's particular strengths and weaknesses. In general, the higher the child's level of intelligence, the higher his reading level will become. And without question, the younger the child is at the beginning of therapy, the better his chances of overcoming his problem. In the case of older students who have been damaged emotionally, there is no way of knowing what the results of therapy will be. The same applies to young adults who have given up entirely.

2. Parents should hope but not expect that the child will become a normal, average reader.

Bright LD children often become good readers; those with more modest mental ability usually learn to read adequately. But the learning-disabled child seldom learns to read as well as non-LD individuals of the same age, intelligence, and education. An eighteen-year-old high-school graduate with an IQ of 140 should be an excellent reader. But if that person is LD, he will probably be just better than average at reading. Either way, the student can get through college. If he is LD, he'll have to work harder.

No matter how smart the person or how successful the therapy, most of the learning disabled will always be slow, inefficient readers. They may become skilled enough to read accurately and to understand anything they see, yet continue to feel frustrated that it is impossible for them to read rapidly. (Speed-reading courses usually lead to frustration and confusion, rather than improvement.)

Children with disabilities in areas other than language often become excellent readers. Bright youngsters with writing disabilities or math difficulties are often avid readers from a very early age.

Those who are diagnosed as having an attention deficit disorder are often excellent readers, even as young children. They usually have trouble with spelling and mastering certain aspects of written language, and they often have the kind of word-attack-skill weaknesses that make reading lists of words in isolation difficult. But as long as there is story and context to hold their interest and provide clues to unfamiliar words, they tend to find great pleasure in the printed page.

3. Parents should not hope or expect that the child will ever become a good speller.

Males with attention deficit disorder and/or learning disabilities almost never become good spellers. With intensive instruction and serious effort, some of them become adequate by learning to rely on phonics rules and spelling generalizations. But since English is only about 80-percent phonetically predictable, this method leaves a lot of room for error. However, a high level of skill at applying phonetic encoding principles can combine with a good word processor's spell-checker to make competent spellers out of those who would have barely limped along in the days before computers. Of course, secretaries, girlfriends, spouses, dictionaries, and electronic spelling references are generally available to help adults who need assistance. Fortunately, poor spelling is not a particularly great handicap in adult life.

Females with learning disabilities and attention deficit disorder often follow a pattern of weakness different from males. It is not at all unusual for an LD girl to be an "automatic" (or good) speller with lovely handwriting and neat, legible work. Typically, LD and ADD females find their problems clustered more in the areas of reading comprehension, math, and organization.

4. The older a student is before being identified as LD/ADD, the more likely it is that emotional scars and feelings of inferiority will be permanent.

First- and second-graders who are recognized and helped early often develop no feelings of inferiority at all. They learn to read and write and spell when taught by alternative methods that work for them, and they never consider themselves very different. But children who struggle through six or more years of failure and frustration have a poor chance of ever getting over the feeling that they are stupid, inferior, and defective.

Love, understanding, acceptance, patience, instruction, honesty, learning-styles training, praise, guidance, successful experiences, and still more love can sometimes accomplish what at first seems impossible. Even the most severely damaged LD adults and teenagers can be freed from their anger, guilt, and shame. At times, professional counseling helps, provided the therapist has a thorough understanding of learning disabilities and attention deficit disorder. A strong, loyal, optimistic mentor is almost always necessary in order to get these individuals straightened out enough to use their talents wisely and function successfully on their own.

5. Parents should hope and expect that the child will be able to go to college or trade school.

Whether or not an LD/ADD student continues pursuing an

education beyond high school depends as much on the nature of the child as it does on the type or severity of the learning disability or attention deficit disorder. A bright LD/ADD student who becomes discouraged easily will not be as successful in college as a less intelligent LD/ADD youngster who is full of confidence and determination.

Four factors determine how successful an LD/ADD student will be in college: intelligence, disposition, motivation, and the field he chooses to study.

There are many fields in which a learning disability or an attention deficit disorder is not a particularly serious handicap to a student. In fact, there are many areas of study in which being LD and/or ADD is a downright advantage. For those with the intelligence and stamina, it is possible to earn a degree in almost any academic area.

When guiding young LD/ADD children, the two extreme attitudes about higher education should be avoided. A youngster should not be brainwashed into thinking that college is absolutely necessary for survival. Nor should he be told that his learning disability and/or attention deficit disorder makes attending college an impossibility. The severely disabled and those with only average intelligence should not be pushed toward a college education if they don't freely choose it for themselves. All those who commit themselves to post-secondary education should be strongly encouraged to put their energy into an area that is compatible with their natural interests and talents.

6. Parents should hope and expect that the child will be able to live normally as an adult.

There is absolutely no question about it—LD and ADD adults can live perfectly normal lives. They work around their weaknesses just as everybody else does. If their spelling is poor, they avoid jobs as secretaries and use a dictionary or spell-checker often. If they have trouble with math, they keep a calculator handy. Welders, pediatricians, mechanics, architects, lawyers, teachers, coaches, business executives, athletes, sculptors, carpenters, nurses, housewives, engineers, artists, musicians, salesmen, plumbers, judges, movie stars, writers, accountants—successful people with learning disabilities and attention deficit disorder are everywhere.

8

TESTING:
How to Play the Numbers Game

GETTING YOUR MONEY'S WORTH

Some doctors listen to the mother's complaints, ask the three-year-old a few questions, do a simple test or two, and identify the youngster as having a learning disability or an attention deficit disorder in ten minutes or less. Some clinics take a week to have a child tested thoroughly by psychologists, neurologists, psychiatrists, social workers, and an army of others. The quick diagnosis is absurd; the extensive team approach is usually not necessary. Between five and ten hours of testing by a qualified LD specialist or a psychologist trained in evaluating children for the causes of academic and attention problems is usually adequate to determine whether or not a youngster has a learning disability or an attention deficit disorder.

As of 1996, a good professional diagnosis costs between eight hundred and twelve hundred dollars. For most families, that is at least two weeks' wages. If the evaluation includes brain scans, interviews, blood-sugar studies, and other tests that take days to complete, the cost can run well into the thousands of dollars. However, some learning disabilities and attention problems are so complicated and puzzling that such an extensive evaluation is essential. Fortunately, many family health care plans include coverage for these types of expenses, and, by law, testing is available at no cost through the public schools.

In this chapter, the terms *diagnosis, evaluation,* and *testing* will be used interchangeably to refer to the process of identifying a child as having a learning disability or an attention deficit disorder.

Public law 94-142 requires that all public schools provide free testing for learning disabilities to all students who need it. In spite of that, it remains difficult—though usually not impossible—to have a child tested by the school.

The red tape is so thick that it is not always easy to prove that a student is in real need of evaluation. But according to the regulations and guidelines established by the government, parents can now expect results if they *ask* for an evaluation. A written request given to the youngster's teacher or principal is supposed to be enough to start the process.

School psychologists are so overworked that it usually takes months to get an evaluation done. Some states have laws that force schools to complete the diagnostic process within rigid time limits; they usually allow between thirty and ninety days. That is still a bit slow, but much faster than typical.

School psychologists sometimes have limited practical knowledge about learning disabilities. Some, however, are extremely skillful at recognizing and dealing with the problems of LD/ADD children. Colleges are putting greater emphasis on training psychologists in that area of their work.

The situation has improved dramatically. Parents should definitely give the school a chance to come up with a reliable diagnosis for a child who is having difficulty learning and/or concentrating. If the school's evaluation is inadequate, the family will then have to look elsewhere for testing.

ADD OR LD?

Most children who are labeled ADD (with no mention of learning disabilities) have been diagnosed by a process that merely requires the teacher and the parents to fill out a questionnaire based on their observations. This quick and reasonably priced type of evaluation is often initiated by the school. Once the survey questions have been answered, there is usually enough evidence of an attention deficit disorder to convince the family physician that a prescription for stimulant medication is called for. Teachers are usually greatly relieved when a youngster's rambunctious behavior tones down in response to medication. When the drugs have the desired effect, that is considered proof that the child does indeed have an attention deficit disorder, and in most cases, the matter is considered settled. Some teachers take the initiative in creating appropriate classroom adjustments for newly recognized ADD students. When parents insist, some modifications may be required in order for the school to comply with the guidelines specified in section 504 of the 1990 Americans with Disabilities Act. Students who are labeled ADD are not likely to get much special help from the public schools.

Any child who is having trouble concentrating or learning in a regular public-school classroom should be tested for a learning disability. The family may not want special services, but it does need answers. Once the difficulty has been evaluated, decisions about adjustments or special help can be based on information and understanding, rather than assumptions and emotion.

Students who are suspected of having an attention deficit disorder should also be tested for learning disabilities. For the majority of youngsters labeled ADD, problems with concentration and impulse control are the most easily noticed symptoms of an unrecognized learning disability. Current federal guidelines do *not* require public schools to provide the same services for ADD children as those that are mandatory for LD students. Under PL 94-142, youngsters who have a learning disability are entitled to remedial services from a specially trained teacher and appropriate adjustments within the regular classroom, as established in a contract called an Individual Educational Plan (IEP), created by the parents, specialists, and teachers. For students who are only diagnosed as having an attention deficit disorder, classroom adjustments must be made in accordance with section 504 of the 1990 Americans with

Disabilities Act, but no special teachers are provided, and an IEP is not required.

For those who wish any kind of special services from the public schools or government agencies, a thorough evaluation is essential.

IS A DIAGNOSIS ALWAYS NECESSARY?

There are some situations when a thorough evaluation is just not realistic. Although current legislation makes it look like children are tested in quick response to a written request from the parents, there are many youngsters who fall through the cracks. Students who are not part of the public-school system seldom get the chance to take advantage of the free evaluations done routinely by school psychologists. Some families do not have coverage for such testing in their health insurance and cannot afford a private diagnosis. And there are a number of parents who are philosophically or morally opposed to any practice that "labels" children. It is the parents' right to make the final decision about whether testing will be done or not. Their needs (both present and future) are best served when the experts they consult make it a point to provide them with the information they need to make a sound decision.

Some private schools have developed their own screening and testing for learning disabilities and attention deficit disorder. They always include an individual IQ test, but they rarely examine mental ability with such a highly specialized IQ test as the Wechsler Intelligence Scale for Children-III (WISC-3) or the Stanford-Binet Intelligence Scale. The batteries done by independent schools almost always evaluate the full array of academic skills with recognized achievement tests. The results are generally reliable, but they do not provide the "official label" that qualifies a student for special services in the public schools or adjustments in the standardized tests required for admission to colleges and graduate schools. As long as the youngster stays within a network of independent schools that honors this simplified identification process, the student will qualify for whatever services are available. In cases where this inexpensive, streamlined form of testing does not produce a definitive diagnosis, the school can be expected to advise the family to seek a more complete evaluation from a psychologist or other qualified professional.

Homeschooling parents usually prefer to avoid any kind of diagnostic evaluation. They do not want to label their children, and they are not interested in any of the special services available through the public schools. However, the knowledge gained through testing can be particularly valuable to parents who are educating their children at home. Although they do not find numerical test scores and official labels useful, they need guidance in choosing a curriculum and developing effective teaching techniques. This kind of advice is available from certified teachers and psychometrists (testing specialists) who are experienced with homeschooling and are well informed about learning disabilities and attention deficit disorder. The battery of tests they administer is much less expensive than the full-scale diagnostic process preferred by psychologists. It usually includes some form of individual intelligence test (but not the WISC-3 or Stanford-Binet) and a full series of standardized achievement tests. Most specialists who work with homeschooling parents make it a point to investigate the child's learning style. (Several organizations and references can guide homeschoolers in finding qualified experts to provide these services. Two that are particularly well known are the Home School Legal Defense Association and the *Christian Home Educator's Curriculum Manual,* by Cathy Duffy.) Knowing that their youngster learns in a manner similar to LD or ADD children can be tremendously helpful to homeschooling families.

The teaching parent needs information about how the child learns and what types of alternative instructional methods are likely to lead to success. The family needs advice in deciding which issues can be remedied at home and which areas require services from a professional. With close supervision and the right materials, most homeschooling moms can successfully teach their LD/ADD offspring to read, and many can develop effective techniques for improving handwriting, reading comprehension, and math. With special training, homeschoolers can help LD and ADD youngsters overcome many of their problems with spelling and expressive writing. Remedial programs like speech therapy are best left to the experts.

GET SOME ANSWERS

All legitimate forms of evaluating LD and ADD youngsters offer advantages: they let the parents know whether or not the child *could* qualify for special services through the public schools or other agencies within the community; they give the family the assurance that the youngster is not mentally retarded or somehow defective; and most important, by providing a label, they tell the parents exactly where to look for guidance. Libraries are full of books on learning disabilities and attention deficit disorder. And most communities have several organizations ready to provide support services and advice.

Regardless of who conducts the evaluation or what it costs, a professional diagnosis should answer the following questions about a child who does not learn normally:

1. Is the child physically able to learn?

Most children are given routine physical examinations every year. Records from such checkups often contain enough information to answer questions about physical factors that might be preventing a child from learning. It's a good idea to have vision and hearing checked by a specialist, in case there is a subtle problem that doesn't stand out in the simple once-over a youngster gets during the annual physical. Some children who have twenty-twenty vision cannot get their eyes to work together or cannot keep them focused for long periods. Small problems with hearing can cause big problems in school.

Parents need to use caution and common sense when getting expert opinions about physical conditions that might be hampering their child's ability to learn in school. A large assortment of specialists is all too eager to provide training to correct problems that are either insignificant or nonexistent.

For years, a group in California had youngsters drawing circles and squiggles as part of a therapy program designed to retrain handwriting and spelling. A lot of children spent a lot of time drawing loops and filling large sheets of paper with geometric patterns. A lot of parents spent large sums of money thinking their children were being taught by the most highly effective techniques available. Unfortunately, after several years of analyzing the results of this training, researchers found that learning to do all the pencil-control exercises in this specialized remedial program did not help youngsters improve their handwriting, expressive writing, or spelling. In much the same way, correcting a "physical problem" in some area underlying the academic difficulty does not always produce an improvement in schoolwork.

2. Does the child have enough mental ability to learn?

Learning disabilities are often mistaken for mental retardation. Only a good individual intelligence test can definitely eliminate retardation as a possibility in a child who fails to learn. WISC-3 and Stanford-Binet are the most highly recognized instruments for testing mental ability (see pages 193–97). In recent years, the Woodcock-Johnson Psychoeducational Battery-Revised-Cognitive Scale has become recognized as a reliable instrument in establishing an IQ score for LD/ADD children (see page 197). Other individual IQ tests are adequate, but no one of them should be trusted to supply a true measure of the youngster's mental capacity.

Some psychologists believe in telling parents the child's IQ score; some do not. Either way, a number or set of numbers is not enough. Parents should be given a detailed explanation of what the intelligence testing reveals. They definitely need to be told the "range" of their child's mental ability.

3. Is there an emotional problem preventing the child from learning?

Most psychologists give a few tests to be sure that a student's basic problem with learning is not emotional. However, such tests are not always administered as part of a routine evaluation. In any case, the specialist conducting the other tests will be alert to signs that might indicate an emotional disturbance. Most LD specialists are not qualified to test for emotional problems, but they are trained to recognize symptoms of those difficulties and to refer the youngster to a psychologist for examination if there is any cause for concern.

If the diagnosis does not mention the child's emotional health, the parents should ask whether or not there is any sign of a psychological problem. A "yes" answer should not strike terror into the heart. It is quite common to have behavior disorders in conjunction with a learning disability. Many of the characteristics of an attention deficit disorder overlap with those typically seen in children who are emotionally disturbed. Some LD/ADD children have an "oppositional," or defiant, nature. This makes them hard to manage but is not always a handicap. Almost all older LD children are emotionally damaged. The important questions are these: Is the student so severely disturbed that the psychological difficulties must be addressed before there can be any hope of academic improvement? Did an emotional problem cause the learning failure in the first place?

4. How much has the child learned?

Grades on a report card are not enough to tell what a child has or has not learned in school. In evaluating a child who has trouble learning, standardized achievement tests are absolutely essential to determining exact grade level scores in silent reading comprehension, silent reading vocabulary, silent reading speed, oral reading, word recognition, spelling, and math. Many other areas can be tested, but those seven are almost always checked. (See page 188 for an explanation of standardized tests.)

5. Is the child learning disabled?

A psychologist trying to determine the cause of a student's learning problem should always test for the symptoms of learning disabilities discussed in chapter 2. In addition, the specialist should have the youngster produce a sample of handwriting, a simple drawing, an original paragraph or story, and some copying work. A visual/motor perception test is also usually part of the evaluation.

6. What kind of learning disability does the child have?

Knowing that a youngster is learning disabled is not enough; the exact nature of the disability must be determined. Fancy names are not necessary. What parents need is a full explanation of the areas in which the child is handicapped, as well as knowledge of the areas in which there are no learning problems. The parents, the teacher, and the LD therapist must have this information to guide them in working with the student.

Unfortunately, experts often have a difficult time explaining this part of a diagnosis to parents. Few doctors and psychologists are able to present their test findings in words that nonexperts can understand. (Pediatric neuropsychologists are best at talking to each other. Some are almost entirely incapable of communicating their findings to anyone outside their narrow, highly specialized field.)

Nevertheless, parents should keep asking questions—some of which may sound foolish—until they get answers that make sense to them. Technical language sounds impressive, but parents need a translation into standard English.

7. What kind of therapy does the child need?

The original evaluation of a child's learning problem should include recommendations for the kind of therapy the youngster needs. These recommendations should serve two purposes: the parents need the names and addresses of several specialists who can provide the type of instruction the student will find most helpful, and the therapist needs guidance in planning a program suited to the child's particular disability.

8. Given the child's special needs and abilities, what school is best able to provide the appropriate help?

Public-school psychologists hesitate to suggest that a student could be served best by some private school; teachers and administrators at independent and church-related schools are reluctant to advise that a youngster would be better off somewhere else; and many specialists do not want to go out on a limb and name particular schools at all. Getting opinions about schools is a tricky task, but it must be dealt with. Parents need to be given recommendations concerning what school would be most helpful to their child.

Parents should ask four kinds of questions as they go about choosing a school for their LD child:

A. What type of school would be best? Does the youngster need to be challenged by a high-powered college-preparatory program? Would a relaxed, flexible atmosphere work best? Would a special low-level environment for slow learners be helpful?

B. Which local schools offer the kind of program and atmosphere the youngster needs?

C. Is there a particular class or teacher that might work wonders for the youngster?

D. Is a special school for the learning disabled necessary? If so, which one?

Larry was a fifteen-year-old nonreader. His hometown did not have a single school in which he could learn. But his parents could not afford to send him to a special boarding school.

The psychologist who had tested Larry came up with a solution to the problem. First, she convinced the state's educational authorities that Larry should be allowed *not* to attend school for the rest of that year. Second, she got Larry started at once on a good program of therapy with an LD specialist. Third, she found ways to get the cost of the therapy down to a level the family could afford. Fourth, she joined the parents in fighting for money from the state to pay for Larry to attend a special school the following year. Fifth, she guided the parents in selecting the special school that would best fit the boy's needs.

Less than six months after his disability was diagnosed, this teenager was attending a fine private school for the learning disabled. And since it had no appropriate services available, the public-school system was paying the bill.

This case is not really unusual. Good psychologists often become deeply involved in helping families fight for the best school placement for their LD child.

The question of which grade the student will enter is no less important than the question of which school. Many educators no longer believe in having a youngster repeat a grade, no matter what the situation. Some grim statistics add weight to their position. Research studies have found that about half of those children who repeat a grade never graduate from high school—and for those who are held back twice, 100 percent drop out!

Some states have competency tests that determine whether or not a student is qualified to move from one level to the next. Youngsters who can't achieve the required numbers on the mandatory tests cannot go on to the next grade no matter what the family says. Summer school is usually offered as an alternative to retention in the same grade, but at the end of the special session, the student still must pass the test to go on. Unfortunately, summer programs almost never offer any classes appropriate for LD students. It's a brutal system that is probably one of the factors pushing our illiteracy and dropout rates ever higher.

Most LD specialists see retaining a youngster as an action that can be helpful in some cases. Repeating a grade must not be viewed as punishment. "You messed up the first time, so now we're going to make you do it again!" is *not* the proper attitude to express to the student. Unless getting a second try at a grade will increase the child's chance for success, retention is pointless.

> After one year in a self-contained LD class, Doug was ready to try his hand in the regular classroom. As a twelve-year-old with a September birthday, he could have been either an extremely young sixth-grader or a slightly old fifth-grader. He was small for his age, and his reading skills were at the high fourth-grade level. It was decided that he was ready to succeed as an average student in a regular fifth-grade class.
>
> Doug was not thrilled with the decision. He was in his sixth year of school and wanted to be in the sixth grade with all his friends. His teachers and his family sympathized but put him where they felt he belonged.
>
> Under the supervision of an outstanding teacher, Doug positively blossomed in his new fifth-grade class. By Christmas, he was the top math student in his room, was doing satisfactory work in all his other subjects, and was happy as a clam. He was definitely in the right place.

Sometimes, it helps to hold a child back a year. Sometimes, another year in the same grade makes matters worse. As part of the evaluation, the diagnostician should give a definite opinion concerning the grade in which a particular student should be placed.

9. How should parents deal with the child at home?

A happy, healthy life at home can be the key factor in helping LD and ADD children. Yet their parents usually moan, "How do we live with that kid? He's impossible. Our family life is a mess."

Parents need guidance with questions of discipline, curfews, chores, homework, recreation, and the like. Does their youngster need set rules enforced with a firm hand, or is it better to be more easygoing with discipline? What kinds of activities should be encouraged? How much sympathy should be given because of the learning disability or attention deficit disorder? What should the other children in the family be told about their LD/ADD brother or sister? Should Aunt Maude be told? What about the kids in the neighborhood?

More than anyone else, the parents need help with these matters. And the specialist who makes the diagnosis is the ideal one to provide that help.

10. What does the future hold for the child?

Making an educated guess about what the future holds for a patient or student is a routine part of an evaluation.

Once parents know what their child's learning problem is, they need to be told what to expect. What are the chances of overcoming the problem? Are there more difficulties ahead? Can they be avoided? Is college a possibility? Will the choice of a career be affected?

THE SPECIALIST'S ROLE

Any good professional evaluation of a child's learning problems will answer most of the parents' questions in each of the ten areas discussed above. When the diagnostic workup is finished, the parents should be given a detailed explanation of the findings in a face-to-face conference. In that conference, all test results and recommendations need to be thoroughly discussed.

Many specialists do a poor job of explaining their diagnosis to the youngster's parents. They simply are not able to put their ideas into language that a nonexpert can understand. Many don't have the time for long explanations. (It takes two or three hours to discuss thoroughly all the topics that should be covered.) Parents need not be embarrassed to ask questions during this conference. It is reasonable for them to insist on clear answers to all ten of the items discussed above.

In addition to having a conference at which the doctor or psychologist reports on the test findings, parents should be given a written report that includes all test results, conclusions, and recommendations. The report will probably be written in jargon. This need not bother the parents, since the report is intended for use by the schools. It is important that the parents have a copy of this report for use by a therapist if they decide to call on one, or for use by a new school system in case the family moves to another town.

A final word of warning: After parents have chosen an individual or institution to test their child, they must make sure before setting up an appointment that they're going to get their money's worth. They should not take their child to anyone who doesn't (1) interview both parents as part of the evaluation, (2) spend at least an hour explaining the test findings when the evaluation is completed, (3) see to it that the child is given a good explanation of the problem, and (4) provide the parents a written report on the test results within thirty days of the testing.

HOW TO GET REAL INFORMATION OUT OF A MAZE OF TEST SCORES

In considering test scores, it must always be remembered that they tell only how well an individual performed at one particular time and place. Had the tests been given one day earlier or one day later, the scores would not have been exactly the same. The specialist doing the evaluation does take this into consideration. Occasionally, the diagnostician will feel that a child's test results do not give a true picture of the youngster's abilities. When that happens, it will be noted in the report and an explanation will be added. But professionals are usually extremely adept at getting children into the right frame of mind so that they do as well as possible on the tests.

STANDARDIZED TESTS

Most tests used to measure intelligence and academic achievement are *standardized tests.* A standardized test is put on the market only after years of research, during which the test is given to thousands of different subjects. The scores are then studied and compared to produce a set of *norms.* Norms are figures that tell how well a typical group of children of the same age performed on the test. In that way, it is determined just how well a child of a certain age and grade can be expected to score.

Those who administer the standardized test are supplied with information, usually in the form of graphs and charts, about the norms that have been established for the test. With that information, the test results of an individual child can be compared with the scores of a huge number of other youngsters of the same age and grade.

For example, eight-year-old Betsy is given a standardized spelling test in September of the year she is in the third grade. It is hoped she will spell enough words correctly to be ranked as an average speller or better. Betsy spells twenty-three words correctly, and the norm charts show that most beginning third-graders get only twenty correct. Then it is known that Betsy is a better-than-average speller. She is a better speller than the typical child of her age and grade placement.

Standardized tests are based on comparing one particular individual with a large group of individuals, all of whom are of the same age or in the same school grade.

STANDARDIZED TEST SCORES

Results on standardized tests have no meaning in terms of "raw" scores that tell how many answers were right and how many were wrong. To be of any value, the raw scores must be converted to either *percentile scores* or *grade level scores*. These types of scores tell how a child's performance compares with that of others.

Percentile scores place the youngster in an imaginary group of a hundred typical children who are exactly the child's age or in the same grade in school. Picture a hundred little third-graders lined up against the wall, arranged according to how well they did on a standardized test. The norm charts tell us that Betsy's score of twenty-three puts her in the sixty-fourth percentile. Starting with the child who scored the lowest, Betsy will be the sixty-fourth youngster in the line. The sixty-three children below her didn't do as well as she did; the thirty-six above her did better. Or to take it one step farther, 36 percent are better spellers than Betsy, while 63 percent do not spell as well. Betsy is not an amazingly good speller, but the standardized test results indicate that she's better than average. Percentile scores tell where a student's performance stands in comparison with that of others.

Grade level scores tell how much a child has learned. They are expressed as decimal numbers and are easy to understand. The numeral to the left of the decimal represents the grade level at which the student is working; the numeral to the right indicates how many months into the grade the child has progressed.

In the example above, Betsy did as well on the spelling test as most children who are in the fifth month of the third grade. So her grade level score is 3.5. Since the test was given in September, when Betsy was zero months into the third grade, a grade level score of 3.0 would be expected from an average speller. Betsy, then, is five months ahead of the average child in her class in spelling.

A youngster who works at the same level as an average student in February of the sixth grade would be given a grade level score of 6.5; a child working at the level of an average student in May of the tenth grade would be given a 10.8; and so forth.

Grade level scores are especially useful in watching a student's progress. A tenth-grader who scores 2.3 on a reading test is reading at the level of a typical youngster in the third month of the second grade. This child has a serious problem. When compared with other students the same age, a student with scores this low would rank down at the first or second percentile; almost all tenth-graders read better than that. If, after a year of therapy, this youngster's reading score rises to 3.9, there has been wonderful progress. There has been a gain of one year and six months in the level of skill. On the percentile charts, this student would still be classified as a very poor reader; the percentile score serves as a reminder that he is still one of the poorest readers in his class. But the grade level score shows that he now reads almost as well as the average child just beginning the fourth grade. He is a lot better off than he was last year.

INTELLIGENCE TESTS

Intelligence tests measure brain power. *IQ test, test of mental ability*, and *intelligence test* are interchangeable names for tests that measure mental horsepower. *IQ test* is the term used most often. The letters stand for *intelligence quotient.*

IQ tests measure a person's ability to think *in areas that would lead to success in school.* They tell little or nothing about creativity, disposition, artistic talent, athletic ability, social skills, musical gifts, and a host of other factors that make up the personality and nature of an individual. Mostly, an intelligence test score tells how well an individual can reason, remember, and understand. It is supposed to determine how "smart" a person is. Those who have strong verbal and mathematical skills tend to do well on IQ tests.

All intelligence tests are standardized. They work by comparing one person's mental ability with the mental abilities of others the same age.

INDIVIDUAL INTELLIGENCE TESTS

Most schools give group IQ tests to all their students. For this type of test, each child is given a test booklet. The directions are given to the whole class at once. Then each pupil must read and answer as many questions as possible in the time allowed. Those who can't read well can't score well. Those who have trouble concentrating often score poorly. For the average youngster, the results of a group test are accurate enough to provide a pretty reliable measure of mental ability. Unless there is some special problem, the vast majority of children never need to be given an individual IQ test.

An individual IQ test is more thorough and accurate than a group test. Since these tests are given orally, one-to-one, by a psychologist or other trained professional, they do not require the subject to do any reading or writing. For some children—the emotionally disturbed, poor readers and nonreaders, the gifted, the learning disabled, those with attention deficit disorder, etc.—only an individual intelligence test can be trusted to give a true measure of mental ability.

INTELLIGENCE TEST SCORES

Intelligence test scores are usually expressed in one of three ways: as a percentile, as an IQ, or as a mental age.

As in the case of achievement tests, a percentile score ranks the child in an imaginary group of a hundred children. Since it can be easily illustrated with stick figures, it is an excellent tool in explaining test findings to children.

A mental age (abbreviated *MA*) is used less commonly than an IQ to indicate the level of a child's intelligence. The MA score works in much the same way that grade level scores do. Two numbers are given, separated in this case by a dash. The first number represents the year of the mental age of the individual; the second number represents the month. For example, regardless of chronological age, a child who scores as well on an intelligence test as the average child who is nine years, four months old has an MA of 9-4. If this youngster scores as well as the average child who is just about to turn ten, the score is 9-11. If the student scores as well as the average child who just turned ten, the MA is 10-0. MA's are read without pronouncing the dash: 9-4 is read "nine four" or "nine years, four months."

Mental age scores are useful in that they allow one to compare the chronological age of a child with his mental age. A seven-year-old with an MA of 10-6 can think as well as most fifth-graders, even though he is only in the second grade. The youngster is unusually bright and should be working at a level well above that of most classmates.

Mental age scores are very helpful in some situations, especially with children who are mentally slow or retarded. But in general, an intelligence test score expressed as an IQ gives more useful information. An MA score can easily be converted to an IQ score by, first, changing the years and months in the MA and the chronological age to a decimal system (10-6 would become 10.5 and 7-0 would become 7.0); second, dividing the mental age by the chronological age (10.5 ÷ 7.0); third, multiplying the resulting quotient by 100 (1.5 x 100). The result, 150, is the IQ score.

The vast majority of IQ scores fall between 80 and 120, with a score of 100 being the perfect average.

To be considered as having "normal" or "average" intelligence, a person's IQ must be between 90 and 109. Obviously, an individual with an IQ at the low end of the range won't be quite as smart as someone whose IQ is close to the high end.

Since the learning disabled by definition are of at least average intelligence, the IQ score of an LD child will be 90 or higher—and it can be a lot higher. For youngsters with an attention deficit disorder, the IQ score can fall in any range, from the very highest to the very lowest. Most youngsters classified as ADD—with no mention of other handicapping conditions—have average or better intelligence, but that cannot be assumed to be the case.

Some specialists believe in giving parents their child's IQ score; some do not. (Federal laws state that parents have a right to see any test scores or files concerning their children.) But the exact number that represents a youngster's intelligence is not at all important. In most cases in which a specialist prefers not to give out an IQ score, parents should not insist.

The range of an individual's intelligence is much more meaningful than the actual score yielded by a test. A youngster who is "low average" or "dull normal" is very different in ability from one who is "high average" or "bright normal." The chart below should clarify these and other terms used to describe intelligence. Since the words *normal* and *average* are used as part of the labels for three different ranges of intelligence, the terms can be confusing.

TWO INTELLIGENCE TESTS WORTH KNOWING ABOUT

The Stanford-Binet Intelligence Scale, highly respected among psychologists and educators, is one of the two individual IQ tests best suited to testing LD and ADD children. It is designed to give only two scores: a mental age and an IQ. Most specialists who use the Stanford-Binet to report on a youngster's ability in each of the different areas of intelligence tested will take the time when explaining their findings to point out areas of unusual strength or weakness in the child's ability.

Only a registered psychologist is qualified to administer and interpret the Stanford-Binet. Giving the test requires at least an hour, and usually longer. There is no limit to how high the score may be. Any IQ over 140 is that of a genius, but it is possible for the Stanford-Binet to yield an IQ as high as 200 or 300.

The Wechsler Intelligence Scale for Children-III (WISC-3) is more commonly used than the Stanford-Binet and is ideally suited to testing LD and ADD children between the ages of six and a half and sixteen. For young children four to six and a half, the Wechsler Pre-School Primary Scale of Intelligence is used. The Wechsler Adult Intelligence Scale is for those over sixteen years of age. Since most schoolchildren are between six and a half and sixteen, this discussion is confined to the WISC-3. Vast amounts of research have been done on this test; shelves of books have been written about interpreting the scores it gives. When used by a real expert, the WISC-3 can provide information that is much more valuable than mere numbers as a measure of mental ability.

The test is so difficult to give and interpret that only a qualified psychologist can use it. It has the advantage of requiring a bit less time to administer than the Stanford-Binet, and the child being tested usually thinks that taking the WISC-3 is fun.

Scoring the WISC-3 is a very complicated process. The test is designed to yield three different IQ scores and as many as twelve

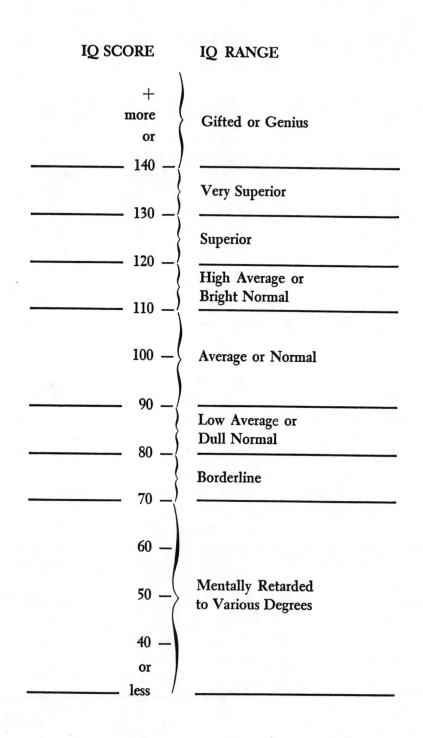

subtest scores. A wealth of information can be gained through the use of this one test.

The twelve subtests that go together to make up the WISC-3 are divided into two categories. The *verbal* tests require the use of language. The psychologist giving the test asks the subject questions; the youngster must then figure out the answers and explain them to the psychologist. In all the verbal tests, the child has to *say* the correct answer. The *performance* tests do not require the subject to use language. Once the psychologist has explained what it is she wants the child to do, he does his part by arranging blocks or pictures or pieces of a puzzle in the way he thinks is correct. The youngster may talk as much or as little as he wants; what counts is how he performs in figuring out what to do with the objects given him.

Thus, the WISC-3 gives both a verbal IQ score and a performance IQ score. For LD and ADD children, those two scores provide the most important information that can be gained from the test.

Usually, the performance IQ of a child is not much different from his verbal IQ. But the two scores are rarely identical. One of the two—and it can be either one—is typically between three and ten points higher than the other. The differences between the two scores in the following examples are common: verbal IQ, 82, performance IQ, 85; verbal IQ, 103, performance IQ, 98; verbal IQ, 128, performance IQ, 134.

A learning-disabled child, on the other hand, often has a verbal IQ and a performance IQ that are greatly different from each other. As in the case with youngsters who are not learning disabled, either score can be higher. These sets of scores might belong to LD children: verbal IQ, 112, performance IQ, 90; verbal IQ, 98, performance IQ, 115; verbal IQ, 114, performance IQ, 134. Anytime there is a difference of more than sixteen points between an individual's verbal IQ and performance IQ, a learning disability should be suspected. (Caution: When measuring the difference between a verbal IQ and a performance IQ, one should make certain that the scores being compared are expressed as IQ scores, *not* as percentile scores.)

When dealing with a psychologist who does not believe in

giving out IQ scores, parents should ask, "How big a spread is there between the performance IQ and the verbal IQ?" Any specialist will gladly give that information. (Another caution: Some individuals who are clearly LD do *not* have a difference of sixteen points or more between their verbal IQ and their performance IQ.) This pair of test scores can provide a major clue as to whether a child with ADD is also LD. It is not very common to find a large discrepancy between verbal and performance IQ for those who are not learning disabled.

The *full-scale IQ* is the third important score given by the WISC-3. It is this full-scale score that tells whether a child's mental ability is average or better. On the WISC-3, there is a limit to how high the full-scale IQ can be. Any score over 140 is fantastic; a score of about 160 is the highest possible.

The twelve subtests that make up the WISC-3 are divided into six verbal tests and six performance tests as follows: the verbal tests cover information, vocabulary, comprehension, math, similarities, and digit span; the performance tests cover picture arrangement, picture completion, block design, object assembly, coding, and mazes.

Few psychologists give all twelve subtests to any one child. The WISC-3 is designed in such a way that several subtests can be left out without harming the reliability of the IQ scores yielded. Three subtests are often not given: the digit span test, the coding test, and the mazes tests. The mazes are rarely used, and for LD and ADD children, that's fine. But the digit span and coding tests can be extremely useful in evaluating the problems of youngsters with learning disabilities and attention deficit disorder. Even though many good psychologists do not normally use those two tests, they (and all the other subtests except mazes) should be given to any youngster suspected of being LD.

Psychologists charge a lot to give and interpret the WISC-3. For families with a modest income, having just this one test administered could cost between one and two weeks' wages. Clients whose children are learning disabled do not get their money's worth when any test other than the mazes test is left out. There are a few specialists who give only two or three of the subtests, charge for the full test, and come up with only a full-scale IQ score. To parents who complain that such a procedure is inadequate, these psychologists shout, "Balderdash!" Their claim that a reliable measure of full-scale IQ can be gained through the use of just a few subtests is supported by research. But in using only two or three subtests, they're not getting the whole picture of mental ability that is available through correct use of the WISC-3.

A third individual IQ test is growing in popularity among psychologists who do a lot of work with children who are experiencing LD- and ADD-type problems in school. The Woodcock-Johnson Psychoeducational Battery-Revised-Cognitive Scale (see page 181) is gaining a reputation as a highly useful instrument in determining the mental ability of school-age children. In the hands of a thoroughly trained psychologist, it yields a full array of scores that can be very informative when testing a youngster for a learning disability or an attention deficit disorder.

PARENTS CHOOSE THE SPECIALIST, THE SPECIALIST CHOOSES THE TESTS

There are many fine tests on the market. Their use allows doctors, psychologists, and educators to measure and study almost everything imaginable that pertains to children and learning. Some are very, very complicated; others are quite simple. And while no two are exactly alike, many are similar. In deciding which tests to use, each expert has those she prefers. Some people like chocolate ice cream, some like strawberry. Some psychologists prefer to use the WISC-3, others like the Stanford-Binet or the Woodcock-Johnson. In *all* areas of testing, it is up to the specialist to decide which tests will give the information she needs and which ones she prefers to use. It is important to realize that in almost all cases, there are several equally reliable tests available for measuring the same thing. Two experts may use entirely different tests, yet if they use the tests as designed, they are both likely to come up with the same correct diagnosis.

Parents need to understand that experts cannot know beforehand exactly which tests will be used in making a diagnosis. Like a detective, the specialist starts by looking for leads. The information gained from one test gives clues about areas that need further investigation. Until the snooping and probing actually begin, there is no way to tell which tests will be required or what they will reveal. Some areas of the child's ability will always be tested. Others will be studied only when the need is indicated.

Keeping in mind the basic format of good testing discussed earlier, parents should find a specialist they can trust, then let her do the testing in her own way.

9

TYPES OF LD PROGRAMS IN THE SCHOOLS:
Variations on a Theme

Think up a fancy term and everybody jumps on the bandwagon to try out the new idea. Teenagers, politicians, and educators are always "into" some new fad. It seems that each year, a new craze develops, complete with its own "with it" vocabulary. In the field of education, the last twenty years have seen a variety come and go: *new math, team teaching, homogeneous grouping, prescriptive teaching, open classrooms, individualized instruction, mainstreaming, outcome-based education, back to the basics, inclusion.* Inclusion and outcome-based education haven't left us yet, but they, too, will pass. As has been true with educational fads of the past, they are not *the* answer.

The jargon sounds impressive; polysyllabic words in pairs always do. Such high-sounding phrases are fine for college professors, textbook writers, graduate students, public speakers, and school superintendents. But parents and teachers need to talk about real situations and real children.

At different times and in different places, each of the "variations" discussed in this chapter has had some kind of impressive name.

But the labels used to describe programs for teaching LD and ADD youngsters are not very helpful to parents. What they need is a basic understanding of what can be done within a school to help their child learn.

THE THEME

In light of all that's been discussed in this book about discovering children's special needs through testing, conferences with teachers, recommendations from psychologists, and considerations of the individual child's personality, it's nice to think that all learning-disabled children will be given the type of instruction that is best suited to their particular disability, talents, personality, and level of intelligence. Unfortunately, that is not quite how it works.

Each school system designs its own program for LD students. (Unless they are diagnosed as having a learning disability, ADD children do not get full-fledged programs complete with specially trained teachers and an IEP.) Although these programs are intended to provide special instruction for youngsters with a wide variety of problems, they are always limited by the availability of money, space, and trained specialists. With budgetary restrictions forcing schools into a rapid adoption of inclusion, many LD programs are being revised in ways that make them more practical but much less effective.

There are several variations on this theme of using the school's resources to the best advantage of LD and ADD students. The degree of success that can be expected from each depends on several key factors.

VARIATION I
NOTHING IS DONE FOR THE CHILD.

The student's teacher does not talk about his learning disability. She does not treat him any differently from the way she treats his classmates. The youngster is not labeled; he is not made to stand out.

That, of course, is not really a variation on the theme of helping the child as an individual. Yet it is alarming how many schools ignore the LD student's problem completely. His learning disability may be so mild that a therapist is not required. Nevertheless, if a youngster has had learning difficulties to such an extent that he needed an official evaluation, and it was found that the problem was a learning disability, then he does need some kind of special assistance and classroom modification.

VARIATION II
THE CLASSROOM TEACHER DOES THE BEST SHE CAN ON HER OWN.

It is possible for a good teacher to work successfully with an LD/ADD student without any outside guidance. But that is likely to happen only in a situation in which the child is mildly disabled and the teacher is unusually creative, intelligent, dedicated, and energetic—and has time to spare. An instructor working alone cannot be expected to do much to help a severely disabled youngster overcome his learning problem. The best she can do is to avoid hurting him. By adjusting the child's assignments and using some of the other guidelines discussed in chapter 6, she can encourage him to learn as much as possible while helping him avoid emotional damage.

VARIATION III
THE CLASSROOM TEACHER DOES THE BEST SHE CAN UNDER THE SUPERVISION OF AN LD SPECIALIST.

In this type of program, the specialist does not come in direct contact with LD children. She helps regular teachers find ways to teach them within the regular classroom. The LD students never get any therapy.

When this program works as it is supposed to, much of the schoolwork assigned to disabled students is adjusted to fit their problems and needs. Sadly, it usually turns out that the special materials designed for them are merely used as "busywork" to keep them out of trouble.

The more severely disabled the students are, the less likely it is that Variation III will help them.

VARIATION IV
THE LD SPECIALIST WORKS WITH STUDENTS IN THE REGULAR CLASSROOM AND PROVIDES GUIDANCE AND SUPERVISION FOR THE CLASSROOM TEACHER.

Programs of this type keep LD specialists in direct contact with students right in the schoolroom while regular class is going on. Sometimes, this model of service delivery even makes special help available for youngsters who are only classified as ADD. Since the LD teacher is already in the room, it's easy to expand her list of pupils to include all the students who could benefit from her assistance.

Variation IV depends heavily on the ability of the specialist and the regular teacher to work together with an attitude of trust and cooperation. Those who make it work successfully usually find some very creative ways of teaching in close collaboration. LD specialists sometimes take over the entire class to demonstrate a new instructional technique. Often, the two instructors take turns observing a particular student in order to evaluate progress or behavior. Sometimes, the pair ends up doing some team teaching as well.

When it works, this variation can create a wonderfully healthy classroom environment where all the students are highly motivated by the success they are achieving with work they find challenging. This idyllic scene is what many educators picture when they refer to "inclusion." Rarely does the reality come even close to the dream.

Despite the diagnostic process, the IEP, and the design of programs based on inclusion, no teacher can be all things to all students. There are limits to how many individualized modifications can be successfully carried out within a regular classroom taught by a regular classroom teacher.

Variations I, II, III, and IV have one fault in common: they rely too heavily on the classroom teacher. In some cases, methods that depend so much on the regular teacher *can* work; in a few cases, they *do* work. Most of the time, they do not. It will take a dramatic change in teacher training to make the lofty ideals of inclusion a reality.

VARIATION V
STUDENTS ARE REMOVED FROM THE CLASSROOM FOR LD THERAPY.

When this method is used, children go to the "resource room" for special lessons with an LD teacher. The therapy may be done one-to-one, but it is usually done in small groups. The students are not tutored in school subjects or helped to catch up with their reading. They are given highly specialized instruction aimed at helping them overcome their learning disabilities. Such therapy does not replace the students' regular reading classes (or math classes, etc.); it is given *in addition* to the regular instruction. When LD children are given at least three hours of help a week by a good specialist, they usually make progress.

When ADD youngsters are classified as having a "behavior disorder," they often get assigned to a resource room for instruction by a specially trained "BD" teacher. In that quiet environment, they are taught to observe and take charge of their patterns of thinking and acting in order to develop the self-control they need to function more successfully in the regular classroom.

VARIATION VI
(VARIATIONS III, IV, AND V COMBINED)
THE LD SPECIALIST GIVES THE CHILD THERAPY AND WORKS WITH THE CLASSROOM TEACHER.

When variations III, IV, and V are combined, great things can happen. LD students go to a resource room, as in variation V. In addition to that, the regular classroom program is adjusted to fit their special needs, as in variation III. If there is an attitude of trust and cooperation between the LD specialist and the classroom teacher, a joint effort on their part can produce remarkable results for their students. For the majority of LD youngsters, such a combination of therapy and classroom modification is the ideal approach.

Unfortunately, LD and BD teachers often *cannot* work with a student's regular teacher. Three common problems can prevent them from developing a satisfactory working relationship:

1. LD specialists are often assigned to several schools. They almost always have to spend a great deal of time screening and testing children suspected of having a learning disability or an attention deficit disorder. It is also common for them to have too many students, too few materials, and too little time for preparation. Paperwork, reports, government forms, long conferences with parents, school-based committee meetings, placement committee meetings, consultations with psychologists and principals—their days are so tightly scheduled that they often don't have time to work with a pupil's classroom teacher.

2. School systems usually have policies that limit the activities of LD and BD teachers. Their territory is clearly defined, and they are not allowed to step outside the area in which they are given authority. One rule is very common: LD and BD teachers are not to become involved with any child who has not been through all the committees and been officially classified as LD or ADD. Other restrictions vary. Resource room teachers are often told, "You do your job and leave everybody else alone. Stay out of the classrooms." Teachers of self-contained LD classes are often warned, "Do not touch *any* child who is not specifically assigned to your class."

Good LD specialists and BD teachers try to work around such regulations by making themselves available to help teachers through casual conversations. At the lunch table, in the teacher's lounge— anywhere paths cross—they try to answer questions and make suggestions to classroom teachers. Small, unofficial exchanges of information have to be used in place of detailed consultations and conferences. But even these little conferences are often made impossible by school policy!

LD and BD teachers are often treated as "different" from the other teachers in the school. The projectors and special equipment on hand for the regular teachers are not available to them; theirs must come from the special education storerooms downtown. The books and materials on hand for the other teachers are not available to them; theirs must be ordered from the special education department. Often, services and materials available to the rest of the school are off-limits to LD and BD teachers.

The principal isn't really their boss. And since they must go to their own special education meetings, they often do not attend faculty meetings in the school or schools where they work. Sometimes, the situation is so bad that LD and BD teachers never even get to know the rest of the faculty in their schools. They work among strangers. They don't have enough contact with other teachers to do much good through casual conversations with them. (Understanding principals tend to ignore rules that make their special education people outsiders. But in many ways, their hands are tied.)

To start my self-contained LD class for fifth- and sixth-graders, I needed materials.

The principal wasn't supposed to make his regular supplies open to my class. But Mr. Northrup personally took me down to the storeroom. In the large collection of textbooks provided by the state, I found what I needed for social studies and science. Mr. Northrup called downtown to have them send out some math books that were not kept in our building. And he sent me to the reading coordinator to search for the right reading books.

She wasn't supposed to waste her time with special education people, either. But she generously spent several hours working with me. We dug through shelves and shelves of state-supplied reading texts. Try as we might, we could find nothing in her huge selection that would suit the needs of my LD students. Every single series used the whole-word or whole-language approach. I was looking for phonetically based materials that could be taught by multisensory methods. Nothing on the reading coordinator's shelves came close to what I was after.

I reported my lack of success to Mr. Northrup. He advised, "You'll have to order some books. Get in touch with the LD supervisor." And so, caught in the trap of which-budget-will-pay-for-this-one, I began six weeks of being shuffled back and forth. Here's how it went:

[late August] SUPERVISOR: Can't your principal find you some books?
[early September] PRINCIPAL: I've checked all the supply areas available to me. Nothing like what you need could be found.
[early September] SUPERVISOR: Get your principal to order what you need out of his budget.

[mid-September] PRINCIPAL: Get your supervisor to order what you need out of her budget.

[late September] SUPERVISOR: There is nothing in my budget to cover reading books.

[early October] PRINCIPAL: There isn't anyplace in my budget where I'm allowed to take money to buy reading books for special ed. They've got $250 set aside for you to buy materials. Ask them to give you that.

[early October] SUPERVISOR: I can't release your $250 yet. It's not supposed to be used for reading books anyway. I'm sure if you really looked, you could find what you need down at the main repository.

[mid-October] PRINCIPAL: This is ridiculous. Order what you need. I'll find the money somewhere.

No principal or LD teacher can totally overcome school policies that separate special education teachers from regular faculty members. The official rules create an atmosphere that prevents cooperation and good working relationships between all categories of special education teachers and the classroom teachers they should be helping.

3. Most teachers do not want "outsiders" meddling in the way they run their classes. There is much distrust of LD and BD teachers because of their lack of contact with regular teachers. Further distrust is caused by the fact that most specialists walk into a classroom and give criticism, rather than help. LD specialists are famous for blaming teachers for all of a child's learning and behavior problems. And they are notorious for coming up with suggestions that are completely unworkable. The problem is that most LD and BD teachers have no experience in regular classroom teaching. They have no conception of what the regular instructor is up against. When they step into a classroom, they cause hurt feelings by asking the impossible.

Good therapy combined with a carefully adjusted program in the classroom is the best solution for most LD and ADD students. It is unfortunate that schedules, rules, and a lack of cooperation among teachers often cheat LD/ADD youngsters out of their best chance for real success.

VARIATION VII
STUDENTS ARE REMOVED FROM THE CLASSROOM FOR LD THERAPY AND INSTRUCTION IN THE AREAS DIRECTLY AFFECTED BY THEIR DISABILITY.

Some children are so weak in one or two subjects that they cannot learn those subjects in a regular classroom. Students who have no chance for success in a given subject should be removed from the classroom so it can be taught to them by a specialist. In this type of program, a youngster with a math disability, for example, would never be part of regular math classes. All his math would be taught to him by an LD specialist. Such a program is most often used to teach language arts or math.

Classroom teachers tend to like variation VII because it makes their jobs much easier. In this program, the regular teacher has to provide instruction for only two reading groups, instead of three; the LD therapist ends up with the bottom group and leaves the two good ones in the classroom. Also, the LD pupils get therapy without missing a lot of classwork that the teacher would have to help them make up later. Principals like this variation, too. Therapy is easier to schedule if it can simply replace a whole subject, rather than being squeezed into some other time during the school day. But the students are often not very fond of such a system. They don't seem to mind being in a special group for instruction, but they often complain because they're not in the "regular book." Not using the same text that everybody else is using leaves LD students open to laughs, teasing, and other put-downs.

Regardless of who likes it and why, variation VII is often the ideal approach for helping LD students in middle and high school. Also, for "high-risk" first-graders and LD youngsters in the primary grades, variation VII can be extremely effective.

> The Greenway School is a private school designed to meet the needs of average children in grades one through nine. It has an outstanding LD program.
> Greenway has a high-risk program (essentially like variation VII) for grades one, two, and three. All children in kindergarten and first grade are carefully screened and tested. Those recognized

as needing preventive help are put into high-risk groups at the beginning of the first grade and are kept there until the end of grade three. All their basic language-arts skills are taught to them by an LD specialist. They spend two hours a day in small groups taught with special materials and special methods. Each child is part of a regular class for the rest of the school day.

As students enter the fourth grade, the LD program shifts to become much like variation VI. Except in special cases, youngsters become part of regular reading and math classes. If their therapy needs to be continued, they go to a resource room. The therapist guides the classroom teacher in adjusting the regular work.

The Greenway School's approach to dealing with learning-disabled children is unusual in several ways:

1. LD students are discovered before they have a chance to fail. This means that most of them do not become freaks with behavior and social problems.

2. The program is flexible. The structure of a child's therapy can be adjusted to fit his changing needs.

3. All therapy is done by highly skilled professionals.

4. Every member of the faculty, staff, and administration is well informed on the subject of learning disabilities and attention deficit disorder. They all understand LD and ADD students and their special problems.

5. Classroom teachers work closely with LD teachers in helping the disabled children.

The key ingredient in Greenway's LD program is the high level of cooperation and understanding that exists between the regular classroom teachers and the LD specialists. They work together in an atmosphere of mutual trust and respect.

Variation VII is sometimes carried out by having LD and ADD students attend a special school for half the school day. In addition to being given LD therapy and appropriate learning-styles training, students are placed in small classes for instruction in subjects affected by their areas of weakness. The logistics of moving youngsters back and forth from one campus to another can be quite inconvenient, but the results of the therapy can be very impressive.

VARIATION VIII
CHILDREN ARE GIVEN ALL THEIR INSTRUCTION IN A SELF-CONTAINED LD CLASS.

Most youngsters with a learning disability and/or attention deficit disorder can function in a regular classroom for at least part of the school day. If only for art, music, physical education, and lunch, LD and ADD children should be given the chance to be with "normal" students.

But there are some LD and ADD students who truly cannot succeed at any of the things done in regular classes. They can't do the classwork because of their learning difficulties; they can't take part in other activities because they have severe problems with concentration, hyperactivity, and impulsive behavior. They fight, sulk, skip school, cry, destroy things, run away, steal, hide, and keep the whole class in an uproar. When LD and ADD children get to the point that they can't even eat lunch in the school cafeteria without ending up in tears or in a fight, it's time to consider placing them in a self-contained class.

In a self-contained LD class, the students spend all day with one teacher—a specialist in learning disabilities. She is the class's only supervisor and teaches all subjects, often including art, music, and physical education.

Three types of children need self-contained LD classes: those with very severe learning disabilities, those whose learning problems are compounded by a severe attention deficit disorder, and those who are defiant, oppositional, or troubled by serious emotional problems related to their disabilities. (LD/ADD children who quietly fade into the woodwork are not likely to be placed in a special LD class. Yet they need it just as much as the ones who break windows and shout curses at teachers.)

Self-contained LD classes are designed to serve three functions:

1. They provide LD and ADD students with a place where they can learn. Because these youngsters are so easily distracted and have such a short attention span, they can work only in small groups. Because their needs are so special, they are better off in a class with other children who have similar needs. Because they must have so much personal attention and close supervision, they need a teacher who has the time to work with them. In some ways, they must be allowed extra freedom; in other ways, they must have unusually strict control. A small, quiet class and a teacher and classmates who understand their problems give LD and ADD students a chance to learn.

2. They provide LD therapy and self-awareness training. In other programs for teaching LD and ADD students, it is impossible to give a pupil more than about five hours of LD instruction per week. The student in a self-contained class may get as much as fifteen hours of such work in a week. Since the therapist is always there, every learning activity can be a part of LD therapy. Only huge amounts of specialized training will give some severely disabled youngsters a chance to learn successfully.

3. They provide an atmosphere in which the child can learn factual information. LD students fail in regular classes because they can't read the books. If they're lucky enough to have someone read their books to them, they still can't pass the tests because they can't read *them* either. In an LD class, the teacher finds ways of getting the information into the children's heads. She teaches them the same material but by totally different methods. The youngsters are in a small class taught by a teacher who knows how they can learn. The approach is one of showing them, telling them, and letting them do it and learn from a real experience.

> My self-contained class of fifth- and sixth-graders was studying explorers. Because of the students' learning disabilities, they all had a poor concept of time. There was no way to get them to really understand Christopher Columbus's incredible voyage by simply telling them, "He spent more than eleven weeks at sea." To them, eleven weeks meant nothing.
>
> To get the point across, we elected one boy to be Columbus, and we launched three imaginary ships.
>
> Every day right after lunch, we had a report from Columbus. Our captain would rise, then make his announcement in a serious voice: "Today is our thirty-third day at sea. The weather

is stormy; the sea is rough. We've run low on water, and some of the crew want to turn back. No land has been sighted." Our Columbus did a great job of coming up with a logical report every day.

The rest of the class loved to grumble about the voyage and the living conditions on the ship. They put their hearts into being a miserably unhappy crew.

Week after week, our skipper gave us his daily report as he marked off another day on the calendar.

By the end of the fourth week, we were all tired of the whole thing. We were sick of reciting the little rhyme, "In fourteen hundred and ninety-two, Columbus sailed the ocean blue." We were tired of talking about our three ships. We hated to hear the name of the queen who had financed the ghastly adventure. But like the great explorer we were following, we kept on.

For eleven solid weeks, we continued. It nearly drove us crazy!

When land was finally sighted, we were overjoyed. We were so relieved to have it over with that we had a party to celebrate.

At five minutes a day for over eleven weeks, our class spent about five hours studying that famous trip of discovery. Yet no historian will ever understand the voyage of Christopher Columbus better than those boys and I do. We learned about it through a shared experience.

Self-contained LD classes, special schools, and homeschooling are the ultimate weapons for those situations when all other methods of therapy have been tried and have failed. The student who *can* function in a regular classroom should be allowed to do so. On the other hand, teachers and parents should not hesitate to place a youngster in a self-contained LD class if he truly needs it. Likewise, special schools should not be avoided just because the child shows no enthusiasm for the idea. Where the student *wants* to be should have no effect on the final decision of where he is placed.

I've never met a student who entered a special LD class or school on the first day of the semester looking as if he wanted to be there. Parents and principals drag them in, push them in, force them in. But once the children find out what it's like to succeed, once they discover they're not alone, once they taste the feeling of being understood, once they're removed from the teasing and criticism they got from students in the regular classroom, then their parents start calling to say, "This is the first time he's been happy since he started school." Soon, the student tells the teacher, "You're the first nice teacher I've ever had." Friends and neighbors notice the difference in the child's attitude and behavior. A former teacher will stop the youngster in the hall to say, "Oh, Billy, you used to be such a devil. I'm glad to see you doing so well."

A student who truly needs to be in a self-contained LD class or a special school for the learning disabled will be very happy there, in spite of the resistance displayed at the beginning.

In situations where homeschooling is a viable option, it is typical for the child to undergo a tremendous transformation in the first year.

It's not just the specialized therapy that helps LD and ADD students regain their confidence and optimism. Getting them out of the regular classroom—and sometimes out of the regular school altogether—can be the first step in a major healing process. It's too bad inclusion doesn't take this fact into consideration.

With *inclusion* as the buzzword, self-contained LD and BD classes are being eliminated. The number of such programs is diminishing rapidly, and those classes that are still in operation are reserved for children who are absolutely nonfunctional in regular classrooms *and* are so disruptive that they prevent other students from learning. It has become extremely difficult to get a youngster placed in the few self-contained classes that remain. Exceptionally persistent parents can occasionally get a severely disabled offspring assigned to such an environment (particularly if they go through "due process" backed up by lawyers and outside specialists), but the chances of success are very limited. An hour or two a day in the resource room is pretty much the maximum level of service available, no matter how much pressure the parents exert. Many families with children who need more than that are turning to homeschooling.

AND THE BRIGHT LD AND ADD CHILDREN GO UNHELPED: INJUSTICE UNDER THE LAW

The law says that all children must be given a free education appropriate to their needs. Most state guidelines specify that students cannot be considered learning disabled unless they fall two years below grade level. The laws are set up to help those who would never learn at all if they didn't get special attention. They are aimed at getting help for the youngsters who are in critical condition.

And that's great. Most schools would not do much for LD children if they weren't forced to do so; history proves that.

But the laws also mean that a whole group of LD students does not get much help in the public schools. Sadly, it is the youngsters with the most potential whose mental talents are allowed to go to waste. LD children with high IQs seldom get into special LD programs!

Learning-disabled students with an IQ over 120 can have severe difficulties yet still not fall two years behind the rest of their class. Their natural intelligence allows them to do passing schoolwork. On their own, they can find ways to work around their disability. They won't be able to perform as the bright children they are, but they will be able to survive in school.

Look at the figures. A youngster with a full-scale IQ of 125 has a mental capacity that is 25 points higher than that of the average child. He should do about 25 percent better in school. As a fourth-grader, he should read at the fifth-grade level. In the eighth grade, he should work at the tenth-grade level. If he's doing just average work, he's not doing as well as he should. He is two years behind where he *should* be. And he's frustrated. He's just as frustrated as an eighth-grader of average intelligence who is working at the sixth-grade level. In fact, he is probably more frustrated.

He feels that something is wrong. But nobody will listen. He knows he's having difficulty, but the adults in his life will not take his complaints seriously. He is likely to get lectures about not putting forth enough effort, not paying attention, or not being organized or disciplined enough. He will probably be blamed, rather than helped. This very bright child is headed for serious trouble.

> Thirteen-year-old Raymond came from a prominent family and attended the most respected private school in town. Usually quiet and gentle, he had always had a temper. People thought he was a bit odd. But he was not a troublemaker or a "punk."
>
> When he was in the seventh grade, Raymond got into trouble

for theft. After he was caught, it was discovered that he had a habit of sneaking out at night after his parents thought he'd gone to bed. The parking lot at a nearby country club held special appeal to him. He loved to steal the flashy hood ornaments from expensive cars. He had quite a collection stashed in a box in the attic.

Although Raymond's family was horrified when his late-night banditry was discovered, he was not treated as the juvenile delinquent that he appeared to be. Instead, he was taken to a psychologist for testing. His parents hoped that the cause of their son's antisocial behavior could be determined.

The testing revealed two important facts about Raymond: he was extremely bright, and he was learning disabled. He had managed to learn to read and do math well enough to get by in school. But even his high level of mental ability did not enable him to overcome his weaknesses in spelling and writing. He could do all his other schoolwork successfully. But with a pencil in his hand, he fell apart!

Raymond was lucky. His parents were interested in his problem, and they had the money to provide him with testing and therapy at a clinic. His school cooperated by adjusting his work and his schedule. Raymond got the help he needed, and certain disaster was avoided.

If Raymond had been in a public school, he would *not* have gotten therapy. (He probably wouldn't even have been tested.) His parents would have been told, "Look at his grades. He's doing average work in everything but spelling—this child doesn't have a problem." Or they might have heard, "Yes, he is learning disabled, but since he's not two years below grade level, we can't place him in any of our LD programs. His problem is mild—he's getting along fine."

That is where the laws work against bright LD children. Even when a public school does want to help, the guidelines make it impossible. School officials shrug their shoulders as they turn desperate parents away. "Sorry," they say, "but we have to abide by the regulations. Unless a child is two full years below grade level, we can't touch him."

Guidelines—poppycock! What is needed is a whole new approach to reaching out to children who can't live up to their full potential without special assistance. Some states have revised their guidelines a dozen times, but none has yet developed a method that gives bright LD/ADD students a realistic chance of being noticed and helped. Children with a high IQ *and* a learning disability have their best chance of getting therapy *if* they have serious behavior problems and disrupt the classroom constantly, *if* they have parents who are willing to fight vigorously and persistently, or *if* their families can afford private therapy.

Carl was having serious difficulties in junior high school. His story was almost identical to Raymond's, except that Carl was in a public school and his behavior problems had not yet gotten him into serious trouble.

Since Carl was not working two years below grade level, the school refused to test him for a learning disability. So his mother paid to have the evaluation done at a private clinic. The test scores showed that the boy was definitely LD. He had a severe writing disability. He also had a very high IQ.

Even when faced with the test results, the school still refused to provide Carl with any therapy. His mother tried everything she could think of to find help for her son. But the answer was always the same: "No. He's not two years below grade level."

In her desperation, Carl's mother returned to the clinic where the boy had been tested and asked what she should do. The clinic had two suggestions:

1. Fight against the laws cheating Carl out of the education he needs. Write your congressman, the newspapers, the state superintendent of schools. Complain and keep complaining. Scream bloody murder if necessary.

2. Get Carl into a private school with a good LD program. If you can't afford it, remortgage your house. But get this boy the help he needs *now*.

10

HOMESCHOOLING LD/ADD CHILDREN:

Great Idea or Big Mistake?

Homeschooling is rapidly becoming recognized as a reasonable option for disgruntled parents who can't get their local schools to provide the special services their LD/ADD children must have in order to succeed. To these families, home education is the last resort—something to be considered only after all other options have failed.

It's becoming increasingly common for parents to pull a miserable LD or ADD youngster out of school in the middle of the academic year. It's as though something suddenly snaps. The family may have quietly endured years of IEP's, long conferences, tears from the child, notes from the teacher, promises from the administrators, and bad report cards, in spite of all the energy they put into running a nightly study hall. They may have come to think of it as normal to feel trapped and helpless. But one day, in a sudden moment of clarity, they realize that their child's curiosity has disappeared, that he no longer has the impish zest for living that used to be such a charming part of his personality. When that moment of truth arrives, parents have no trouble severing their ties with the schools with just one word: *Enough.*

The decision is terrifying, but it is usually based on one absolute certainty: "Surely, *we* can do better than this!"

Homeschooling is not for everybody. But in the hands of the right kind of family, it can prevent many painful and destructive situations from developing and can bring healing to children who have been all but crushed by the system.

Many parents shy away from the thought of educating an LD and/or ADD child at home because of the horrible hassles they've had trying to help the youngster with homework. Homeschooling LD and ADD children is *not* as hard as helping them with their homework. Homework is always tackled at the end of the day when the child has already had all he can stand of teachers and books and frustrations. It's usually conducted by a parent who is tired from a long, hard day of responsibilities. As often as not, the parent and the child both resent the fact that they have to get enmeshed in assignments that are inappropriate, with directions that are not clearly understood, in books that are too difficult. There's almost always more work than can be accomplished in a reasonable length of time, and half the time, the necessary book gets left at school.

HOW DOES HOMESCHOOLING WORK?

Those who are unfamiliar with homeschooling picture a mother locked in the house all day with a brood of listless youngsters plugging along through an endless series of boring workbooks. Others imagine homeschooling to be an excuse to let children run wild with no discipline, no formal instruction, and no prospects for success in the future. To the unfamiliar, educating children at home is thought of as second best—an option chosen by religious fanatics, antisocial bigots, and those who live so far from civilization that normal educational opportunities are unavailable.

This may have been true in pioneer days, and it may apply to some home educators today, but in general, those who choose to educate their offspring take the job very seriously. They make it their business to get the training and guidance they need to provide a strong background in the basic skills, while also nurturing and developing special interests and talents in their youngsters. Through conferences, book fairs, catalogs, and support groups, homeschooling parents make it a point to determine which materials are best suited to their children. Through workshops, seminars, consultants, college courses, and a variety of homeschool support services, they receive the special training they need to master the instructional methods most appropriate for their children.

> A Utah mother of six assumed full responsibility for teaching her LD children to read. With the first one, it took some experimentation before she found a method that worked. Once she established a routine combining effective techniques with the right materials, she believed she had "the answer."
>
> Much to her surprise, the closetful of expensive materials that had worked so beautifully for her eldest didn't do a thing for the next in line. In order to get her number-two son reading, she had to go through a whole new process of exploring materials and trying out alternative methods. By the time the second child was learning successfully, number three was ready to start.
>
> Fully trained and experienced in two methods for teaching reading, the mom figured that introducing the third child to the printed page would be a breeze. Not so. Neither of the approaches she had so carefully developed brought the desired results for the newest first-grader. It was back to the catalogs.
>
> By the time LD child number four reached first-grade age, this family knew what to expect. As with the siblings who had gone before, a completely customized reading program had to be created just for this one little beginner.
>
> It was labor-intensive and quite expensive, but the results were outstanding. One by one, each of the six LD children in the family entered the regular neighborhood school in the third grade, fully functional at grade level in all subject areas.
>
> Highly trained, fully certified LD specialists rarely have a record that good!

Successful homeschoolers come in all flavors. The United States and Great Britain have a long history of educating children at home. The practice has helped produce outstanding adults in many fields. Among United States presidents, George Washington, James Madison, John Quincy Adams, Woodrow Wilson, William Henry Harrison, Abraham Lincoln, and Franklin D. Roosevelt benefited from homeschooling. Other well-known statesmen with similar schooling were William Penn, Winston Churchill, Patrick Henry, and Benjamin Franklin. Many great military leaders received some homeschooling, among them Robert E. Lee, George Patton, and Douglas MacArthur. Many successful composers, writers, and artists were given homeschooling: Johann Sebastian Bach, Wolfgang Amadeus Mozart, Irving Berlin, Hans Christian Andersen, Pearl Buck, Noel Coward, Charles Dickens, Agatha Christie, Helen Keller, George Bernard Shaw, Laura Ingalls Wilder, Claude Monet, and Andrew Wyeth. Great innovators and inventors have benefited from homeschooling: Alexander Graham Bell, George Washington Carver, Pierre Curie, Leonardo da Vinci, Thomas Edison, Cyrus McCormick, Andrew Carnegie, Orville and Wilbur Wright, Albert Einstein, and Charlie Chaplin. Two particularly well-known women who received homeschooling were Florence Nightingale and Eleanor Roosevelt. The explorers Lewis and Clark were both homeschooled.

The one thing all homeschooling parents have in common is a total commitment to providing their children with an education of the highest quality. They truly believe they can arrange for or provide such an education themselves, at home and in conjunction with resources available in their community. In most cases, their belief in their ability is well founded.

A multitalented high-school student was extremely active in a number of theater groups in his city. He had major roles in at least five or six productions every year. He took dance lessons, guitar lessons, voice lessons, gymnastics, art lessons, and acting classes. He was also interested in video and made dozens of productions in his basement studio.

Ideally, this fifteen-year-old should have been at some expensive school for the performing arts. But Cal had a severe learning disability, along with a troublesome attention deficit disorder. It would have taken a highly specialized (and extremely expensive) LD school to create classes where he could be successful. Through homeschooling, the boy's parents provided him the advantages of a school of the arts *combined with* a specially modified academic curriculum to accommodate his learning difficulties. No amount of money could have purchased an education more appropriate for this particular student. By educating their gifted son at home, Cal's family created the ideal program to fit his unique strengths and weaknesses. Few children are so fortunate.

CONTACT WITH SCHOOLS

Many homeschoolers maintain a connection with the schools their children might otherwise attend. Whether parochial, public, Christian, or independent, if approached creatively, most educational institutions will develop a cooperative, helpful relationship with homeschooling families and make parts of their programs and facilities available to part-time students who do the bulk of their work at home or on some other campus.

A particularly persistent New England father enrolled his seventeen-year-old son in the state university system as a special student. Twice a week, the youth commuted to classes. The boy also took an advanced electronics course at the local community college. And he had art and an advanced-placement history course at the local high school, where he was captain of the football team. As for homeschooling, his mom was his instructor and partner for world literature and foreign language. The two of them were finishing up the fourth year of their mail-order Spanish course. For their literary studies, they were reading the works of contemporary Central and South American authors in the original. In addition to the book learning, they spent half an hour a day stretching their vocabulary by working in the garden or cleaning up the kitchen with no English allowed. Once a month, they spent the day with a group of Hispanics. Every summer, they went to Central America on a two-week mission for their church. These two became very skilled at using their foreign language. No nearby school offered training any better than what they were getting at home. This young man had it all!

USING PROFESSIONALS

Other homeschoolers use professionals to do some of the teaching. No matter how remote the area, there is almost always somebody available to provide instruction in the subjects in which the mother feels inadequate. LD specialists in private practice can do therapy with homeschooled youngsters or coach and instruct the teaching mom. High-level math courses, advanced lab sciences, art, music, and foreign language are commonly taught by paid professionals. Sometimes, a group of homeschoolers bands together and hires a certified instructor to teach a whole class of students.

Guidelines that set limits on homeschoolers vary from state to state. Homeschooling is generally done any way the family sees appropriate. It's just a matter of dreaming up what is ideal for a particular child, then making it happen.

> The father of a youngster who showed talent in creative writing let his son do the regular college preparatory program at the local high school—except for English. That instruction was provided by the parents, who were both English teachers.
>
> It was an extremely successful venture. The young scholar matured into an internationally recognized poet when still in his twenties!
>
> Through homeschooling, this family found a way to give its son a language-arts program of outstanding quality. Judging from the outcome, the energy invested paid off well.

FLEXIBILITY

One of the beauties of teaching children at home is the flexibility that allows families to design their own schedule. There are no fixed rules. Many ADD youngsters are "night people" who just start coming to life when other children their age are turning in for the night. Even when they don't stay up as late as they like, it's extremely difficult to get them out of bed at the crack of dawn in order to dive into the books. Their brains just don't perk up until the middle of the day. For them, a school day that starts around ten in the morning (or after lunch) makes more sense. With older children who have a job or talented youngsters who need the daylight hours to practice music or sports, academics can easily be postponed until late in the day. And for those who really want to be free from the restrictions imposed by schedules, there's nothing to say that homeschooling has to be done at home. One California mother takes her three students to the beach twice a week. She says their best discussions take place during the commute.

Since homeschooling is done in a quiet environment where there are few distractions, youngsters with an attention deficit disorder find it easier to concentrate. Children with a learning disability have all their assignments tailored to fit their abilities and needs. Under the watchful eye of a truly dedicated teacher, students with a low tolerance for frustration can avoid the aggravations that lead to tears and outbursts of temper. Thus, by making it possible for children to work at full capacity and at top speed, most homeschooled LD/ADD students get all their work done in three to four hours a day.

Freed from the restrictions imposed on those who work with large groups, homeschooling parents can turn almost any corner into a good study space. Gathering around the kitchen or dining-room table is popular. Some families give up the den or the living room in order to make it into a classroom. Kitchen counters are great places for working on projects, and front-porch swings are ideal spots for reading. Parents who work with ADD students often do a lot of teaching outside. They'll chant arithmetic facts with a youngster who is rhythmically bouncing on a trampoline, or call out spelling words while the child shoots baskets. When a quiet environment is necessary, public libraries are available.

Some homeschoolers believe in teaching through real-life experiences. In using the instructional methods they refer to as "unschooling," they rid themselves of the stifling effects of structure, eliminating anything that even vaguely resembles schools, schoolrooms, and schoolbooks. To those who see all activities as part of learning, the whole world becomes a classroom.

WHO WILL DO THE TEACHING?

What kind of qualifications must parents have in order to successfully teach their children at home? In some states, a high-school diploma and a willingness to give it a try are considered sufficient.

Other states require close supervision from the public-school system or special training for the teaching parent. A few states only allow those with a college degree and a teacher's certificate to educate their offspring at home. A call to the state board of education or department of public instruction can clarify the legal restrictions involved. But that information only tells parents what the local laws allow. Other issues also need to be considered.

The one ingredient absolutely essential is total commitment. Without enthusiasm and cooperation from every family member, educating children at home is not likely to be successful. In most homeschooling families, the mother does the bulk of the day-to-day instruction, but fathers are often actively involved in the teaching of a subject or two. The men often volunteer for math or science and do their part in the evening after they get home from work.

Most families that are providing school at home are quick to point out that homeschooling is a lifestyle—an undertaking that involves every member of the family every day of the year. By making such a commitment to the process of educating children, every family activity takes on meaning as part of the teaching. Vacations become field trips where new skills can be applied and developed. Hobbies and leisure activities become elements of the academic program. There is no such thing as a day off. Everything that happens to a child is seen as educational.

The traits that make a parent suited to the task of homeschooling have more to do with temperament than background or education. Planning and carrying out a good educational program for a child requires patience, courage, creativity, determination, persistence, energy, enthusiasm, optimism, and more patience.

PARENTAL PITFALLS

Some people are not cut out to be teachers. They have the wrong temperament for the day-to-day supervision of those who are struggling to master a new skill. They want to be helpful, flexible, encouraging, inspiring, and kind, but some part of their makeup prevents them from doing so.

Perfectionist parents make terrible teachers. They fail to allow beginners to make the mistakes necessary for the gradual development of skills and understanding. Students don't learn everything all at once; it takes practice and experience. When there is no tolerance for errors, learning becomes a slow and painful process. Those who can't bear to let up on the pupil until an exercise is letter-perfect are best advised to leave the teaching to someone else.

> A homeschooling mom and her twelve-year-old LD/ADD daughter were at each other's throats constantly. The girl had been in and out of several schools. Her lack of social skills made her classroom experiences a horror story of humiliation and rejection. She was also hyperactive, extremely distractible, poorly coordinated, and disorganized. This young girl and her mom had been homeschooling for over a year, and both of them hated it!
>
> The mother was a registered nurse and a perfectionist. By training and temperament, nothing ever suited her until it was accurate, neat, and complete. Directions had to be followed to the letter. No work was ever finished until it was perfect.
>
> A parent with unreasonably high standards is not a good match for a student with a serious attention deficit disorder.

Disorganized parents are also likely to have serious difficulties being in charge of an educational program. Even the unstructured approach of "unschooling" requires a certain element of control over the learning process. Unplanned, random events do not work together to expose a youngster to all the basic skills necessary to thrive in the real world. Successful teaching requires goals and a process of deliberate preparation. Someone has to decide on the activities used to expose learners to information and ideas, supervise day-to-day practice of skill development, and take responsibility for time-management techniques that establish realistic schedules and deadlines. Parents who want to homeschool youngsters with learning disabilities and attention deficit disorder must be willing and able to maintain an orderly environment where such children can be productive in spite of their tendency to be disorganized.

On the other hand, some parents are *too* organized to manage a homeschool program. "Neat nuts" who try to impose their orderly preferences on LD and ADD students usually end up creating a contest of wills that is very destructive.

> Harry was an unusually disorganized teenager. From long-overdue library books to moldy sandwiches, he carried just about everything he owned in the huge backpack he used as a book bag.
>
> Most parents would not have been particularly bothered by his slovenly habits. But Harry's dad did not hold with standard views on cleanliness. The man was a "neat nut." It was always easy to tell when the father had packed this eighth-grader's lunch: the brown bag was creased as precisely as the pants in a general's dress uniform, then the top of the sack was folded twice, pressed to a crisp, sharp edge, and fastened in the exact middle with a staple.
>
> In his attempts to force his untidy offspring to adopt his own orderly ways, the father's persistence evoked angry responses in the boy. There must have been some awful scenes; the father referred to his son's attitude toward neatness as "combative."

Parents with a short fuse often have serious trouble homeschooling. They find it extremely difficult to listen compassionately as a frustrated child complains about school being stupid and boring. Quick-tempered adults usually have limited tolerance for careless errors. And LD/ADD youngsters make lots of them. It takes self-control and a great deal of patience to successfully teach any student who has difficulty sitting still, paying attention, and learning.

One other potential pitfall involves learning styles. Teachers tend to gravitate toward the methods and materials they found interesting and helpful when they were students. It's natural for visual learners to assume that everybody needs lots of illustrations, charts, and diagrams. Likewise, auditory learners tend to rely on long explanations without realizing that many LD/ADD students find lectures exceedingly boring and confusing. Homeschooling parents need to make it their business to find out about learning styles—their own as well as those of all the children they'll be teaching. Homeschooling is not much of an improvement over the regular classroom if there is no attempt to customize the curriculum to fit each student's individual talents, interests, limitations, and needs.

WHAT IF BOTH PARENTS WORK?

Working parents who are truly committed to homeschooling usually find ways to work around their scheduling limitations. Students who are doing a mail-order program, a videotaped curriculum, or workbook-style courses require little supervision; they only need to confer with their teacher for brief periods a couple of times a week. As long as they can be trusted to get their work done and stay out of trouble, being home alone allows them the freedom to be fully in charge of their academic activities.

Sixteen-year-old Mike had lost interest in academics in the seventh grade. For four years after that, he slept through classes, refused to do homework, and hung out with troublemakers. He smoked cigarettes, came home drunk on a number of occasions, and did more than a little experimenting with drugs. He was on the verge of dropping out of school.

Out of desperation, Mike's mother and father gave in to their son's pleas and arranged for homeschooling. Since both parents had full-time jobs, the boy would have the house to himself all day long. From his past performance, he certainly did not look like an ideal candidate to be trusted with so much freedom. But his parents had tried everything else and were willing to give such a radical measure a try.

Much to everybody's amazement, Mike settled into his new homeschooling routine like a hand slips into a glove. Every day, he happily completed all of his assignments. His work was of good quality, he did well on tests and reports, and his attitude was excellent. Without the constant contact at school, his old party-loving crowd lost interest in him. He got more active in the youth group at his church and made new friends. By the middle of the fall, he was looking into colleges.

In early February, Mike's mother lost her job. While she was unemployed, she spent a lot of time around the house. Mike found her presence a terrible disruption to his concentration. Just as he'd sit down to the computer to write a book report, the whine of the vacuum cleaner would claw at his mind for attention. Every time he took a break, he'd get parental reminders about the need to do schoolwork. He even viewed sweet, motherly invitations to share a gourmet lunch on the patio as in invasion of privacy.

Mike was tremendously relieved when his mom got a new

job. He was pleased to get her "out of his face" so he could get back to work!

Although the unsupervised approach is best suited to older students, there are a number of families who find that their nine- to fourteen-year-olds have the maturity to act responsibly while left unattended to do their schoolwork. One such family is homeschooling two boys, ages thirteen and nine. The youngsters get up and get their day started before their parents leave for work. They do their assignments independently of each other. The younger son relies on his brother for assistance when needed. The older boy uses E-mail when he needs help. When there are decisions to be made, the teenager is in charge. During breaks, the two shoot baskets or play computer games or tinker with their bikes or work on projects or do their chores. When the mother gets home, the boys get free time until dinner. In the evening, each son gets one hour of private homeschooling instruction. Both parents participate in the process of checking work, teaching new concepts, and making assignments. Not every pair of brothers could handle so much responsibility, but for this family, it works beautifully.

LD and ADD youngsters are notorious for daydreaming or piddling around when left to study alone. Yet when they are given assignments they can successfully complete without assistance, and when they are placed in an environment where they are free from interruptions and distractions, some of them blossom into contented independent learners.

WHAT ABOUT SOCIALIZATION?

There are young people who crave solitude. Our culture tends to fear any kind of isolation that might turn a child into a "loner." Yet for some children—particularly those with poor social skills—it is a kindness to remove them from the constant burden of having to interact with their peers.

Children who have trouble paying attention cannot tune out the activity going on around them. They notice everything. Only a handful of teachers present their lessons with such dynamic energy that *all* the students in the class keep their minds riveted on their schoolwork. Thus, in most classrooms, children with an attention deficit disorder spend most of their time with their eyes on their classmates, rather than their teacher. If there's any horsing around going on, they are likely to be in the middle of it. Sometimes, they are the ringleaders; often, they are mindless followers. All too frequently, they are the victims.

When families switch to homeschooling, this entire social problem is eliminated. The distractions caused by the presence of other children no longer pull attention away from schoolwork. By placing LD and ADD youngsters in an environment where they cannot be influenced by the actions of other children, their tendency toward impulsive behavior can no longer get them classified as lazy students, stupid kids, troublemakers, outcasts, or nerds.

For children with a learning disability or an attention deficit disorder, that's one of the biggest advantages of homeschooling. By not forcing them to blend into the general mix, parents get control over who will have the opportunity to influence their children. During their formative years, children learn by emulating the behavior of those around them; the little kids copy the big kids. Those who wish to be sure that their youngsters are not exposed to role models who will lead them toward violence, drugs, foul language, sexual promiscuity, and other undesirable behaviors see homeschooling as an affordable option. Homeschooling allows parents to be selective about the company their children keep.

CUSTOM-DESIGNED PROGRAMS

Those who successfully homeschool LD and/or ADD youngsters tend to design programs that are child-centered. If the student has special interests and talents, they get top priority. Also, there is a strong commitment to teaching the basic skills; most homeschooling families are absolutely adamant in their belief that all children *must* master reading, writing, spelling, and math. The time schedule might not coincide with the sequence set out by regular schools, but teaching parents rarely give up until the goal is achieved.

It's not unusual for home educators to postpone formal reading instruction until a child is eight or nine. On the other hand, many teaching mothers introduce phonics to four-year-olds. It's a matter of readiness and a personalized curriculum that fits the student's capabilities and the parent's teaching style. Faced with an area where a youngster's development is slow, many homeschoolers have the courage to wait for a window of opportunity where interest and desire motivate the child to leap into the subject with enthusiasm and optimism. It's the teacher's job to be alert to the subtle signals that indicate when a new stage of development has prepared a youngster for success in previously unexplored territory.

> Alice, a pert little ten-year-old, had not mastered even the most basic elements of mathematical computation. She'd gotten stuck somewhere in the first grade and never progressed. Every year, her mother introduced her to a new book and a new set of teaching techniques. Every year, the child resisted instruction and gained no new skills. As a youngster, her mother had been slow in catching onto arithmetic. She had complete faith that her daughter was merely following the same pattern and would catch up.
>
> In the summer vacation between fourth and fifth grade, Alice ran across an old first-grade math workbook. One rainy afternoon, she curled up in the porch swing and worked her way through all the problems. She had so much fun that she asked her mother if they had another book of "number games." By bedtime, the child finished the material in the second-grade book. To finish the third-level workbook, she needed a little instruction. With her mother providing guidance when needed, Alice played with her math books for the rest of the summer. By the time the family resumed homeschooling in the fall, Alice was doing fifth-grade arithmetic, just like she should have been. Somehow, over the summer, reasoning with numbers came to make sense to her.

Many homeschoolers have had similar experiences. Some children just can't seem to learn to read when the basic literacy skills are introduced in first and second grade, then suddenly catch on somewhere in their early to mid-teens. Although they get a late start, it all comes together for them, and they're on grade level within a few years.

That seems to have been what happened to Winston Churchill. He was a nonreader until the age of thirteen or fourteen. He was well versed in the classics and world history, because he was homeschooled and his family read *to* him. In his mid-teens, he was sent to a military academy, where he learned to read and write and spell well enough to become a war correspondent when he was only nineteen. In his mature years, Churchill wrote several highly respected volumes on the history of World War II.

Albert Einstein followed a similar pattern. As an adult, he often referred to his "retarded development." Although he did not learn to read until he was a teenager, he was a successful student in a major university in his early twenties and was a prolific letter writer throughout most of his life.

Many students have trouble when forced through a fixed curriculum at a predetermined pace. For those whose intellectual growth does not progress in accordance with standard developmental patterns, homeschooling has the flexibility to let the student's readiness be the determining factor in deciding which skills and topics are introduced. When a student is really ready, learning is a natural, spontaneous, pleasant process.

CAN PARENTS REALLY TEACH LD AND ADD CHILDREN?

Families who make the choice to homeschool their LD and/or ADD children get the information they need about materials and instructional methods through support groups, conferences, and a network of specialists who help home educators develop the skills they need to successfully teach their children at home. LD children will still have trouble learning to read and write and spell when schooling is done at home. In most cases, the teaching parent keeps changing the curriculum until one is found that works. Homeschooled youngsters with an attention deficit disorder still have difficulty sitting still and paying attention. Through patience, determination, a thorough understanding of the child, and a commitment to providing everything necessary for successful learning, most homeschoolers figure out ways to keep ADD students organized, on task, and energetically involved in academic activities.

In the hands of the right parents, LD/ADD students thrive in the quiet, noncompetitive environment outside the regular classroom. When asked if such a radical commitment was worth it, these parents usually beam with delight as they say, "We've got our child back."

11

THE LD/ADD CHILD'S ROLE IN THE FAMILY:

Square Peg in a Round Hole?

First and foremost, children with an attention deficit disorder and/ or a learning disability are children. They have exactly the same hopes and needs as any other human being their age. They want to be warm and fed and cared for. They want to feel that they are important. They want to feel happy and safe. In order to live peacefully with others, they need to learn discipline and responsibility.

Parents would like to be able to give their offspring all the things they need and desire. But no one can give children happiness; no one can give them a feeling of security; no one can give them a sense of self-worth. Parents can make it possible for youngsters to achieve those ends, but they can never present them to their children as gifts.

It is like the process of baking a cake. You can mix flour and eggs and sugar and milk and so forth. But no amount of effort will turn the mixture into a cake without the process inside the oven that works magic on the soupy batter.

Raising children works in much the same way. The family can

provide the right ingredients. But youngsters must use those ingredients to develop feelings of happiness, security, and self-worth.

THE INGREDIENTS EVERY CHILD NEEDS

1. All children need love. From the words, actions, and attitudes of others, youngsters need to feel that they are loved. This goes far beyond the simple expression of affection (although that is very important). A genuine interest in children and their activities shows love. A willingness to give them time and attention shows love. The patience to try to understand, the strength to enforce discipline, the determination to teach responsibility—all the things that are done to help children develop into the best adults they are capable of becoming—all these can be expressions of love.

2. All children need to feel accepted. Youngsters need to feel that those near them think they're okay, even with all their imperfections. They need to be able to sense that others are glad they're around.

3. All children need success and genuine praise. To become a "can do" person, children need to be successful in at least some of the things they attempt. Seeing their accomplishments makes them feel good about themselves. It helps them develop pride. It encourages them to try other new things despite the risk of failure. And the joy of receiving praise at the end of a job well done can make the whole struggle worth the effort.

4. All children need to be protected. As much as possible, youngsters should be made to feel safe. They should be able to trust that others will take care of them when they are not able to take care of themselves. From *real* threats to body, mind, and life, they should be protected. But they do *not* need to be protected from situations and experiences that they must eventually face on their own.

By the age of ten, Zeke had been playing Little League baseball for two years. Suddenly, his mother had doubts. Other parents didn't let their sons participate because they felt that the children were put under too much pressure.

Seeking an expert opinion, Zeke's mother called the pediatrician. She was given excellent advice. This is the essence of what the doctor said: "Zeke is going to be living in the real world. And in the real world, there is pressure to perform. You can't protect a child from life until he's eighteen, then suddenly turn him loose and expect him to be able to deal with reality. Pressure is one of the things that Zeke must learn to deal with. Don't overprotect him. Just see that he isn't put under more pressure than he's ready to handle."

Zeke continued to play baseball every spring all the way through the twelfth grade. He loved it. The pressure was there, but it didn't seem to bother him. He had some great moments of success and some horrible times of failure. He always made the team, but he never got to be the star player.

Some of Zeke's finest qualities were developed through his participation in sports.

5. All children need freedom to learn and grow. Youngsters learn from experience. It's in the process of solving real-life problems that mental development takes place. Parents should encourage their children's natural tendency to be curious and venturesome. They should allow them to discover and pursue their interests and talents. And equally important, they should allow them to take *reasonable* risks and make mistakes. The process of trying and failing is part of learning. But in doing these things, parents must be careful not to use criticisms such as, "See, I told you that wouldn't work," or "What'd you try a dumb thing like that for?" when children fail. Failures must be expected sometimes and dealt with in an understanding way.

A friend of mine let her teenage daughter, Marion, drive the family car to school. The girl was supposed to be home in time for dinner at six-thirty. At seven o'clock, she still had not arrived.

When Marion finally walked in at seven-thirty, she was as pale as a ghost. "I *lost* the car," she gasped. "I parked in the faculty parking lot. They towed the car away, and I can't find out where they took it."

Marion was really upset. She felt terrible for having gotten into such a mess. There was no need for anyone to tell her she had done something dumb. She already knew.

My friend did not get angry at her daughter. Instead, she did what she could to help solve the problem. She made some phone calls and finally located the car. Marion paid the hefty towing fee to get the car back. Punishment was unnecessary; the expensive tow-truck cost took care of that.

6. All children need healthy outlets for their energy and creativity. Youngsters need to explore and develop outside interests. Children need free time to amuse themselves and play with friends. They must be encouraged to devote time to hobbies and other activities they enjoy. Swimming, rock collecting, Scouting, music lessons, raising hamsters, team sports—fun and success in such activities put sparkle in the eyes and a bounce in the step. If youngsters are to become enthusiastic participants in life, their days must include more than school, chores, video games, and TV.

7. All children need discipline. Youngsters need to live in a world in which there are definite limits on their actions. The real world is that way. If you lean too far back in a chair, you *will* fall. That is the law of gravity. "If you play with matches, you *will* be punished." That is one of the rules for young children. If the rule is absolutely enforced, youngsters will quickly learn to live within its limitations. The objects of discipline are to keep children safe and to teach them to be considerate of others. The ultimate hope is that they will develop habits of reasonable behavior and maintain them through self-discipline.

Firm discipline seems to make youngsters feel loved and secure. Children who can get away with almost anything usually feel that their families don't really care about them.

8. All children need responsibility. Youngsters need to be taught that they are accountable for their actions, and that they must think *before* they act. At any age, children are capable of accepting responsibility for what they say and do.

A teenager caused an automobile accident and was charged with drunk driving. The driver of the other car was killed.

The boy's lawyer, in pleading his client's case, told the judge, "He's young. He used poor judgment. This is the first time he's gotten into trouble for driving under the influence."

The judge's unsympathetic response was, "It was the victim's first time, too."

Children need to develop another aspect of responsibility as well. If they are not given specific duties for which they alone are responsible, they will not feel like full-fledged members of the family. Even a four-year-old is able to clean the ring off the tub after taking his bath. Most five-year-olds can be trusted to take out the garbage. Children are not servants, but they must not be treated as guests either. When youngsters are given duties that they are capable of handling on their own, they will develop a sense of responsibility and a feeling that they belong.

In meeting the needs of their children, parents supply them with the ingredients that make it possible for them to feel happy, secure, and valuable. Families do not give happiness itself. All they can do is provide what youngsters need so that they can develop happiness within themselves.

MEETING THE NEEDS OF LD AND ADD CHILDREN

The parents of an LD and/or ADD child usually center their thoughts on how the youngster is different from other children. But in doing so, they are starting from the wrong position. They must change their thinking.

A youngster with a learning disability or an attention deficit disorder must be thought of first as a child—a young person with the same basic needs all children have. The learning disability may become a complication. The attention deficit may be a challenge. But the youngster's basic needs remain the same.

When things go wrong, parents must not look first to the child's learning disability or attention problem. In dealing with a difficult situation, the first thing to think about is the youngster's needs as a *child*.

Bob, who is LD and ADD, starts a fight with one of the children in the neighborhood. If his parents assume that his angry outburst was caused by impulsive behavior related to his attention deficit disorder, they will believe it's part of a problem that cannot be changed. Therefore, they will either make no attempt to change his behavior or punish him for his bad behavior while ignoring the real cause of the problem. Neither approach will be effective.

The parents need to shift their attention from the child's learning and attention difficulties and focus on Bob's needs as a child. Once they recognize the real nature of the problem, they can deal with it creatively. In this case, the youngster doesn't feel accepted; he has rarely been successful at anything; and he was not protected from the pain of being teased. A logical solution would be for the family to see to it that his needs are met. Bob should be led to activities at which he can be successful, guided toward playmates who are not quick to tease, and helped to feel accepted. Then he won't have such a chip on his shoulder.

Before taking any action to solve a problem that an LD and/or ADD youngster is having, parents should ask themselves what is causing the problem. It could be the learning disability and/or attention deficit, but more than likely, the real cause has to do with an unsatisfied need. Very few of the troubles LD/ADD children have are caused directly by their disability. Their difficulties are almost always a result of the way that the child and others respond to the disability.

SQUARE PEGS IN ROUND HOLES

No child fits anywhere until *taught* to fit. And children with learning disabilities and/or attention deficit disorder are no exception.

However, LD/ADD children do have special problems that sometimes make it difficult for them to adjust to the people and situations they encounter. In many ways, they are not very different from other youngsters. But for parents, raising an LD and/or ADD child *is* different.

The traditional approaches used in rearing children simply do not apply to LD and ADD youngsters. Granny's stern philosophy, modern notions of unlimited freedom and self-expression, systems that the neighbors use with their children—these don't give parents

ideas that work very well with children who have a learning disability or an attention deficit disorder.

> Tuesday was Linda's day to take out the garbage. She forgot
> to do it. In our society, tradition says her parents could (1)
> punish her, (2) bribe her to do better, (3) sit down and have a
> talk with her, then select one of the first two choices, or (4)
> forget it.
>
> Tuesday was Sally's day to take out the garbage. Sally has an
> attention deficit disorder, and she forgets to do her chores. None
> of the ready-made responses that parents usually rely on in such
> situations is appropriate this time. The parents are on their own.

As problems arise, parents of "normal" children can look to accepted patterns, respected traditions, and their own personal experiences for guidance. From what they've heard and seen, they can
choose a solution that should work to settle the matter at hand.

But even when faced with standard problems, the parents of LD
and/or ADD children have nothing to fall back on for help. What
do you do when an LD child comes home with a report card full of
F's? How do you deal with an ADD youngster whose teacher complains that he daydreams and wastes time? Punishing isn't going to
help. Bribes aren't going to do much good. Reasoning with the
child might help a little, but it won't solve the problem. And ignoring the matter will definitely not make things better. For the parents
of LD and/or ADD youngsters, there is no list of tried-and-true
solutions. When traditional methods don't apply, solutions must be
created.

CREATING SOLUTIONS

In developing the ability to create solutions, the parents of LD
and/or ADD children must remember that there is never just one
way to solve a problem. It is never a matter of finding the *right* answer. It is a question of figuring out the *best* answer. From several
possibilities, one should be chosen that seems the most promising.

The process of creating solutions should always begin with these
two questions: What are the needs of the youngster as a child? How

can those needs be met when the learning disability and/or attention deficit is taken into consideration?

For example, take another look at Sally, the ADD girl who could not remember to take out the garbage. Which of her needs as a child are involved?

1. She needs responsibility.

2. She needs the freedom to learn and grow.

3. She needs to feel accepted.

4. She needs success and genuine praise.

What aspects of her attention deficit are involved?

1. She cannot deal with time; she never knows what day it is.

2. She is forgetful.

The task is to create a solution so that the garbage is taken out and Sally can have the feelings of success and recognition that come with doing a job well, and on her own. Her parents might come up with several plans, some better than others.

According to plan A, Sally's father could take the garbage out on his way to work and save everybody the hassle. But then Sally wouldn't experience responsibility, success, praise, or acceptance as a regular member of the family.

According to plan B, Sally's mother could put a flag in her oatmeal every Tuesday morning. That would remind her. But then the garbage wouldn't be just *Sally's* responsibility.

According to plan C, Sally could be given the added responsibility of bringing in the newspaper every morning. She could read the day and date off the front page as a general announcement of interest to the whole family. That way, she would notice what day it was every day. She would get the garbage out because she'd know when it was Tuesday. Also, she would develop the habit of checking the day and date every morning as a help in working around her difficulty with time. In this way, many of her needs would be met.

(What if Sally announced the day every morning, but the mention of Tuesday sometimes didn't ring a bell? One of her parents could say, "Tuesday, huh?" as a gentle reminder. But if Sally needed to be reminded every Tuesday, a different plan would be needed.)

According to plan D, Sally could be given her own calendar. At the beginning of every month, "Sally—Take out garbage" would be written in the spaces for all the Tuesdays. Each morning, she would announce the day and date to the whole family. As she checked the calendar, she could either remind everybody of scheduled appointments or just watch for her own. In addition to having all the advantages of plan C, plan D would help Sally remember her mother's birthday, cheerleading practice, and her tuba lessons.

The possible solutions for Sally are endless, right up to plan Z, in which she makes a deal with her brother: she takes over his paper route, since she tends not to forget things that have to be done every day; she pays him ten dollars a week to take out the garbage and keep track of her appointments for her; and she uses the rest of her earnings to make a down payment on a CD player.

Situation by situation, the possible solutions to the problems of LD/ADD children are endless. By thinking first of the child's needs as a child, by considering special needs caused by his disability, and by being open to nontypical possibilities, parents can find an unlimited number of ways to deal effectively with problems as they come up. There is never just one solution. But the *best* solution can be found through creative thinking and the proper attitude.

12

GETTING ACTION:

Harnessing the Power of the Hysterical Mother and Big Daddy

"Back when my son was in the first grade, I knew something was wrong." Mothers of learning-disabled children make that statement with frightening regularity. Often, the child was taken to the family doctor, diagnosed with ADD, and put on medication—but still the mother knew something was very, very wrong. It's not at all unusual for such youngsters to go through four, five, six, or more years of suffering and failing in school. Yet nothing is done. In the first conference after an eleven- or twelve-year-old student has finally been identified as learning disabled, the mother's attitude is usually expressed with a sigh of relief and a tired, "Thank God, help at last."

How can this happen? Or, more realistically, how can it happen so often? What keeps parents from doing something? What are they waiting for? Why don't they speak up? And if they are ignored, why don't they shout? A child with learning problems needs strong support from someone who is willing to take on the whole system, if necessary. Usually, that support comes from a hysterical mother.

The hysterical mother can almost be considered a symptom of a learning disability. And it is definitely a symptom of an undiagnosed attention deficit disorder. Hysteria in the mother of an LD and/or ADD youngster is logical. And it can be productive. True, a frantic mother often makes life unbearable for herself, her offspring, and her entire family. But the power of the hysterical mother, if used creatively and to its fullest extent, can be effective in getting help for an LD or ADD child.

MOTHERS DO KNOW WHEN SOMETHING'S WRONG

Anyone who has spent six years raising a child can trust her own judgment as to whether or not that youngster is behaving as he always has. If the child has always had a cheerful disposition, entering school should not change him into a whining complainer. Once a father told me that, as a preschooler, his son had lots of playmates and was the wrestling champ of his neighborhood. But after a few months in the first grade, the boy withdrew into a shy, lonely world where he had no further contact with children his age. The parents did not trust their suspicion that something was wrong. They should have. Their son spent fifteen miserable years trying to get through twelve years of school before he finally gave up without a high-school diploma. And this young man had an IQ over 120!

Educators—teachers, counselors, psychologists, principals, school superintendents—often try to convince parents that there is no way to predict how successful a youngster will be in school. They say, "The fact that your child's achievement level does not meet your expectations doesn't mean something is wrong. The youngster does not have a problem. *You* are the problem." In some cases, this is true. But more often than not, a mother does have a pretty realistic idea of what her offspring can be expected to do. From toilet training to bicycle riding, she has watched the pattern of learning. She knows how he approaches a new task, how much curiosity and determination he has, how he handles failure, what he thinks of himself. From firsthand experience, she knows whether the youngster is bright or lazy or slow or moody. So when a mother feels that her child is not as successful in school as he should be, she *is* qualified to make the judgment that something is wrong.

> At the age of three, Charles could name the make and model of every car on the road. But when he was in the third grade, he still could not identify the letters of the alphabet. Obviously, he was not learning to read as well as he should have. His mother knew it. But she didn't do anything helpful with her knowledge.
>
> On a fluke, Charles was identified as learning disabled by a visiting consultant. At that time, he was failing the fourth grade for the second time.

Parents *do* know when something is wrong with their child. No one should be able to convince them otherwise without overwhelming proof.

MOTHERS USUALLY FAIL IN THE FIRST GRADE

A mother who knows that her child is not learning as he should—and who is on the verge of hysteria for that reason—usually fails to make creative and effective use of her hysteria. When she goes to confer with her child's first-grade teacher, the teacher offers one or more of these reasons for the youngster's failure to learn: he's lazy; he's wiggly; he never pays attention; he causes trouble; he doesn't try. Then she tells the mother, "He's just immature; there's nothing to do but wait. Don't worry, he'll grow out of it. Lots of children have these problems. Leave him alone. He'll be fine."

Since the teacher is the expert, since the teacher has so much experience with children of that age, since the teacher is so sure of herself, the mother makes her first big mistake: she holds back her hysteria. She is calm. She is polite. She forces herself to trust the teacher's judgment rather than her own. She *wants* to believe that her suspicions are wrong, so she goes home to wait and hope.

Sometimes, the child is seriously disruptive in the classroom and the teacher has had some experience with attention deficit disorder. In such cases, the teacher might suggest that the family check with a doctor about trying the youngster on medication. Most teachers and many physicians operate on the theory that if stimulant medication will help the child settle down in school, then there will be no further problems. The fact that the drugs don't help the student learn to read and write and spell is rarely taken into consideration. Once a youngster is given drugs to promote concentration and control impulsive behavior, any further difficulty with academic achievement is blamed on the child.

THE HYSTERICAL MOTHER IN ACTION

The mother of one of my former students is a good example of a parent who fought for her offspring from the start. Her son had been in the first grade for only a few months when she became convinced that something was wrong. The boy's teacher insisted there was nothing to worry about. Not satisfied with the teacher's assurances, the mother requested testing. That brought the school's principal into the picture. He refused to request an evaluation by the school psychologist and tried to discourage the mother from pushing the matter further. Nevertheless, she made arrangements to have her son tested at a private clinic. Unfortunately, the clinic came up with a classic example of a wishy-washy diagnosis. Without even using the terms *learning disability* or *dyslexia*, the specialist recommended a wait-and-see attitude. So the boy finished the first grade as a nonreader, the family was frantic, and the mother was labeled a troublemaker.

But this woman was tough. The public schools and a private clinic had not resolved the problem. Next, she turned to an independent school. At the admissions interview, she told the director about her child's learning problem. She was told that the school would make its own decision on the matter. After the admissions testing was completed, the mother asked that her son be allowed to repeat the first grade. The school placed him in the second grade.

In mid-September, both parents went to confer with the boy's teacher and the school's LD specialist. Everyone agreed that something was indeed wrong. A new evaluation determined that the child was severely learning disabled. He was given one-to-one therapy, and conferences were held regularly; the solution to his problem seemed close at hand. But he continued to fail in the second grade, and his behavior problems were increasing both at home and in school. The frustration continued to build.

In many such situations, the youngster's school difficulties would have been discussed with the family doctor, medication would have been prescribed, and no further options would have been explored. In this case, even though the boy was indeed hyperactive and inattentive, everyone was convinced that his classroom behavior was only a small part of the problem. At the mother's insistence, the school kept working with the family to find a long-term solution to the second-grader's difficulties with behavior and learning.

Finally, in midwinter, it was agreed that the boy would be put back into a first-grade class and that the LD therapy would continue. The effect was traumatic for the entire family. Every day, the child came home from school crying because his parents had "ruined his life." The mother cried for weeks. She would go into the school's office and sob hysterically. But at home, both she and her husband were positive and supportive of their son. It was rough—really rough.

The crisis did not pass until well into the spring. But by the end of the school year, everyone was relaxed. The boy was happy—and he was learning. Three years later, his classmates considered him the brain of the fourth grade. Ironically, the child's mother still does not seem to recognize the part she played in getting the help her son needed so desperately.

Beginning with the first conference in the first grade, this mother who used her hysteria effectively was the key to finding a solution to her son's problem. She had many chances to settle for defeat; she could easily have adopted the "it's best to be reasonable" role. But nothing shook her belief that her son could be helped if only she kept fighting. Her hysteria made her stubborn and unwilling to give up.

Any parent can use hysteria as well as she did.

THE HYSTERICAL MOTHER ON A BUDGET

Mrs. Williams fought the schools for five years before her son, Ken, was finally identified as learning disabled. During that time, she got him eye training, counseling, and perceptual/motor therapy. When the boy was finally placed in a self-contained LD class, he absolutely blossomed. After two very profitable years of special instruction, he was placed in a regular seventh-grade program—for which he was not ready.

Ken quickly fell back into his old pattern of failure, misery, and anger. Mrs. Williams tried to get her son placed in a more appropriate class. She was given the brush-off by the principal, the social worker, the counselor, several teachers, and a long list of others.

It was financially impossible for the Williams family to enroll Ken in a private school or clinic. In desperation, the mother called me and begged for suggestions. I gave her a list of people within the school system I thought might be able to help. She spent another day on the phone. This time, she talked to supervisors, administrators, psychologists, other principals, social workers, and more teachers. Some gave her sympathy, but all agreed that nothing could be done. There were no LD classes available at the junior-high level.

Mrs. Williams realized that she would *have* to work through the faculty and administration at her son's school. She had already tried to get them to understand the situation, and no one had been willing to listen. But she called the principal again and demanded a conference with all of Ken's teachers. Then she called me and asked that I go to the conference with her. Reluctantly, I agreed.

We were met in the school's library by the principal, fifteen teachers, an LD specialist, the assistant principal, the football coach, and a counselor. There were many of "them" and few of "us." If we had thought of that group of people as the opposing team, we'd have been too frightened to say a word.

The principal introduced everyone. Faculty members, teaching aides, and members of the staff—each of them had direct contact with Ken.

Mrs. Williams is a gentle, shy person. In a few brief sentences and using simple words, she explained the reason for our visit. The warmth of her personality and the love she felt for her son showed very clearly as she concluded by saying, "We're here because we want to work *with* you."

Since no one at the meeting (with the exception of the LD specialist) had any knowledge about learning disabilities, I began by explaining the LD symptoms that are listed in chapter 2. To my delight, the teachers were so interested that they took notes. Some of the symptoms were particularly important in understanding Ken's problem. I gave those special attention.

The teachers asked many questions and sought advice from us. They genuinely wanted to understand Ken and help solve his learning problems. Long past the time when they would usually have gone home for the day, they kept the discussion going. "How do I treat him?" one asked. "Is he embarrassed about his learning disability, or can I talk to him about it?" Others wanted to know such things as, "What kind of work can I expect from him?" "How much pressure should we use?" "What kind of discipline will work best for him?" "What can I do in my class to give him a chance to succeed?"

One by one, Ken's teachers committed themselves to making specific adjustments within their classes. All of that was done voluntarily. Once those teachers recognized and understood Ken's problems, they wanted to be part of the solution. (In my experience, that is almost always the case. The enemy is ignorance, not teachers who don't care. Teachers who truly understand an LD student's situation usually want to do everything in their power to help.)

When the meeting finally broke up, the principal, the shop teacher, and the football coach stayed to talk further. The coach was especially interested in Ken's directional confusion and his poor eye/hand coordination. He'd hoped that the large, muscular seventh-grader would be one of the stars of his team. But Ken's performance had been very puzzling. "He's one of the biggest boys, and he's one of the best players," the coach explained. "But he runs plays to the wrong side a lot, and I can't seem to get him to handle the ball properly. Can you give me some ideas? How can I work around the fact that he can't tell right from left?" Together, we figured out some adjustments that we thought might work. Then the coach realized that he was late for practice. But he was not concerned. He chuckled as he told us, "Ken is the captain of the team. I don't need to worry about what they're doing out there. He's got them organized and doing their warmup drills."

Mrs. Williams and I had been at the school for nearly three hours. As we left, the principal shook our hands and thanked us warmly for coming. He asked if I would return sometime and lead a workshop for his entire faculty. After I agreed to do that, he turned to Mrs. Williams and thanked her again. "By coming here to talk with us, you have done me and my faculty a great favor," he explained. "I've been teaching for over twenty years, and I've never seen a child who couldn't tell right from left. I never knew there *were* such teenagers."

We left the school knowing that our visit had done more than just help Ken. In fighting for him, we had also helped stamp out the ignorance that hurts all LD and ADD students. Without name-calling or accusations or rage, one mother using controlled hysteria had accomplished some very important things.

A month later, I went back to the school to watch Ken play football and to find out whether or not our conference had really helped him.

Mrs. Williams and I huddled on the bleachers yelling, cheering, and talking about Ken. She told me that every teacher had followed through with the adjustments that had been promised. For two or three weeks, the school had experimented to find the best way to deal with all the different problems involved in teaching Ken. In less than a month, he had begun learning satisfactorily in every subject. His attitude had improved right away. He had quickly returned to his normal, happy, pleasant self.

In fact, life was better than ever for Ken. He was passing all his classes. He was the captain of the football team and had been named Most Valuable Player in three straight games. All the students recognized him as a natural leader. The boys looked up to him and wanted his friendship. The girls stopped him in the hall to talk and flirt. He was popular with his teachers, too. They admired him for being hardworking, honest, cheerful, cooperative, and well mannered.

Hysterical mothers don't just get action—sometimes they get miracles.

The events described above happened prior to the original publication of this book in 1980. It was tempting to omit Ken's story as outdated. After all, we now have better-trained teachers and many years of experience in meeting federal and state mandates designed to force schools to provide appropriate learning environments for all types of exceptional children. Yet even in 1995, a highly qualified psychologist got involved in a case similar to this one. Unfortunately, the outcome was not at all satisfactory. After several meetings, the school still made none of the promised—and legally required—modifications, and the family went home to debate between litigation and homeschooling.

BIG DADDY: THE ULTIMATE WEAPON

Nothing can beat the power of an irate father. When he enters a school to fight for his child, teachers listen, counselors pay attention, principals stand up and take notice. A hysterical mother backed and supported by a strong, forceful man—together they make an unbeatable team. The family that has a man leading the fight for an LD and/or ADD child rarely fails!

After over thirty years of women's lib, this statement offends many people. It is true nonetheless. Mothers are seen in schools all the time. As room mothers, they bake cookies and dish out ice cream. At football games, they run concession stands and take tickets. They are frequently seen assisting in classrooms, libraries, and lunchrooms. They provide transportation for field trips and act as chaperones for dances. Their presence is neither unusual nor threatening.

Fathers, on the other hand, do not grace corridors and classrooms often. When a father makes an appearance in a school, his mere presence is noticed. Students whisper. Teachers comment. Just by being there, he commands respect and attention. Gender-based status may be changing, but there is no doubt about it: in American schools of the twentieth century, men are taken seriously.

That seems unfair to the many fatherless families. But it needn't work against them. School conferences commonly include an amazingly varied assortment of father figures: grandfathers, uncles, older brothers, ministers, family doctors. *Any* man standing firmly behind the mother can have a tremendous effect.

A fine private school spent two years trying to help Bruce. Yet at the end of the sixth grade, his situation was worse than ever. The group LD therapy provided by the school was doing no good, because the boy's disability was too severe. He refused to cooperate in any attempt to solve his difficulties with paying attention. In all of his classes, he had serious problems with behavior.

Mrs. Miller, Bruce's mother, had been to the school for several conferences. She wanted help for her son. But none of the school's suggestions ever seemed to be carried out.

For weeks, the school's administrators struggled to decide what to do with Bruce. The child couldn't possibly succeed in the seventh grade. He'd already repeated a grade and couldn't be held back again. There seemed to be no choice; Bruce would have to be denied admission the following year. Any answers there might be for him simply were not going to be found in this particular private school.

Firm in their resolve, the headmaster, the director of the lower school, the LD specialist, and all of Bruce's teachers faced the Millers over the conference table. With heavy hearts, they slowly and carefully presented the situation. Bruce's mother cried softly. His dad listened in stony silence. Finally, the headmaster took over. As gently as possible, he told them the school's decision. "Bruce may not return here next year," he announced. The words rang firmly, leaving no room for further discussion.

Mr. Miller was stunned. He did not lean over to comfort his sobbing wife. For a long time, he did absolutely nothing. Then he slowly rose up tall in his chair, leaned forward, and with deep emotion said only one word: "No." There was no anger and no explanation.

The rest of the group sat there aghast. Mr. Miller's face and that one word said it all. He was *not* going to let his son be removed from the school.

Then, with the careful control of a businessman attacking a problem, Bruce's father began to speak. "You say my boy has a severe learning disability and needs help you can't give him. What does he need and where can we get it?" he asked.

The boy's teachers recommended intensive LD therapy at an excellent clinic nearby. Three times a week, somebody would have to pick Bruce up at school, drive him ten miles to the clinic, wait an hour while he had his lesson, then bring him back. Someone was going to have to make a huge sacrifice transporting the child back and forth.

Mr. Miller did not bat an eye. He looked directly at his wife. "It'll be rough, but we'll do it. I'll help out as much as I can. And if we have to, we'll hire a cab."

Having settled that issue, he moved to the next point. "You say my son is headed into deep emotional trouble. I don't see it. But if you will help us find a good psychologist, we'll take Bruce in for a professional opinion. If counseling is needed, we'll see that he gets it."

No one could argue with that. Some well-qualified psychologists were recommended, and it was agreed that an evaluation would be undertaken immediately.

Then Mr. Miller faced the last point. "With counseling and LD therapy, can Bruce succeed in the seventh grade here next year?"

Faculty members and administrators agreed completely: the answer was no. The child was nearly three years behind in every subject. There was no chance that he could succeed in seventh grade.

Not discouraged, Mr. Miller continued, "With counseling and therapy, could he pass the sixth grade if given another chance?"

It was agreed that success in the sixth grade was within the realm of possibility—if the therapy went well.

Mr. Miller concluded with this proposal: "I want Bruce here next year, in the sixth grade. We'll get him the counseling and LD therapy he needs. We'll work *closely* with you for one more year. If at the end of the year Bruce cannot pass the sixth grade, we'll take him out of the school with no further argument. If he succeeds, he'll stay right here and go into the seventh grade."

From the father's first word, there was no question as to whether or not Bruce would be back the following year. Everyone there wanted to do what was best for the boy. By speaking up, Mr. Miller led the school to find a creative solution for his child.

And the solution found that day worked very well. Bruce stayed in that school through high school, played soccer on the varsity team, and went on to college.

That father's "no" was important. When the chips were down, he fought for his son. It's always a privilege to work with courageous parents.

A LONG, TOUGH FIGHT—TOGETHER

It must not be assumed that one success solves all the problems of an LD or ADD child. For example, Ken's "miracle," told earlier in this chapter, lasted for about six months. Then a new difficulty arose. Ken punched a student and was expelled from school for three days. The following year, he got into a scrap in the cafeteria and threw a fork at someone. With each crisis, his mother had to start over. His case is typical.

Each of the stories in this book represents just one episode in the life of a particular LD and/or ADD youngster; each one tells about a single predicament and how it was resolved. But almost always, one crisis is followed by another. The fight seems to be endless. Children are in constantly changing situations—they face different schools, different teachers, different classmates, and differences within themselves. New problems continue to arise. Again and again, the parents must be willing to get the help their children need.

The parents are the key to ultimate success for LD and ADD children. Only they can be counted on to be there, to understand, and to care—day after day, year after year.

Well-informed, forceful parents give LD and ADD children their only real chance for success.

APPENDIX
Useful Addresses

CHADD (Children and Adults with Attention Deficit Disorder)
1859 North Pine Island Road, Suite 185
Plantation, Fla. 33317
(305) 587-3700

FAUS (Feingold Association of the United States)
P.O. Box 6550
Alexandria, Va. 22306
(703) 768-FAUS

Homeschool ADDvisor
P.O. Box 118
Lincoln University, Pa. 19352
(610) 932-4149

LDA of America (Learning Disabilities Association of America, formerly
    ACLD, the Association for Children with Learning Disabilities)
4156 Library Road
Pittsburgh, Pa. 15234
(412) 341-1515 or (412) 341-8077

Learning Styles Network (Drs. Kenneth and Rita Dunn)
St. John's University
8000 Utopia Parkway
Jamaica, N.Y. 11439
(718) 990-6335

NATHHAN (National Challenged Homeschoolers Association Network)
5383 Alpine Road S.E.
Olalla, Wash. 98359   .
(200) 857-4257

*NILD (National Institute for Learning Disabilities)
107 Seekel Street
Norfolk, Va. 23505
(804) 423-8646

NICHCY (National Information Center for Children and Youth with
    Disabilities)
P.O. Box 1492
Washington, D.C. 20013-1492
(800) 695-0285

Orton Dyslexia Society
Chester Building, Suite 382
8600 La Salle Road
Baltimore, Md. 21286-2044
(410) 296-0232

INTERNET ADDRESSES FOR ADHD ISSUES
alt.support.attn-deficit
www.chadd.org

---

* *with a focus on Christian schools*

SELECT BIBLIOGRAPHY

LEARNING DISABILITIES

Brutten, Milton, Sylvia O. Richardson, and Charles Mangel. *Something's Wrong with My Child*. New York: Harcourt Brace Jovanovich, 1973.

Clarke, Louise. *Can't Read, Can't Write, Can't Talk Too Good Either*. New York: Walker and Company, 1973.

Hampshire, Susan. *Susan's Story*. New York: St. Martin's Press, 1982.

*Herzog, Joyce. *Learning without Labels*. Lebanon, Tenn.: Greenleaf Press, 1994.

MacCracken, Mary. *Turnabout Children*. Boston: Little, Brown and Company, 1986.

Osman, Betty B. *Learning Disabilities: A Family Affair*. New York: Random House, 1979.

Schmitt, Abraham. *Brilliant Idiot*. Intercourse, Pa.: Good Books, 1992.

Simpson, Eileen. *Reversals*. Boston: Houghton Mifflin Company, 1979.

* *written from a Christian perspective*

Weiss, Elizabeth. *Mothers Talk about Learning Disabilities*. New York: Prentice Hall, 1989.

LEARNING DISABILITIES COMBINED WITH ATTENTION DEFICIT DISORDER

*Evans, James S. *An Uncommon Gift*. Philadelphia: Westminster Press, 1983.

Levine, Mel. *Keeping a Head in School*. Cambridge, Mass.: Educators Publishing Service, 1990.

McCarney, Stephen B., and Angela Marie Bauer. *The Parents' Guide to Attention Deficit Disorders*. 2nd ed. Columbia, Mo.: Hawthorne Educational Services, 1995.

ATTENTION DEFICIT DISORDER

Armstrong, Thomas. *The Myth of the A.D.D. Child*. New York: Dutton, 1995.

Barkley, Russell A. *Attention-Deficit Hyperactivity Disorder: A Handbook for Diagnosis and Treatment*. New York: Guilford Press, 1990.

———. *Taking Charge of ADHD*. New York: Guilford Press, 1995.

Hallowell, Edward M., and John J. Ratey. *Driven to Distraction*. New York: Pantheon Books, 1994.

McCarney, Stephen B., and Angela Marie Bauer. *The Parents' Guide to Attention Deficit Disorders*. 2nd ed. Columbia, Mo.: Hawthorne Educational Services, 1995.

THE BRAIN, LEARNING, AND CHILD DEVELOPMENT

Armstrong, Thomas. *In Their Own Way*. Los Angeles: Jeremy P. Tarcher, 1987.

———. *Seven Kinds of Smart*. New York: Penguin Books, 1993.

Healy, Jane M. *Endangered Minds*. New York: Simon and Schuster, 1990.

———. *Your Child's Growing Mind*. New York: Doubleday, 1987.

Rose, Colin. *Accelerated Learning*. New York: Dell, 1985.

★ *written from a Christian perspective*

TEXT REFERENCES

American Psychiatric Association. *Diagnostic and Statistical Manual of Mental Disorders.* 3rd. ed. Washington, D.C.: American Psychiatric Association, 1980.

Feingold, Ben F. *Why Your Child Is Hyperactive.* New York: Random House, 1985.

Werner, Emmy E. *Overcoming the Odds: High Risk Children from Birth to Adulthood.* Ithaca, N.Y.: Cornell University Press, 1992.

Witelson, Sandra. "Two Right Hemispheres and None Left." *Science* 195 (1977): 309–11.

INDEX

Italics indicate case histories.